Country Ways
and Wisdom

Country Ways and Wisdom

Rosamond Richardson

Time-Life Books is a division of Time Life Inc.
TIME LIFE INC.
President and CEO: George Artandi
TIME-LIFE BOOKS
President: Stephen R. Frary
TIME-LIFE CUSTOM PUBLISHING

Vice President and Publisher	Terry Newell
Vice President of Sales and Marketing	Neil Levin
Director of Special Sales	Liz Ziehl
Director of Design	Christopher M. Register

TIME-LIFE is a trademark of Time Warner Inc. U.S.A.

Library of Congress Cataloging-in-Publication Data

Richardson, Rosamond.
   Country ways and wisdom: over 400 natural tips and traditions to enhance your life / by Rosamond Richardson.
     p. cm.
  Includes index.
  ISBN 0-7370-0020-1
  1. Home economics—Miscellaneous. 2. Gardening—Miscellanea.
3. Herbs—Utilization. I. Title.
TX158.R56 1998   98-2869
640—dc21   CIP

First published as *Country Wisdom* in Great Britain in 1998 by
Kyle Cathie Limited
20 Vauxhall Bridge Road
London SW1V 2SA

Text © 1997 Rosamond Richardson
Photography © 1997 Michelle Garrett
Designed by Robert Updegraff
Home economy by Jaqueline Clarke and Susie Theodorou

Author's Acknowledgments

This book is dedicated to countless unknown philosopher-magicians, mostly women of intuition, who have practiced country wisdom down the generations across the world.

My thanks to the late Harry Westbury, who suggested the idea for this book to Kyle Cathie in the first place. I deeply regret that he never saw it published. I am indebted to Rafi Fernandez, Chantek McNeilage, Barbara Lumsden, Annie Holland, and Marlise Riding. Special thanks also to E. Barry Kavasch, Yvane, Françoise, Joan, Emanuele, Lionel and Hilda, Jenny, Diana, Angela, Oona, Inge, Robyn, June, Mineke, and Olga. I am grateful to numerous friends and acquaintances who tolerated my endless questions and demands while I was researching this book, and who went to some lengths to find material for me. Thanks, too, to the team at Kyle Cathie Limited who have put so much energy and skill into producing this beautiful book.

Important Notice

This book contains information on a wide range of herbs and remedies that can be used medicinally. It is not intended as a medical reference book, but as a source of information. Before trying any remedies, herbal or otherwise, the reader is recommended to sample a small quantity first to establish whether there is any adverse or allergic reaction. Remember that some remedies, which are beneficial in small doses, can be harmful if taken in excess or for a long period. The reader is also advised not to attempt self-treatment for serious or long-term problems without consulting a qualified doctor or health practitioner. Neither the author nor the publisher can be held responsible for any adverse reactions to the recipes, recommendations, and instructions contained herein, and the use of any remedy or herbal derivative is entirely at the reader's own risk.

Printed in Singapore

Contents

Introduction

Country Ways and Wisdom is a lively and varied compilation of recipes and domestic lore, as passed down through the generations. This practical, common-sense wisdom, collected from all over the world, offers many keys to everyday life, because country "wisdom" is halfway between common sense and science and touches on both. Our grandparents, the wise women and men of the past, were practical philosophers who understood how things work rather than why. Their innate wisdom was grounded in observation and experience. Subsequent generations have made use of this inherited wisdom because it works, and not necessarily—although there are many exceptions—because it has been "proved" by the criteria of science. A certain element of mystery may thus enter into this wisdom: It may not be proven, but it should not necessarily be dismissed either, even by experts in the field. It is in a category of its own and that, along with an occasional flirtation with superstition, is part of its eternal charm.

The response from people whose grandparents or parents have used practical lore in house or garden, sometimes adding the language of symbols, stories, and proverbs, shows vividly how it has become woven into the fabric of everyday family life. I gleaned some of this wisdom in response to a worldwide request on the Internet for personal stories. Other gems were collected from friends and acquaintances of many nationalities, so this book is an accumulation of oral sources, family "commonplace books," small unpublished herbals, and local publications. What became clear is that traditional country wisdom is still very much alive in rural areas, but fast disappearing with the encroachment of city life and the genesis of a new "urban folklore."

This wisdom appears in slightly different but recognizable guises around the globe, and has a universal place in society. One of the great mysteries is that similar ideas and customs occur in distant places among people who have no cultural contact with each other, and spring from entirely different races and civilizations—even in the most remote places on earth. "Truth is one, the sages speak of it by many names," in the wisdom of the Vedas. Identical concepts, astonishingly constant and with roots that go back into antiquity, appear to come from a universal, collective source. The "basic magic ring of myth" has no respect for boundaries. Thus, the wisdom of a Mexican healer mirrors a cure "discovered" by a farm-worker in East Anglia, England: The former used cobwebs to seal the cut umbilical cord after childbirth; the latter pulled curtains of cobwebs from the barn walls when a colleague was badly cut by farm machinery—they stanched the wound, and his prompt action saved a life. These stories, two of many, touch on a vast subject, incalculable in size, infinite and universal, which can never fit between the covers of one book. We can offer but a taste, yet even this is a rich feast.

This book is a celebration of a mostly female culture, of a heritage based on nature and practiced by country women who were closer to the usefulness of plants and the cycle of natural rhythms than we are today. They lived their lives without constant reliance on technology and chemicals, but according to nature and the seasons, using a combination of common sense, intuition, and inherited wisdom. Some might call them witches, but "It behoveth a magician, and one that aspires to the dignity of that profession, to be an exact and very perfect philosopher," according to Giambattista della Porta, an Italian herbalist writing in the seventeenth century. The multi-faceted arts these women practiced offer welcome relief from today's prevailing reductionist approach: Now their wisdom fulfills a need, deeply felt by many, to use fewer chemicals, to recycle material, to "waste-not-want-not," and to be less dependent on processed goods.

Rich with symbols and yet rooted in practicality, this country wisdom, with its awareness of nature and its relationship to folklore, contains the possibility of fulfilling another universal need, that of giving significance to the mysterious, thus empowering us to influence our own lives. So grounded in pragmatic experience is this art that much of the wisdom of our grandparents is still applicable to us today: It works. This collection is no arcane whimsy, but essentially a "how to" book,

translated where necessary into today's terms, although some superstitious touches are included for fun—old wives' tales, love lore, and legends about cats are not overlooked.

The book looks at gardening lore and weather; how herbs can be used as gentle medicines; the use of plants for simple cosmetics and in making traditional wine cups and brews; how certain plants always had their part to play in the household, whether it be for cleaning and fragrances, or for celebrations. And there is a section on how to use many wild plants for the pantry and freezer, making the most of an annual country harvest that is autumn's gift to us all.

This is a book to use, to amuse, to be enchanted by, to enjoy. Its richness lies in its variation as much as its abundance. Fully illustrated with beautiful photography, it offers the key to a magical yet practical world that is ours for the exploring.

Home and Hearth

Mid pleasures and palaces though we may roam,
Be it ever so humble, there's no place like home.
John Howard Payne (1791-1852), from his play *Clari*

Whether your home is ever so humble, or a palace, or something in between, it is your castle. If you live in a city or town, you may dream of making your home in the countryside, with its inky starlit nights and fresh air, to feel the changing climate through the turning seasons, to be subject to the moods of nature to which urban life is less exposed. Whether your home is a refuge from pollution and noise, or looks out onto the lanes and fields, looking after it takes a significant amount of time and energy. We learn some lessons from the experience of our mothers and grandmothers, the rest we pick up as we go along. There is a rich store of wisdom from the days before heavy chemicals were used in cleaning and washing. Some of it is just as appropriate to today's world as it was then, and can be updated to modern needs. I have collected tips from people who live or have lived in far-flung corners of the world—Singapore, Zimbabwe, Brazil, St. Helena, China, Holland, and Germany, as well as the UK and USA. What is surprising is how many of the practical tips overlap, even though they originate from unconnected cultures. For example, the use of salt recurs universally, and lemons are ubiquitous.

Native Americans believed that salt could be used to overcome bad energies in the house: Sprinkling salt in the corners of each room created a protective circle that invited in the Spirit of the Wind. Interestingly, Jews have a custom of presenting salt (and bread) to the new owner of a house on their first visit. And there is an English tradition of sprinkling salt in front of the threshold before you take ownership of a house.

There are endless touches that constitute the art of homemaking. The use of color, or the way you arrange the furniture and ornaments, expresses something about who you are. Rudolf Steiner said that "you never see a straight line in nature, so try imitating the curves of the natural world in your furniture and fittings." Bringing houseplants into the home increases the healthy ions in the atmosphere; candlelight can transform an occasion; and an open fire gives coziness and focus to cold winter nights. The family festivals that punctuate the year have as their focus hearth and home, underlining the central importance of the homemaking aspect of our family life.

The task of keeping the home fresh and clean is eternal. Using natural as opposed to chemical ingredients makes your house smell good, and it will not be polluted by some of the toxic gases given off by synthetic cleaners. Cheap and easy to use, these materials really do work, the natural way, and are just as handy for today's computer keys as they were for scouring the pots before the days of stainless steel. You can control household pests, keep the bathroom spotless, banish unwanted cooking smells, and remove stains without resorting to an array of chemicals. Try it—it works.

KITCHEN

"A general anarchy prevails in my kitchen," wrote the lugubrious Dr. Johnson. Perhaps he needed a touch of *Feng Shui*, which prescribes the kitchen to be airy, spacious, and well-lit. Associated with the health of the family, it should be a calm environment with as many natural materials as possible—cane, raffia, wood, and clay. Green houseplants deflect bad energy and ionize the atmosphere, although spiky cacti are not auspicious (anything with sharp angles on it deflects good energy). Keeping the kitchen clean the natural way, without resorting to heavy chemicals, will keep it smelling good. Friends in the USA, Kenya, Germany, and Holland, to name but a few places, have contributed their tips on how to keep this important center of the home clean, bright, and fragrant using ordinary kitchen ingredients.

Dealing with Strong Smells

To remove strong smells on wooden boards after chopping onions, garlic, or fish, rub the area with the cut side of half a lemon. If your hands smell strongly of garlic, rub some mustard powder into them before washing them; this neutralizes the smell. To clean pans in which you have cooked fish, and which still retain the smell, rub well with a cut lemon after washing, then rinse thoroughly.

If the bread box smells musty, wipe it with a little white vinegar on a damp cloth and leave it open to dry. This will also get rid of any mildew. For smells in the refrigerator, leave a bowl filled with cat litter, baking soda, or charcoal inside: They all absorb smells.

After using the oven, while it is still warm, put some pieces of orange peel in it; these will help get rid of any unpleasant cooking odors. If the microwave gets smelly, half-fill a small bowl with water, add 3–4 tablespoons of lemon juice, or 2 teaspoons apple-pie spice or a few sprigs of thyme, and run on high for 1 minute. Remove the bowl and wipe the oven clean.

Simmering spices gives the kitchen a beautiful aroma and disguises unwanted cooking smells. Simmer cinnamon sticks or whole cloves with a little brown sugar in water over very low heat. Or, squeeze a halved lemon into a pan of water, add the lemon halves, and simmer for 10–15 minutes.

Damp Cabinets

Fill an empty coffee can with charcoal briquets, punch holes in the sides and lid, and place it in the cabinet to absorb moisture. Or, you can tie pieces of chalk together and hang them inside the cabinet. If you have a damp outside wall, plant sunflowers against the wall. A Dutch friend who lived on marshland told me this, and I tried it in a cottage where I used to live. It worked, and the sunflowers gave me a lot of pleasure as I worked in the kitchen.

Cast-Iron Pans

Cast-iron pans rust easily. The best technique to prevent this from happening is to rub them with vegetable oil after washing, and dry thoroughly with paper towels. If, despite this, they do rust, rub the area with a solution of 1 tablespoon citric acid in 2 cups water; this will remove the rust. A Norwegian friend told me that her grandmother boiled pots and pans with horse-droppings to prevent rust!

Aluminum and Stainless Steel Pots and Pans

A woman in the village who has done cleaning work all her life told me that for discolored pans she simply boils up rhubarb or lemon juice to remove staining. If there is burned residue on the bottom, fill the pan with cold water and leave to stand for an hour. Then add some borax powder or cream of tartar and boil up. The burned food will come away quite easily without injuring the pan.

Alternatively, fill the pan with water and add a sliced onion plus a tablespoon of salt. Boil for 10 minutes, then leave to soak overnight. The residue will wash away easily.

For marks on stainless steel, rub with a handful of flour, then polish with a soft cloth. If the pan is badly marked, use a scouring pad and lemon juice.

Copper

When heavily tarnished, an English country remedy is to rub the coat of grime with crushed rhubarb leaves, or use the cut side of a lemon dipped in fine salt. A Belgian friend suggests you fill a plant-spray bottle with vinegar, spray it on, and let it stand for several hours, then rub clean.

If copper turns green, remove this verdigris with a solution of ammonia, using rubber gloves.

Cleaning the Oven

Everyone's least favorite task is made easier if you rub the oven clean with a damp cloth dipped in baking soda. For heavy soiling, mix 1 tablespoon of kerosene with 2 tablespoons of salt and scrub into the staining. Rinse off with hot water and washing soda (wearing rubber gloves).

Pouring salt onto food-spills on the stovetop while you are cooking prevents them from burning. This also works inside the oven and is very useful—I am constantly having overflows in the oven, which burn horribly. This simple treatment prevents the worst of the smells and the spill can be wiped up easily when the oven is cool.

Dishwashing

For coffee and tea stains on cups and mugs, dip a damp cloth into baking soda and rub the stain off. Use the same treatment for a teapot, or, if heavily stained, put in a handful of washing soda and fill up with boiling water. Let stand until cool and this will remove the tannin.

When washing greasy dishes, a useful tip is to add a little vinegar to the water (2 tablespoons per sinkful)—it leaves dishes sparkling clean. You can also use lemon juice as a rinse-aid in the rinsing water.

If you have a porcelain sink that needs cleaning, put layers of paper towel over the bottom, and saturate with diluted bleach. Leave for 5–10 minutes, then remove the paper and rub clean. The even contact of the bleach, plus the length of time it is left in the soaked paper, cleans up all discoloration and brings up the whiteness of the porcelain. For a stainless steel sink, use a damp cloth dipped in white vinegar to remove water spots. Shine by rubbing with soda water.

To keep the sink in good condition, put a cupful of washing soda down the drain once a week, and wash it down with a kettleful of boiling water to remove any blockages and keep it clean. For limescale around the drain, rub the deposit hard with the cut side of half a lemon: The acidity dissolves it away.

To freshen your dishwasher and remove any smells, sprinkle about ¼ cup baking soda over the bottom and turn on to the cold rinse cycle.

My mother always used to clean her copper pans with a vinegar-soaked cloth.

Feng shui recommends that bedroom furniture be kept uncluttered, especially around the door, to facilitate the flow of energy into the room.

BEDROOMS AND BATHROOMS

Weary with toil, I haste me to my bed,
The dear repose for limbs with travel tired.
William Shakespeare (1564–1616), *Sonnet xxvii*

You could say that the bedroom is the most important room in the house: We probably spend more time there than in any other single room. *Feng Shui* calculates the direction that the bed should face according to the year of your birth, whereas Muslims never lie in a bed with their feet pointing toward Mecca, always the head. An English grandmother told me that she had always been told to place the head of the bed to the north and the foot to the south.

In *Feng Shui*, the shape and element of the headboard can make a significant difference to your energy: Rounded metal is good for people engaged in paperwork, rectangular wood for professionals, and oval or wavy shapes for artists and musicians. Don't have too many mirrors in the bedroom—if any—because they attract so much energy into the room that you may have trouble sleeping.

In illness the bedroom becomes a particular focus. Put plants or cut flowers next to the sickbed in order to produce more oxygen during the day, and remove them at night when they put out carbon dioxide. A bowl of water on the radiator will help relieve a dry cough at night; add some eucalyptus oil, if you like. There are some excellent invalid beverages (see pages 178–9), and for a really good night's sleep, drink one of the nightcaps on page 181.

Stains on the Mattress

Moisten 1 tablespoon of dry laundry starch with a little dishwashing liquid and apply to the stain. Let dry, then brush off with a stiff brush. Or, wearing rubber gloves, sprinkle a damp cloth with a few drops of ammonia and apply to the stain.

Cupboards and Chests of Drawers

My American grandmother left me a chest of drawers made from cedar wood, which is a natural moth-deterrent, and I still use it. Line the drawers with fresh paper, and add dried citrus peel, or scented bags (see page 104), to keep them smelling fresh and fragrant. These are also moth-deterrents. Put unwrapped soap into drawers to scent them. Or, make some simple sachets. For a lavender sachet, take a handful of lavender buds and place in the middle of a square of cheesecloth. You can add some dried wormwood, too, an excellent moth-repellent. Gather up the edges and tie tightly with a satin ribbon.

A Dutch friend described how her grandmother aired musty cupboards and drawers. After removing the contents, she hung them up outside on a pleasant day to air. Then she crumpled up newspaper, filled the drawers and cupboards, and left them slightly open for a few days so the paper and ink could absorb damp and smells. Finally, she would wipe them out and, if possible, leave them outside on a breezy day to air thoroughly.

Storing Clothes

The Sultan's clothes from around 1450, kept in the Topkapi Museum in Istanbul, are completely intact and look like new. They are folded in linen and laid flat, kept in the dark, and brought out to air once a year. The embroidered silks, brocades, damask with gold and silver thread, and tapestries remain as pristine as they were five hundred years ago. We can use this simple technique for storing our own clothes.

A Malaysian friend always puts whole cloves—a moth-deterrent—into the pockets of her coat before storing them away for the summer, and into plastic bags with her wool sweaters. Cloves keep them far more fragrant than the horrible smell of mothballs.

Mirrors and the Dressing Table

To clean mirrors, apply a few drops of denatured alcohol on a damp cloth, then buff with a clean, soft cloth. Don't use water, as it may run down into the frame and damage the silvering.

A teaspoon of borax powder plus a tablespoon of washing soda in warm water will keep hairbrushes clean and fresh.

Soak jewelry in a solution of dishwashing liquid for a few minutes before cleaning with toothpaste and a fine toothbrush—this according to an American friend's grandmother in Ohio. Rinse again, and dry off with a hairdryer. Buff with a soft cloth to bring up the brilliance. Diamonds love gin: They sparkle after a good soaking and then brushing with a toothbrush in warm water.

To keep pearls clean, wear them next to your skin as often as possible—the natural oils in the skin polish them.

Bathrooms

Rub liquid detergent on mirrors to prevent them from steaming up. When a natural sponge becomes slimy, soak it in 1 tablespoon of vinegar to 2½ cups water. Clean off hard-water marks on tiles or shower doors with distilled white vinegar on a soft cloth. Leave for 20–30 minutes, then rinse off.

Rub stubborn marks in the bath or basin with turpentine and rinse with soapy water. For old stains on baths or basins, use equal quantities of turpentine and linseed oil on a soft cloth. Clean off with hot soapy water and rinse thoroughly. Use kerosene for the most stubborn stains. Scrub stains from dripping faucets with lemon juice, using an old toothbrush dipped in salt. You can also make a paste of borax powder and distilled white vinegar and brush until the stain disappears.

To remove limescale from faucets, rub vigorously with the cut side of half a lemon. Rinse, then buff dry with a clean, soft cloth. To descale bathtub spouts, tie a plastic bag filled with vinegar over the spout and leave until the scale has dissolved, then rinse. Use an old toothbrush to get rid of the grimy deposits around the base of a faucet using vinegar or lemon juice. To clean chrome faucet handles, rub with a handful of flour, then polish with a soft cloth. If you have a blocked shower-head, soak it in a bowl of warm vinegar, then use a toothbrush or darning needle to clear the holes.

When washing lace curtains, add a spoonful of sugar to the final warm rinse, to keep them crisp. If they become discolored, soak them in cold tea to dye them a creamy-beige. After washing, hang them while still damp so that they don't shrink—pull them gently into shape.

To neutralize smells in the bathroom, strike a match. The smell of the sulfur predominates, and the flame burns away odors. Alternatively, sprinkle a sweet water such as orange-flower water or lavender water (see page 94) into the toilet.

WASTE-NOT-WANT-NOT

From the Garden

If you grow your own herbs, trim them during the summer when they begin to overtake the garden, and dry the trimmings by hanging them upside down in bunches in the kitchen. They add a natural touch and smell lovely, and you can use them for stocks and sauces.

When you have a glut of apples, store them carefully for winter use. I put mine between layers of newspaper, set slightly apart from each other so they are not touching—this slows down the spread of mold. Other people store them in straw. Apples have to be kept in a cool place such as a shed or garage—they will rot quickly in a centrally heated house.

If honesty (Lunaria annua) grows in your garden, don't weed it out. Instead, pick it in the fall, slide off the husks around the flat, silvery-white seed pods, and use in dried-flower arrangements.

Leftover Wallpaper

Use this to line kitchen shelves and chests of drawers. For the pantry shelf, cut 4 or 6 layers to size, and remove a layer regularly as it becomes dirty, so that your storeroom surfaces are always clean.

Keep leftovers to patch any damaged wall areas: Cut out a matching piece slightly larger than the area you need to replace; and if you leave the edge slightly irregular, the patch will be less noticeable. Glue to the spot, matching the pattern carefully and using a roller to flatten the edges.

Old Toothbrushes

These are incredibly useful for a variety of jobs: cleaning jewelry (see page 15), scrubbing limescale and deposits off faucets (see page 15), cleaning grouting (dipped in a solution of chlorine bleach), and polishing intricate woodwork or metalwork. Toothbrushes get into otherwise inaccessible moldings on grates, and into the crannies of complicated kitchen appliances.

Good Housekeeping

You can increase the shelf-life of a sponge-mop considerably by storing with a plastic bag tied around the sponge end to stop it from drying out and warping. You can save on detergent when you are cleaning the house by adding a tablespoon of baking soda to the solution. This also softens the water. And soften dried-out shoe polish with a little turpentine to give it a new lease of life.

Energy-Saving Tips

Re-use foil: Simply wipe clean with a damp cloth on a flat surface to "iron" it and prolong its shelf-life. Use it to save energy in the following ways:

Place foil inside a broiler pan to reflect heat: Not only is this an economy, but it is also useful in that you throw away the foil after use rather than having to scrub grease and other deposits off the pan. You can also economize on heat by placing a sheet of foil under an electric burner. This reflects heat and makes it far easier to keep the range clean—foil wipes clean easily, burned objects don't stick, and you simply throw the foil away when it is heavily soiled, and replace it.

Place a sheet of foil under the ironing-board cover to reflect heat into garments.

Plastic Containers

Keep plastic containers (e.g., from margarine, yogurt, cottage cheese) and use for freezing food. I put soup into large yogurt containers, which conveniently contain one serving. You can also use these as receptacles for cleaning paintbrushes and/or mixing paint.

Linen

Turn old tablecloths into a set of napkins. Make pillowcases from sheets that have worn out in the center, but which are still good around the outsides. Use the un-worn-out parts of flannel sheeting for children's nighties.

Give sheets a new lease of life by cutting the sheet lengthwise through the center where it has worn out, or where it tears, turning the sides to the middle, sewing the outer edges together; make a small, neat French seam for strength and smoothness and hem the outer edges. Make single sheets from double sheets. Keep worn-out sheets to use as drop cloths when you are painting the house, or cut them up and use as polishing cloths.

A needle and thread always come in handy to repair fabric, and can save you a lot of money.

CLEANING

C-l-e-a-n, clean, verb active, to make bright, to scour. W-i-n, wind, d-e-r, der, winder, a casement. When the boy knows this out of the book, he goes and does it. Mr. Squeers in *Nicholas Nickleby,* by Charles Dickens

Cleanliness is next to godliness, or so it is said in more than one culture. Let it be observed that slovenliness is no part of religion, preached John Wesley in the eighteenth century. *Feng Shui* has it that clutter, and by implication dirt, blocks the free flow of energy through the home. Certainly a spring-cleaned house is a pleasure; it imparts a sense of the new, of vitality and freshness. Before the days of chemical cleaners, our grandmothers used common household or kitchen ingredients to achieve this pristine sparkle—lemon,

vinegar, baking soda, and salt all played major roles, alongside the tougher elements of ammonia, denatured alcohol, turpentine, and mineral spirits. Borax, glycerin, and washing soda have been all but forgotten by the modern housewife, yet they are wonderfully effective cleaning agents. Protect your hands by wearing rubber gloves for all these strong substances, to avoid the "hands like bears' backs" so aptly described by a friend's mother, who remembers the days of doing all the family washing by hand. "What's worth doing is worth doing well," was the adage she repeated often to her daughter. The following tips have been gleaned from people living all over the world, in Singapore, Zimbabwe, Canada and the USA, New Zealand, Iceland, and various parts of Europe.

Making homemade beeswax polish

Housework

The maid of a friend in Singapore always used two dusters while she was cleaning—one in each hand—saying that she would finish in half the time. A good general tip is to soak a new duster in equal parts kerosene and vinegar. Store in a tightly closed jar until ready to use. You will find that it really lifts dirt.

Polished Furniture

Use turpentine, an all-purpose solvent, to remove ring marks, rubbing along the grain. A New Zealand friend told me that to remove a watermark on polished furniture, mix a few flicks of cigarette ash with olive oil, rub it in, and leave for 30 minutes. Buff with a soft cloth. A mixture of salt and vegetable oil, left on for an hour, also helps to remove marks from polished wood. Remove after 30 minutes, then rub with a soft cloth.

To revive dull polish on wooden furniture, mix 2 tablespoons each of turpentine, distilled white vinegar, and denatured alcohol, which shifts sticky substances, and 1 tablespoon linseed oil, which feeds and protects wood. Shake well, and apply with a soft cloth. For dirty woodwork, mix 1 part turpentine with 1 part vinegar and enough dry laundry starch to make a paste. Apply with a soft cloth and rub into the grime. Buff with a soft cloth.

Rub linseed oil into lusterless oak to make it shine. When dusting intricately carved wood, use a paintbrush or toothbrush. Remove sticky marks on wood with a little vinegar and water, then apply beeswax, the most nourishing of wax polishes.

Homemade Beeswax Polish

This works beautifully and is far cheaper than buying the polish ready-made.

3 ounces beeswax
5 fluid ounces turpentine
Essential oil of lavender (optional)

Put the beeswax into a bowl and set it over simmering water until the wax melts. Then add the turpentine and stir thoroughly. Pour into a jar, add a few drops of essential oil of lavender, if you wish, and let cool.

Other Surfaces

Marble is porous, so treat stains as soon as possible. For wine, coffee, or tea stains, use a solution of 1 part distilled white vinegar to 4 parts water. Wipe off at once. Or, apply fresh lemon juice to bleach out the stain. You can remove marks on wallpaper by rubbing with a scrunched-up piece of white bread, which also works on burlap.

For grease marks on wallpaper, apply a warm iron over brown paper to absorb the grease. Repeat with clean bits of paper until the stain disappears. For rust on metal furniture, simply use a stiff wire brush. To revive dull ebony, rub in petroleum jelly, leave to soak in for 30 minutes, then rub off with a soft cloth.

To clean phones, radios, clock faces and computer keys, use denatured alcohol on absorbent cotton, and penetrate the inaccessible bits with a cotton swab. Two tablespoons denatured alcohol and 2 tablespoons water mixed together will clean dirty piano keys. Apply on absorbent cotton, well squeezed out. Be careful with denatured alcohol because it is flammable. It is also useful for removing felt-tip ink and sticky labels.

To clean paintwork, mix 1 tablespoon turpentine, 1 tablespoon milk, and 1 tablespoon dishwashing liquid with 5 cups hot water. Apply with a soft cloth. For scuff marks on vinyl, use an eraser; turpentine will also do the job.

Natural Polish for Leather Upholstery

Boil 1 cup linseed oil, cool, and add 1 cup vinegar. Apply with a cloth and then buff to a polish.

Cleaning Bamboo Furniture

From a friend in Germany:

1 tablespoon salt
1¼ cups water
A little lemon juice (or a mixture of warm water and washing soda)

Apply with a soft brush into the crevices, and wipe dry with an old piece of velvet soaked in linseed oil. Leave the coating of oil on for an hour or two, then polish off with a soft cloth.

In Singapore, they spray cane and bamboo furniture with water from a plant atomizer from time to time, to keep it supple.

WASHING

"I have no passion for clean linen," growled Dr. Samuel Johnson. Many would disagree. In the old days a starch was made from the roots of bluebells and arum lilies, and the crushed leaves of soapwort (*Saponaria officinalis*) produced a homemade soap that gave a good lather. It still does. The presence of saponin in the leaves loosens dirt particles and produces a light lubricating froth, which has been used in modern times by specialists to clean fragile antique fabrics.

Recent rust stains on linen can be removed with cream of tartar mixed to a paste with a little water. Spread over the affected area, let dry, and then brush off. You can also try dabbing on lemon juice, covering with salt, and leaving to dry for an hour, in the sun if possible. Rinse off, then wash. Soluble aspirin solution will dissolve underarm sweat stains.

If linen gets marked, dip the stain in buttermilk and dry in the sun, then wash in cold water and dry. For iron molds and mildew, wet the affected part of the cloth and rub with the cut surface of a lemon. My Indian friend uses lime juice to remove ink and other stains from clothes. Beet stains are pernicious: Rinse immediately

You can use simple, natural treatments on many delicate fabrics.

under cold running water, then soak in a borax solution. Borax is a strong detergent that breaks down grease and softens water at the same time. Wash wool sweaters and jersey outfits inside-out, to prevent matting of the pile, and add a tablespoon of vinegar to the final rinse to revive colors.

Add 1 tablespoon distilled white vinegar—one of the most versatile of home cleaners—to a bowl of rinse water for hand-washing, to remove all traces of soap. A teaspoon of Epsom salts added to the last rinse keeps colors bright. Soak well-used washcloths in 1 tablespoon vinegar or lemon juice to 2½ cups water before machine washing, to remove all traces of soap. Soak cloths in cold water prior to washing, to loosen dirt. To keep colors bright, soak clothes in cold, salty water before their first wash.

Special Treatments

When black garments lose their blackness, soak them in water with a little distilled white vinegar, or add water softener to the wash, to remove the build-up of soap that has caused the color to change. To revitalize black silk, a woman in the village who had worked "below stairs" in the manor house in the 1920s, told me to boil and mash ivy leaves until the water is dark. This acts as a reconditioning dye.

A friend, who is one of the few women I know to love housework, and whose home always smells of fresh laundry, gave me these tips: A little denatured alcohol added to the rinse water preserves the sheen of **silk**. Add 2 lumps sugar to the rinse water to give silk body, plus a little lanolin to protect and restore it. Sprinkle **lace** with powdered magnesia and leave for a few days before shaking it out—this works like a dry shampoo, the powder absorbing the dirt. To raise the surface of **velvet**, put a wet cloth over a hot iron and hold the velvet over the steam. Brush against the pile with a soft brush and it will rise beautifully.

Cleaning the Iron

Clean the base of the iron (unplugged) with toothpaste, applied with a soft cloth (unless it is nonstick, in which case you can sponge it with a dishwashing solution, or use denatured alcohol).

Pets in the House

A young puppy can cause havoc with your housework until it is house-trained. Neutralize urine smells on the carpets with a solution of 1 part vinegar to 5 parts water in a plant atomizer. This will help remove the smell and deter the animal at the same time. Blot the area with ammonia solution (wearing rubber gloves) to further deter a repetition. Club soda is a useful instant remedy, too.

Strips of citrus fruit peel deter cats, because they dislike the smell so much—this from a Chinese woman born in Singapore.

Wipe oil of cloves on furniture legs to prevent a new puppy from chewing them—dogs dislike both the smell and the taste.

For pet hairs on furniture, wrap adhesive tape around your fingers, sticky side out, and rub over the upholstery to pick up the hairs.

Carpets

For a "dry shampoo": Sprinkle baking soda liberally onto the carpet. It neutralizes acid stains and counteracts smells. Leave for 20–30 minutes, then vacuum.

Shoe-polish stains can be removed by applying naphtha, a versatile solvent. Allow to dry, then dab out any remaining dye with denatured alcohol. Dampen a cloth with turpentine and rub away grease spots, then rub softly with a clean cloth to remove traces of the turpentine. Weak vinegar solution is also effective for grease and dirt on carpets. If you find dye stains on the carpet, add a few drops of ammonia to some denatured alcohol in a small dish and apply on an absorbent cotton pad until the dye vanishes.

If you find cigarette burns on a carpet, rub them with the edge of a silver coin. For beer stains, use club soda, blot well, and clean with baking soda (see above). For old beer stains, use denatured alcohol. Tea and black coffee also respond to the club-soda treatment, then sponge with borax solution.

To retrieve tiny objects, such as gemstones or contact lenses, lost in carpet pile, fit a stocking over the nozzle of the vacuum cleaner; they will be sucked into the fabric.

Windows and Glass

For grimy windows, rub first with the cut side of an onion. Then make a solution of water and vinegar and put into a spray bottle.

A cut onion is useful for cleaning fly specks from glass.

This solution cuts through grease and brings up a good shine. Wipe dry newly washed windows with crumpled newspaper— the ink gives a good shine.

For any glass with flyspecks, clean with the cut side of an onion. My old cleaning lady's grandmother used to boil up 2–3 onions, and use the water to remove flyspecks. You can also clean up an oil painting with a cut onion.

Glasses

Add lemon juice to the rinse water to bring up a shine. For cloudy decanters and vases, mix a handful of salt (or crushed eggshell) with white vinegar and place inside, then fill with dishwashing liquid. Shake well and leave for several hours. Rinse thoroughly. Or, fill cloudy glasses with water and add 1 teaspoon ammonia to each one. Leave overnight, and wash clean in hot water. For dull glass, make a paste with baking powder and water and rub it in. Wash off and polish with a soft cloth.

For crystal, place 2 teaspoons ammonia inside and fill the vase or decanter with water. Leave to stand for several hours, then wash out thoroughly.

If you spill red wine on the carpet, cover the stain with salt (see Wine below).

STAINS

The golden rule for stains is to treat them as soon as possible. Laundry borax is excellent, and glycerin helps remove old stains. For example, glycerin mixed into egg white in equal proportions gets old grass stains out of whites. The world's most universal and natural stain remover is the cut side of half a lemon—the acid is a bleaching agent that takes out unwanted marks and odors.

Stains on Clothes and Upholstery

Blood: Soak the fabric in cold water.

Chocolate: Sprinkle with borax and soak in cold water before washing.

Coffee: Rub fresh stains with glycerin and rinse out with warm water.

Egg: Soak in cold water with a little salt added before washing. On furniture, sponge with cold salty water.

Fruit juice: Soak in milk for an hour before washing. (This also works for cola stains.) Egg stains flatware black: Wipe off deposits and rub the stains with salt applied on a damp cloth.

Grease: A friend told me she smothered her husband's new silk tie in talcum after it became heavily stained with cooking grease; after brushing it off the next day, the staining had disappeared. Rub suede with glycerin to remove grease; and an emery board will restore shiny patches to their original texture.

Hair oil on a headboard: Rub with white spirit.

Ink stains on carpets: A woman now in her nineties, who lived in Rhodesia in the 1930s, remembers ink being spilled on a pale pink carpet, and the dog proceeding to trot through it. The woman's household servants put milk on the stains and they disappeared without trace. You can also rub such a stain with the cut side of half a tomato, and rinse out well. Scrub ink stains on the hands with a nailbrush dipped in vinegar and salt. Lemon juice also works on this and on other dyes left on the hands. For ink stains on wood, dab with household bleach on a cotton swab and blot with paper towels. When the stain has cleared, apply wax polish.

Mildew: Soak in a diluted bleach solution before washing, and hang in the sun to dry.

Milk: Soak in cold water, then put between paper towels and iron out any remaining grease.

Tar: Scrape off as much as possible, then treat with eucalyptus oil soaked into a white cloth.

Tea stains on upholstery: Sponge with a laundry borax solution.

Wine: Sprinkle salt onto a red wine stain on the carpet and leave to absorb, then brush off. Repeat as necesary. Or, pour some white wine over it as soon as it happens. Blot well, sponge with clean water, and pat dry with paper towels. Or use a glycerin solution. On clothes, rinse in warm water, then soak in borax solution (1 tablespoon borax to 2 cups water) before washing. Old stains may respond to a little denatured alcohol on a sponge.

Silver and Other Metals

For years we lived in a college at Cambridge University, and my mother ran the Master's Lodge with the help of a wonderful couple from St. Helena, an island in the South Atlantic. Here are some of the tips she picked up from them.

Silver: When tarnished, dissolve a handful of washing soda in an aluminum pan, soak the silver in it, and remove as soon as the tarnish has disappeared. Rinse and polish. Or, use a paste of fine salt and lemon juice. Brighten up silver quickly with a drop of denatured alcohol on a soft cloth. **Brass**: Clean off heavy tarnish with a solution of vinegar and salt (1 tablespoon salt to 2½ cups vinegar), or washing soda. Clean up with lemon dipped in salt, and rub vigorously. Then wash with warm water and ammonia solution (1 tablespoon ammonia to 2½ cups water). Dry and buff to a polish. **Pewter**: Mix wood ash to a paste with a little water and rub it in for a dull sheen. Or, rub with cabbage leaves. Or, immerse in leftover egg-boiling water. Remove grease marks by rubbing with a little denatured alcohol on a soft cloth. **Copper**: If copper turns green, remove this verdigris with a solution of ammonia (see above), wearing rubber gloves. **Lead**: Scrub with turpentine. If heavily stained, soak for 5 minutes in a solution of 1 part distilled white vinegar to 9 parts water, with a little baking soda added.

Brighten up silver instantly by applying denatured alcohol and then polish with a soft cloth.

PESTS AND VERMIN

When I was researching a TV series on village life, I interviewed a retired gamekeeper and his wife, Lionel and Hilda, who lived in a cottage just outside a pretty village in Hertfordshire, England. Inside, the house was plain, but immaculately tidy—Hilda had been a cleaning lady for various villagers all her life. The garden was mostly planted with vegetables, with small borders of annuals around a patch of lawn. The old couple came up with these well-tried methods of pest control in the house, which are largely based on natural eco-friendly methods.

Flies

Beer or molasses in a saucer, or smeared onto sheets of paper, will attract and kill flies. If you are eating outdoors and are plagued by flies and wasps, put down a saucer of jam at a little distance

Thyme is an excellent moth-repellent.

away—it acts as the perfect decoy. Pyrethrum powder (from *Chrysanthemum cinerariaefolium*) is an environmentally safe fly-repellent. Scatter it around the windowsills or put onto a plate.

Friends who live in a wonderful house in Pennsylvania, surrounded by woods, use the leaves of black walnut (*Juglans nigra*) to keep ants and flies from the house. Rue repels houseflies: Hilda still grows it in a window-box outside the kitchen, and Lionel remembered it being planted as a border next to one of the barns on the farm. If by any mischance you should swallow a fly, Lionel's grandmother's tip was to drink a little vinegar laced with cayenne. This would kill the insect immediately (but goodness knows what it would do to you).

A Frenchwoman living in Morocco showed me her pot of basil by the door: No country home was without one, she declared, because it kept flies out of the house. Basil is kept in the local bars and stores and all living rooms. I immediately tried this on my kitchen windowsill, and it substantially reduced the number of flies that plague us during the summer. The same woman told me that in her house in France she hangs up large bunches of fresh mint in the kitchen to get rid of flies, pinching the leaves every time she passes. I have found that sprigs of wormwood work well, too, as do rue and tansy.

Moths

Take a handful each of dried rosemary, sage, and mint, and mix with a little grated lemon peel and a pinch of cinnamon. Tie into cheesecloth bags and lay in drawers or hang in cupboards. Dried wormwood and southernwood are effective moth-repellents, too. And if you tie long sprigs of thyme together and hang them in the closet, they will keep moths away as they dry out.

Fleas

According to Hilda, the country tradition is that fleas arrive on March 1st. If you spring-clean that day, early in the morning, the "black army" will not move in, and you will be free from fleas all year. Fleas hate wormwood, and pennyroyal and fennel both repel them. Wash your animals in a strong infusion of walnut leaves. Or, infuse water with wormwood overnight, then soak the animal's coat thoroughly with the mixture; brush and comb when dry.

A woman on Shelter Island, New York, puts braids of pennyroyal into her dogs' beds to repel fleas and ticks, which they do very effectively. Lionel said that giving your dog an unpeeled garlic clove in its food would repel fleas; it worked immediately on my dog. Lionel also said the garlic would get rid of worms.

Ants

My gardener friend Barbara said to pour boiling water on the nest. Or, open it, throw quicklime over it and immediately pour water over the top; do the same with the haunts of cockroaches. A friend who lived in the Bahamas for many years used to do what the natives did, and scattered pennyroyal over the shelves where ant infestation occurred; the ants were gone in no time. Mint planted by the front door will stop ants coming in, as will tansy. The bruised leaves of sprigs of lemon thyme have the same effect. All these are much more pleasant than the toxic substances that you may buy. In the pantry, hang pennyroyal, rue, or tansy, and sprinkle chili powder on the shelves when ants appear. Mineke, who comes from West Friesland, north of Amsterdam, remembers her mother drawing a chalk line across the threshold to stop ants coming into the house. It worked!

Cockroaches

A friend in New York City has found that the best roach repellent is to put down an equal mix of baking soda or borax and confectioners' sugar. It's the borax that gets them. A traditional country roach poison is the black hellebore that grows on marshland. Strew it on the floor. The cockroaches will eat it when they come out at night, and will be found dead or dying the next morning.

For crickets and beetles, place scotch snuff or chloride of lime in the holes that they frequent.

Mice

Leaves of dwarf elder (*Sambucus ebulus*) drive mice away from stored grain. Vetchling or everlasting sweet pea (*Lathyrus latifolius*) repels field mice and other small rodents, and spearmint planted near the house has the reputation of keeping rodents away. The

The arch pest controller

spurges (*Euphorbia lathyrus* and *E. lactea*) repel moles and mice.

An old gentleman in his nineties had a father and grandfather who had both worked as book-keepers. They added powdered wormwood (*Artemesia absinthinium*) to the ink that they used for writing out their figures; this stopped mice and rats eating the ledgers.

"Get a cat," said Lionel.

Rats

Make a thick paste with 3 pounds flour and water to mix. Dissolve 1 ounce phosphorus and 2 ounces turmeric in 3 tablespoons melted butter. Spread this on bread and leave where the rats can get it, or make into balls and roll in sugar. Or, you can impregnate hay with cayenne pepper and stuff it down their holes; they are unlikely to pass through the barrier. Simply sprinkling cayenne down their holes is unpopular enough. and "will certainly send them off at a sneezing pace."

"Get a terrier," said Lionel.

Spiders

The final word comes from a grandmother who said that when big hairy spiders come into the house it means autumn is coming, and they must be left alone. She used to call them "the charladies."

FIREPLACES

Where glowing embers through the room
Teach light to counterfeit a gloom,
Far from all resort of mirth,
Save the cricket on the heart.

John Milton, *L'Allegro* (1632)

There is a brick jutting out near the top of the chimney in my three-hundred-year-old thatched cottage. I am told this was called the witch's seat, provided for her so that she would not come down any farther. The inglenook has a small cavity in the wall that was used to store the household salt, to keep it dry. Witches hate salt, so I have double protection. One old builder told me they used to put salt-glazed bricks into the chimney to keep witches away. Be that as it may, an open fireplace is the heart of the house, a place to gather and gaze into the flames, and talk and listen to stories, and roast chestnuts. A woman now in her eighties, who used to work as a maid in a stately mansion in Oxfordshire, England, was told that the fireplace must be kept spotlessly clean because it was the "altar of the house."

Firewood

My German friend Inge was told by her grandfather never to burn elder wood in the house: This would be very unlucky because the wood spits and could cause a fire, and it brings the Devil down the chimney. Ash is the best wood—it burns hot and long, and doesn't spit. Pine is dangerous because it sends out showers of sparks, so never be tempted to burn up bits of old pine furniture. Cut your wood in the summer and let it "season," or dry out— wood should not be burned while the sap is running as all it does is hiss at you from the grate. Also, well-seasoned wood is less

A log fire burning in the hearth is the heart of the home.

likely to spark. Keep your wood supply under cover to keep off rain and snow falling. If you don't have a wood shed, stack wood under a sheet of plastic, allowing air to circulate from the sides.

If you have a large fireplace and need a lot of kindling to start the fire, tie it in a bundle with a twist of pliant twig (not string, which burns immediately) so that the heart of the fire does not collapse. To add fragrance to the fire, throw citrus peel onto it, or pine cones, which are beautifully aromatic. If you burn hickory wood it will fill the house with its aroma; apple wood smells fabulous. You can make good use of wood ash: Put ashes on the driveway to make a hard core—it packs down gradually. Or, put it onto the garden or the compost heap (see page 51).

Soot Marks

Salt helps lift soot marks from carpets—just sprinkle it over and brush clean. Talcum powder is good, too. For soot marks on brickwork surrounding a fireplace, use a stiff bristle—or even wire—brush dipped in a warm water-vinegar solution. Or, rub with another piece of brick. Thick residues of soot may have to be chiseled off. Use vinegar for scorch marks. On stonework, use dishwashing solution, adding a bit of bleach, if necessary.

Cleaning the Chimney

An old-fashioned way of sweeping the chimney over a wood fire was to drop one end of rope, with a big bunch of holly leaves tied halfway along it, big enough to thoroughly scrape the edges, down the chimney. You have one person at each end, and work up and down until the chimney is cleaned of excess soot.

Toasting Goodies by the Fireside

Get yourself a toasting fork and make toast, holding the bread at a judicious distance from the flame so as not to burn it. Do this with marshmallows, too—get them hot enough and near enough to the flame to give them a crust all over the outside, then remove and cool a little; you will find the inside gooey. You can even try an impromptu "fondue," putting ¾-inch cubes of cheese onto the toasting fork and turning them in the flame until they begin to melt. This takes practice: It is easy to overcook and lose the whole thing with a hiss as it disappears into the flames. When you

Toasting marshmallows on a winter's evening

succeed, however, the smoky flavor and the melting texture are fabulous. But beware of putting anything cooked like this straight into your mouth—you could be horribly burned by the hot metal of the fork. Always remove the hot article to a plate first and cool a little before you eat it.

If you have a big wood fire with a lot of hot ash underneath, bake potatoes there by burying them in the hot ashes and leaving to cook for about an hour. Best of all on winter nights are roasted chestnuts: Wait until the fire dies down, then slit the tops of the chestnuts (which otherwise will explode violently) and put into the hot embers. Leave for 5–7 minutes before removing carefully with tongs. Alternatively, use a chestnut roaster, which is an iron holder with holes on a long handle. Hold it over the fire for 5–7 minutes, then cool slightly before you peel the nuts.

If you put a candle in the freezer for a few hours, it will burn longer.

CANDLES

Absence diminishes commonplace passions and increases great ones,
as the wind extinguishes candles and kindles fire.
Duc de la Rochfoucauld (1613–80)

Candles were invented in the ancient world, as evidenced by Egyptian and Cretan candlesticks dating back to 3000 B.C. There is a legend that King Alfred the Great (849–899) used candles to measure the passing of time. Placed in a lantern to protect them from drafts, each one would burn for four hours. By 1272, there were seventy-one chandlers, or candlemakers, working in Paris, according to a tax list.

The soft light of a candle brings beauty to a room and is flattering to the skin, but its romantic connotations are not without risks: "Choose neither women nor linen by candlelight," says country wisdom. Nowadays there are floating candles, scented candles, and candles of many colors and shapes for creating atmosphere within the home. Modern candles are a composite of paraffin wax and stearic acid, sometimes with beeswax or bayberry wax added.

Candles have been used in religious and spiritual ceremonies and rituals all over the world for centuries. The Roman Catholic Church used to stipulate that candles must be 100 percent pure beeswax, but now the measure is down to only 25 percent. There was a tenth-century Welsh law that stated that a Mass could only be said when bees were present—in the form of beeswax candles. Bees are holy because they swarmed out of Paradise in disgust at the Fall of Man.

The obvious analogy of lighting the darkness made candles symbols for purity and enlightenment:

I shall light a candle of understanding in thine heart, which shall not be
put out. Esdras VIII.25

Practical Tips

Place new candles in the freezer for a few hours to make them burn longer. Dip a candle end in very hot water to soften it before putting into a candlestick: Heating it with a match marks it black. If the holder is loose, wrap the end of the candle in adhesive tape.

To remove wax from pewter candlesticks, place them in the freezer for an hour or two; the wax will peel off easily. Use a hairdryer to melt away any remaining wax. On china candlesticks, remove the excess with a blunt knife, then place in the microwave on full power for 1–2 minutes to soften the remaining wax, which you can then rub off easily with your fingertips. For silver candlesticks, pour hot water over them to remove the wax. Melt the remainder with a hairdryer.

To clean up candlewax on a wood floor, let it harden (speed this up with an ice cube), then ease off with a blunt knife. Rub in some polish and buff with a soft cloth.

Allow spilled wax on the carpet to harden. Gently scrape off what you can without damaging the pile. Then set the iron to warm and blot the rest of the wax through paper towels. Keep changing the paper until all traces of wax have disappeared.

On clothes, treat with denatured alcohol, which will also absorb color dye. On wallpaper and furniture, use the paper technique.

To Make a Rush Candle

Rush lights were once the most economical source of domestic lighting for rural homes. Here is an old-fashioned recipe for making a rush taper, from the days when chandling was a home craft. The taper would be mounted on a piece of tree bark and lit to give a soft light after dark. The great advantage of rush lights is that they do not drip.

Cut soft rushes (*Juncus effusus* or *J. conglomeratus*) when they are fully grown but still green. Cut off both ends, peel off the green skin, and hang up to dry.

Melt some fat—mutton is best, or the fat obtained from boiling beef marrow bones. Add beeswax to make an extra bright flame. Soak the rushes in the fat and take them out and dry until hard. Do this several times until well coated.

Superstitions and Sayings

Candles have given rise to many common sayings. "To hold a candle to the devil" is to assist an evil person. If the "game is not worth the candle," the enterprise is not worth the labor or expenditure. To "burn the candle at both ends" is to be immoderate, wasteful or extravagant. To be "not fit to hold a candle to" means not to be compared with.

It is unlucky to light a candle from the fire on the hearth. The accumulation of wax dripping to one side of a candle foretells death, because it looks like a shroud. To snuff a candle accidentally is a portent of a wedding. An actor friend told me that three candles in the dressing-room, or on the stage, bring bad luck.

How far that little candle throws its beams!
So shines a good deed in a naughty world.
William Shakespeare, *The Merchant of Venice* (1596–7)

The soft light from candles is flattering to the skin.

Common Superstitions

Most cultures have invented superstitions as a kind of accessible everyday magic to protect against unseen forces. This magic is distinctive to its own society, but may also find echoes in another, however distant.

Household

"Touch wood" is said to have come from the old days when relics of the True Cross were kept in churches and solemn oaths were sworn on them. The wrought iron S and X shapes on cottage walls have a superstition behind their obvious practical use: They act as lightning conductors as well as wall props, but the S represents the thunderbolt of Jupiter and the X, or swastika, the hammer of Thor. Acorns used to be hung at the window to protect the house from lightning, and window-blind pulls are still today fashioned as acorns—the sacred nature of the oak, Jupiter's tree, brought into the home. Everyone knows that horseshoes are lucky, but remember that they should be nailed upward, and with their own nails. Upside down, all the good luck spills out. Breakages always come in threes, according to many.

Never hang a garment on a doorknob, my neighbor told me, because a piece of clothing on the outer knob of the door used to tell you that someone inside had died. Never open an umbrella in the house, said a man from Minnesota. Spilling salt is unlucky; to reverse this you must immediately throw some over your left shoulder. My Dutch friend Mineke was told that if you dropped butter on the floor it meant you would have a visitor.

Spiders

Spiders have long been supposed to bring good luck and prosperity:

> *If you wish to live and thrive*
> *Let the spider run alive.*

One legend goes that during the Flight into Egypt, Joseph hid the Holy Family in a cave and a spider wove a web across the entrance. Seeing the web unbroken, the pursuing soldiers concluded that no one had entered.

A young woman who lived in Tahiti for a while told me that there spiders are sacred because they are thought to be "shadows of the gods," and to kill one was extremely unlucky.

Mirrors

Breaking a mirror means seven years of bad luck. But if you wash the broken bits in the stream, or bury them, you can reverse the curse.

Primitive man believed that his reflection was that of his soul, and if anything separated it from his body—by breaking the mirror, for example—he would die. Something dreadful would happen if you looked in a mirror where a dead person lay because you would see the reflection of the deceased looking over your shoulder. So a custom arose of veiling the mirror. If you look into a mirror and see no reflection, that is the worst of all: Death is certain, for the soul has already departed. Napoleon believed these superstitions—during a campaign in Italy, he broke the glass over a miniature of Josephine that he carried with him. He could not sleep until the courier returned assuring him that no ill had befallen his beloved.

My Russian friend Olga used to love looking at her distorted reflection in the curves of her grandmother's shiny teapot. Grandmother would take the pot away saying: "Never look at yourself in a mirror at table—it will eat up your beauty!"

Cats

A local thatcher told me that his grandfather used to put a dead cat into the thatched roof as he worked, to protect the house from evil spirits and fire.

A three-hundred-year-old mummified cat—buried alive in the brickwork of a fireplace to ward off evil spirits—was found in the Mill Hotel in Sudbury, Suffolk, England, by builders doing renovations. They tossed the gruesome object into a bag. Over the next four years, the mill's foundations started to sink and its fabric to crumble, and a major fire broke out. The builder, knowing something about cat superstitions, had not dared throw the cat away, and the manager persuaded him to retrieve it from his yard. It is now restored to pride of place in a glass case in the hotel entrance and no further harm has come to the building.

LOVE LORE

Gather the Rose of love, whilst yet is time,
Whilst loving thou mayst loved be with equal crime.
Edmund Spenser, *The Faerie Queene*, (1596)

Around the world, love lore centers on aphrodisiacs, some less grounded in fancy than others. The most famous, rhino horn, is aphrodisiac by sympathetic magic only—not for any special chemistry, but because of its hardness. On the other hand, ambergris, taken from the intestine of the sperm whale, has a seductively strong, musky smell, and has been used for centuries to oil the path of love (or lust). Hippocrates claimed that asses' meat with milk and honey was aphrodisiac, and until not so long ago this was fed to the harems of Istanbul to keep up the women's stamina. Brides in the Balkans used to have their faces smeared with honey, which is thought to be aphrodisiac—indeed, so much so that the Magyars smeared the sex organs of young men and women with honey to ensure their mutual attraction.

St. Valentine's Day, February 14th, is, and has been since time immemorial, the moment to choose a sweetheart and exchange gifts, although the saint himself is obscure and seems to have had no connection with romance other than dying for his faith. Chaucer, in *The Parlement of Foules*, refers to a belief that birds choose their mates on this day.

When I was visiting Sicily, I was introduced to an Italian woman who told me of a most bizarre matchmaking custom. Her grandmother had saved her mother's umbilical cord, which over the years had dried out. When the time came to make a good match for her daughter, she powdered it into the cake and wine that she gave to the man she wished her daughter to marry. The idea was that the man would be so overcome with love that he would propose marriage immediately.

Some Aphrodisiacs

Absinthe

Contains absinthine and thujone—which is also found in vermouth in small amounts—and these have an aphrodisiac effect.

Banana

Contains the alkaloid bufotenine in its skin, which is a hallucinogen found in some magic mushrooms (and the skins of toads, so beloved by witches).

Jamaican Banana Power

Fill a baking dish with ripe bananas, the skins slit lengthwise, and bake at 350°F for 20 minutes. Carefully remove the cooked fruit from the skins. Scoop out the inner linings of the skins along with the juices, mix these with rum, and pour over the fruit with a sprinkling of allspice. Serve with cream . . . and so to bed.

Chocolate

Waxy beans from the cocoa pod contain phenelethylamine, a mood-altering chemical with orgasmic effect. Aztecs offered cocoa as food for the gods for this reason and also used it as an aphrodisiac. Montezuma would drink 50 cups of chocolate a day and make love to as many women. Chocolate was introduced into Europe by the returning Conquistadores in the sixteenth century. Today's researchers find that chocolate is a mild genital tonic due to its diuretic action. (But huge amounts are required.)

Chestnut Blossom

This contains a combination of chemicals also found in the seminal secretions of the male. Socrates taught the young men of Athens under a chestnut tree, and the Marquis de Sade noted its aphrodisiac effect. You can use the blossoms in sachets or soak them in the bath water (see page 92).

Herbs

Green coriander's lovely scent and flavor is so pleasing to the senses that the Crusaders brewed it with honey and water to make a love potion. Ginger, a "hot" herb, enhances sexual excitement. Arugula used to be banned from monasteries in France and England because it "excited the games of love."

"But alas! There are no herbs to cure love." Ovid

Angel Water

An eighteenth-century English recipe suggests mixing rose water, myrtle water, and orange-blossom water with some distilled spirit of musk and a dash of ambergris. This was often presented to the happy couple at country weddings to get the couple off to a flying start.

There are hundreds of superstitions and divinations in love lore, enough to fill books. I was brought up with this, among others:

> *Monday for wealth*
> *Tuesday for health*
> *Wednesday best day of all*
> *Thursday for losses*
> *Friday for crosses*
> *Saturday no luck at all.*

It was advice I failed to hear—a doomed marriage took place on a Thursday.

> *If you change the name and not the letter*
> *You marry for worse and not for better*

This turned out to be true in my case. I should have listened. It coincided with another warning:

> *Marry in Lent*
> *Live to repent.*

I did.

In India, arranged Hindu marriages will only go ahead if the horoscopes match. The art of synastry is practiced on the two charts. If a very rich man wants a particular daughter-in-law and knows that the stars don't work, he will bribe the astrologer to get his way.

Some Love Proverbs

> *A maid that laughs is half taken.*
> *Love is like linen, often changed, the sweeter.*
> *A woman that cries hush, bids kiss.*
> *A woman kissed is half won.*

Frosted holly leaves make an unusually pretty (but inedible) cake decoration.

FESTIVALS IN THE HOME

The great religious festivals of the world bring families and communities together to perform traditional rituals, often residues of pagan ones, which include feasting. The bonding effect of these events makes it an important time for the family, in whatever part of the world. For Diwali, India's Festival of Light, small earthenware lamps are filled with oil, then placed in temples and houses and set adrift on rivers and streams. At the Jewish Passover, bitter herbs are eaten, symbolizing the harsh life of the Hebrews under the Egyptian yoke. Nowadays, celery, romaine lettuce, parsley, Belgian endive, and horseradish root are served. The Chinese celebrate their New Year with colorful pageantry and feasting, the Mexicans their Day of the Dead, the Druids the Summer Solstice, the Irish St. Patrick's Day. Easter is a major festival in the Western world, whereas Japan celebrates the Buddha's birthday at Kambutsue. And so on. Human beings love to celebrate, and no more so than at Christmas and Thanksgiving.

Many people feel that Christmas is over-commercialized. But you can still make your own cards and decorations and wreaths— I shall never forget one beautiful wreath made by an American friend, using the evergreen herbs rosemary, thyme, rue, winter savory, and sweet laurel. Certainly your own homemade food, made in the tradition of our mothers and grandmothers, gives Christmas that personal touch and family feel. This tiny selection gives a flavor of the charm of an old-fashioned Christmas.

Christmas

Frosted Holly Leaves

This old-fashioned and very pretty notion was given to me by a lady approaching her hundredth birthday, who told me that she remembered her grandmother making them, for decorating the Christmas fruitcake.

Pick the leaves from their stems and wipe them clean, and dry. Hang up in a warm place to dry for 2 days. Then dip them first into melted butter and then into sugar and put them on a tray. Return them to the warm place to dry for 2 more days.

Cranberry Rope

This Christmas decoration using cranberries was described to me by a woman living in New York City, who remembered picking cranberries as a child in the bogs near her home in Massachusetts.

Pick the cranberries and clean them. Thread a medium needle with waxed thread and thread the cranberries carefully onto it, making the rope as long as you need. You can also alternate the berries with popcorn to make a red and white rope. The berries dry out over the days and end up like beads, which makes the rope shorter when the spaces are closed up—so allow for this by making the rope extra-long. The occupational hazard of this is that your hands get stained red (remove the stain with lemon juice, see page 22). This rope looks extremely pretty twisted around the light wires on the tree.

Christmas Cookies

These are the Proustian madeleines of my life. My American mother used to make "sugar cookies," as she called them, and they are an integral part of my childhood, bringing distant memories into focus.

MAKES 24	
½ cup all-purpose flour	½ cup (1 stick) butter
½ cup granulated sugar	Grated zest of ½ lemon
	2 teaspoons vanilla extract

Preheat the oven to 350°F.

Mix the flour with the sugar and rub in the butter until it is like very fine bread crumbs. Add the lemon zest and vanilla. Knead on a wooden board to a soft dough. If you want the cookies to hold their shape, add a little more flour (2–3 tablespoons) to make a stiffer dough.

Roll out fairly thin and cut into rounds or other shapes—either make up your own and do them freehand, or use cutter shapes (stars, trees, angels, etc.). If you are going to hang the cookies on the tree, puncture a small hole near the top edge before baking. Bake for 8–10 minutes, until a light golden color. Let cool for 3–4 minutes, then lift off carefully and cool on a wire rack.

Luxury Wassail Cup (see also page 169)

This celebratory cup for Christmas is steeped in tradition. If you are pouring the hot liquid straight into glasses, put a metal spoon in first to conduct the heat so that the glass doesn't break in your hand.

SERVES 15	
1–2 tablespoons (¼ ounce) whole cardamom, cloves, nutmeg, mace, ginger, cinnamon and coriander	4 bottles port, sherry, or Madeira
	4 cups granulated sugar
	12 egg yolks and 6 whites
	12 apples, baked until they burst

Simmer the spices in a little water, covered, for 15 minutes. Strain into the wine. Add the sugar and dissolve over a low heat. Leave on a low heat for 30 minutes, not allowing it to boil. Beat the eggs in a large bowl and pour over a cupful of the hot wine, beating well. Gradually add the remainder of the wine, whisking all the time until frothy.

Add the apples, which will float like froth on the top, and serve.

Thanksgiving

The North American tradition of Thanksgiving goes back to the autumn of 1621, when the Massachusetts Bay Governor, William Bradford, invited neighboring Indians to join the Pilgrims for a three-day feast, in gratitude for the harvest and the blessings of the past year. It caught on. Thanksgiving Day was proclaimed a national holiday by Abraham Lincoln in 1863, and Canada adopted it in 1879. Roast turkey, cranberry sauce, and pumpkin pie are the order of the day.

Stuffed Acorn Squash

A wonderful dish to serve alongside the roast turkey and cranberry sauce.

SERVES 8–10

5 pounds acorn squash

STUFFING

¾ cup wild rice

1 teaspoon salt

2½ cups minced mushrooms

¼ cup minced red onion

2 tablespoons butter

½ cup grated cheese

2 teaspoons ground ginger

Salt and pepper

1 cup brown bread crumbs

3 tablespoons olive oil

Preheat the oven to 400°F. Put the squash on a baking sheet and bake for 50–60 minutes, until a sharp knife inserted into the center goes in easily and all the flesh is soft. Cool, then cut in half horizontally and scrape out the seeds and fibers.

Cook the wild rice for 30 minutes in boiling water, or until tender, adding the salt during the last 5 minutes. Cook the mushrooms and onion in the butter for 4–5 minutes until softened. Mix into the cooked wild rice with the cheese and ginger. Season to taste. Preheat the oven to 350°F.

Pile the filling into the cavities of the squash. Crisp the bread crumbs in the olive oil, tossing until coated all over. Sprinkle the squash with the crumbs. Bake in the bottom of the oven (to prevent the crumbs from burning) for 35–40 minutes.

Old-Fashioned Cranberry Sauce

This recipe was given to me by the grandmother of a large family. She has been making this sauce since the 1940s. She used to make it with canned cranberries, but I used fresh. The sauce is absolutely brilliant, and it freezes well. You've got enough to do preparing all the rest of the food for Thanksgiving dinner, so the simplicity of this labor-saving recipe is a godsend.

2½ cups cranberries, fresh or frozen

1½ cups canned mandarin orange sections, with juices

½ cup granulated sugar

½ cup walnut pieces

Simmer the cranberries with the mandarins and their juices, the sugar, and the walnuts until they are mushy, about 5 minutes. Then crush lightly with a potato masher, and the sauce is ready to serve.

Pecan Pumpkin Pie

A great finale to the feast. This is the best recipe for pumpkin pie I've ever tasted—it will dispel all doubts that non-Americans may have about this delicacy. It is scrumptious, light, and mouthwatering with its creamy, golden filling and the crunch of nuts on top. You will find it unforgettable.

Pie dough for a 9-inch pan

1-pound slice of pumpkin, seeds and fibers removed

⅔ cup light cream

3 eggs, lightly beaten

¾ cup packed brown sugar

2 teaspoons ground cinnamon

½ teaspoon each ground allspice, ginger, and nutmeg

Pinch of salt

2–3 tablespoons brandy (optional)

½ cup pecan halves

Preheat the oven to 325°F. Roll out the dough and use to line a 9-inch pie pan. Line the pastry with foil, fill with ceramic baking beans, and bake for 20 minutes. Remove the foil and beans, and leave to cool.

Preheat the oven to 400°F. Wrap the pumpkin in foil and bake for 25–30 minutes until tender. Cool, then remove the skin. Blend to a purée in a food processor, and add the cream. Beat the eggs with the sugar, spices, and salt until they are thick, and fold into the pumpkin mixture. Flavor with brandy. Pour into the prepared pie shell. Decorate the top with the pecan halves.

Bake the pie at 400°F for 40 minutes, or until a knife inserted into the center comes out clean. Cool on a wire rack. Eat warm, served with whipped cream and a cup of the very best coffee.

Originally, Thanksgiving was celebrated on the last Thursday in November, but in 1941, it was set on the fourth **Thursday of that month.** The Canadians celebrate it on the second Monday in October. Thanksgiving brings families together around the **traditional food-laden** table. Eating, drinking, and talking take up most of the day, and old bonds are renewed in an atmosphere of **feasting and celebration.**

GARDENING MAGIC

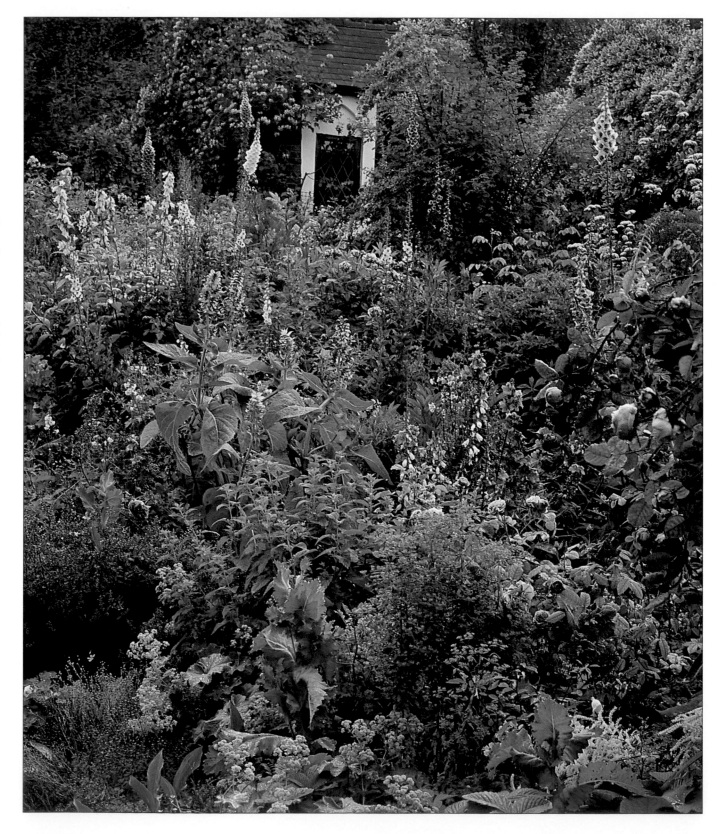

The gardener half artist must depend
On that slight chance, that touch beyond control
Which all his paper planning will transcend;
He knows the means but cannot rule his end;
He makes the body: who supplies the soul?
Vita Sackville West, *The Garden* (1946)

F rom earliest civilization, mankind has engaged in the engrossing activity of cultivating a small enclosed piece of ground called a garden: A personal paradise—a green thought in a green shade—to fulfill practical or esthetic needs, or both. From sacred groves and a vision of an archetypal Eden have evolved flower and fruit gardens, kitchen gardens, rose gardens, pleasure gardens, landscape gardens. As men and women planted and toiled, knowing success and failure, a vast tradition of gardening wisdom, both oral and written, began to grow. It is immense, international, and universal.

I have gleaned some of this traditional wisdom by talking with many gardeners, who have contributed their common-sense experience to this book. Other knowledge I picked up in childhood from my mother's gardener, Mr. Williams, who became my personal archetype. He worked for us for many years, and our garden was, to me, the magical place of childhood. I loved to follow after him, watching what he did and pestering him with questions. His way of speaking and turns of phrase are lodged in my memory. He seemed very old indeed to me then, a tall stooping man who always wore a cap and an old tweed jacket. He was forever dropping wise remarks about the wind or the weather, the phases of the moon, or which plants to put next to each other, all of which he had learned from his grandfather. Most of it went over my head then, but, as I started to tend a garden myself, much of it resurfaced, and it appears here in its inherited version.

Making a complete collection of the country ways and wisdom of the garden is a well-nigh impossible task. Enough books to fill libraries have been written through the ages on such fascinating topics as divining weather, planting at the correct phase of the moon, enriching the soil with compost, companion planting, the work of bees and butterflies, the curse of insect pests, and the microlife of a garden. Likewise, the folklore of flowers and trees, steeped as it is in a fascinating mixture of science and superstition, is impressive in its immensity. A few pages can claim only to give the reader a taste of this universal practical wisdom, with its delicate touches of fantasy.

Red sky at night, Shepherd's delight

WEATHER LORE

Those that are weather-wise
Are rarely otherwise

So Mr. Williams, my mother's gardener, used to observe. Although much traditional weather lore is unsubstantiated, it is still widely believed, and in many cases, meteorological science has not come up with anything better. Man has always sought to control or predict the weather, in an eternal attempt to understand and come to terms with the environment. It is in the temperate countries, where the climate is most variable and the seasons least dependable, where weather lore has flourished: It is relatively rare in the tropics and sub-tropics, where the climate is more stable.

The roots of weather lore lie in early religion. Its first exponents were priests or wise men who decided the all-important dates of sowing or harvest. Fertility of the crops, on which survival depended, meant the accurate interpretation of weather signs. Sailors and navigators became adept at this, because failure could lead to certain death, so much of their lore is reliable. For example, an oncoming gale can set up a rolling swell that travels rapidly ahead, giving warning of bad weather to come, before any other indicators such as cloud or rain.

Fine Weather

Year after year, I remember Mr. Williams saying the weather would be fine if swallows, martins, or skylarks flew high, and he never tired of repeating: "Red sky at night, shepherd's delight." A friend who lives in northern California quotes this version: "Red sky at night, sailor's delight."

Common as this saying is in its various forms, it is not always trustworthy, although the next part of it ("Red sky at morning, shepherd's [sailor's] warning"), found in various forms throughout the world, reflects a scientific reality: The scattering of light rays linked to thermal stratification or the formation of atmospheric currents. It is generally accepted as a reliable piece of weather lore.

Clouds and Wind

Clouds may indicate weather changes: "Mackerel sky, twelve hours dry." My neighbor used to call it a "cruddly" sky. In meteorological terms, this sky, dappled with small, white fleecy clouds, is a cirrocumulus formation marking the end of unsettled weather. Looking at the movement of upper layers of clouds can tell you if a change of weather is imminent, if their direction is very different from the winds blowing clouds below. A Moroccan woman told me a famous legend, that locusts know where it will rain in the Sahara. In fact, swarms fly downwind until they meet an area of convergent winds, where rain is most likely.

Virgil said that "rain and wind increase after a thunderclap," and this appears to be borne out as an accurate observation throughout the centuries. The Zuni Indians of New Mexico had a saying: "If the first thunder is from the east, winter is over." This is also grounded in generations of experience and found to be true. But probably the best guide to weather prediction, grounded in careful observation by men and women close to the cycles of nature, is in the wind. Francis Bacon said: "Every wind has its weather," a belief shared by many cultures, from the ancient Greek to the Native American. "Do business with men when the wind is in the northwest," goes an old saying from the north of England. This wind, usually accompanied by a rising barometer, has been shown to be related to such diverse events as increased activity on the New York Stock Exchange, and a greater success rate in the artificial insemination of ewes in France!

Looking at the movement of clouds can tell you if a change in weather is imminent.

Rain

Many persistent country sayings about the weather are not grounded in science, but they have not been disproved either. If ants retreat into their nests, rain will not be far behind. If a candle will not light easily, it means rain; a wavering flame means windy weather is on the way. If the down flies off dandelions, coltsfoot, or thistles when there is no wind, it is a sign of rain. "Rain from the east, two wet days at least." These are mere observations, but they may contain some truth. An Irish musician told me that the call of a curlew predicts a downpour, and that horses get restless and shake their heads just before rain. One of the most prevalent beliefs is that it will rain if cattle lie down in the fields. Possibly cattle have learned, and passed on through their genes as an adaptive process, to find a dry spot before it is too late. The most that can be said is that animals do indeed behave in particular ways under certain meteorological conditions, and so can be said to provide a forecast of sorts. Bees fly home if bad weather is coming. Many insects hatch in the humid weather before a storm, and swallows fly low to catch them. Owls hoot more at night, and cocks crow more frequently when there is rain about.

My German friend Inge's grandfather worked on the land all his life. He swore that he could predict rain by his corns and rheumatism. Widespread as this lore is, there is no evidence to prove the connection. Men, like plants and animals, react quickly to climate, but other factors, such as diet, temperament, and anxiety levels, also have to be taken into account.

An old lady from deepest Herefordshire, England, told me that in her experience beetles always come out of their haunts before rain, and worms, too, presumably to escape drowning. On the other hand, "Fine weather next day if bats or beetles fly late in the evening" is a common country saying in East Anglia, England. My friends from Oregon mentioned trees, such as poplar and silver maple, turning up their leaves when it starts to rain, an observation also well known in Europe. Scientists now know that plants react quickly to their environment, and their survival depends on the genetic transmission of safety responses, so they can be read as consistent weather indicators.

I was brought up with the dictum from my American mother, "rain before seven, dry before eleven," and learned early to distinguish a rain cloud—the cumulus cloud:

A round-topped cloud with a flattened base
Carries rainfall in its face.

Many people, myself included, take a rain check on St. Swithin's Day (July 15th): "If it do rain, for forty days it will remain." This piece of lore has entered commonplace wisdom, based on long-term observations and passed on down through generations. Science has not been able either to prove or disprove it. Likewise with this well-known piece of country weather lore that Wilf, my beekeeper neighbor, used to come out with every year:

If the oak's before the ash
There will only be a splash
If the ash before the oak
Then we're sure to get a soak.

"Rain before seven, dry before eleven."

The moon is an enduring focus of weather lore.

The Moon

The moon features large in weather lore, in spite of the absence of scientific explanation. The nearest is the "ring around the moon," a white halo sometimes tinged with red, formed by refraction through ice crystals in the clouds and often seen when rain is approaching. It is not, however, infallible. A woman from Oregon told of her mother's dictum that a ring around the moon means rain next day—a well-known saying all over the world:

If the moon shows like a silver shield
You needn't be afraid to reap your field;
But if she rises haloed round,
Soon we'll tread on deluged ground.

Some country folk say that a new moon brings a change in the weather, that sharp horns mean windy weather, and that the full moon clears the sky and brings good weather:

The moon on its back
Holds rain in its lap

Emanuele, living in rural France near Vaugines, has noted that when the weather turns bad at the start of the new moon, it will stay bad for the whole lunar cycle.

Cold Weather

When I was a child, my best friend's grandfather always used to say, "If the cat turns her back on the fire there will be frost," while my old neighbor Wilf, in his best Essex dialect, used to say: "An east wind is a lazy one; it will go through you before it goes round you." These signs were immutable—if nuts or berries hang on the branches after leaf fall, it means a hard winter ahead: "Many haws, many sloes, many cold toes" and "When the oak wears his leaves in October you can expect a hard winter."

Holly berries shining red
Mean a long winter, 'tis said.

There is always one fine week in February in England, or later if winter is late, but beware the "blackthorn hatch." This warm weather brings the sloe into blossom, but spring is not just around the corner—it is immediately followed by a patch of very severe weather. Ever since Wilf, sadly now departed, told me this, I have observed it happen unfailingly each year.

We all know that if March comes in like a lion, it goes out like a lamb, and vice versa. And "cast not a clout till May be out" because "in the middle of May comes the tail of winter," according to the wise.

"Sow seeds in the afternoon," they say, "as the earth draws in."

PLANTING WISDOM

The phases of the moon are closely associated with fertility, and their importance in planting lore occurs so often all over the world that it is hard to dismiss this as superstition.

The Moon

Traditional wisdom has it that the time when you put the seed into the ground is of utmost importance for its success: Root crops should be sown when the moon is waning, while a new moon is auspicious for crops that grow above ground, so that the waxing moon influences them. I am convinced that there is something in this—as is an Indian friend who has the greenest fingers of anyone I know.

"Sow corn when the moon is waxing, never when it is waning," goes an English saying. The exceptions are watery plants such as cucumbers and summer squashes, which are best sown at full moon. A gardener in Shropshire, England, who had worked the land all his life, quoted this:

Cut all things or gather, the moon in the wane,
But sow in increasing, or give it its bane.

The mother of an Indian friend who lives in Jaipur told me that onions are much larger and better nourished if sown during a waning moon. She also said to plant potatoes with a rising tide so they grow with it, and to sow all kinds of leguminous vegetables with the moon in Cancer.

A Dutch friend's grandmother has a saying: "Trees are not to be grafted the Moon waning, or not to be seen."

The Seasons

Mr. Williams used to say:

Drunk or sober,
Sow wheat in October

and

Who in January sows oats,
Gets gold and groats

He would always sow garlic and fava beans on the shortest day, advice I successfully followed in the days when I had a vegetable patch. Sow onions, he said, on St. Gregory's Day (March 12th) for a good crop. To do well, shallots should be sown on December 21st, along with the garlic, and pulled on the longest day (June 21st). Other pearls of wisdom included sowing potatoes when the yellow wagtail arrives in spring, usually March.

The Weather and Time of Day

Thomas Hyll, in his mid-sixteenth-century *The Sowing and Care of Seedlings*, tells us that "seed must be sown on a mild, clear day and not when a north wind is blowing, nor the day verie cold, for in such seasons and dayes (as all the skilful report) the earth as then timorous and fast shut, hardly receyueth and nourisheth the seedes committed to it."

Sometimes, however, country lore contradicts itself—hedging its bets perhaps: "Sow dry and set in the wet," yet "sow beans in the mud and they'll grow like a wood" and "sow in a slop, 'twill be heavy at top." "If you can squeeze a handful of soil together and it sticks, it is too wet to plant." And "Sow barley when the sloe is white."

Sow seeds in the afternoon when the earth is drawing in, and don't water newly set plants too late in the day—"they don't like to be shivering in their shoes," as my gardener tells me.

Superstitions

Sowing seed can be a wasteful and expensive business when birds and other creatures think that we are providing for them: The son of a gardener in Lincolnshire, England, quoted his father's sayings:

Four seeds in a hole:
One for the rook, one for the crow,
One to rot and one to grow

and

One for the birds
One for the mice
Two for the master

Thomas Hyll, the sixteenth-century English gardener, suggests mixing seeds with soot before planting them, to protect them from birds and other predators. This is surely worth a try to avoid disappointment.

For hundreds of years, almanacs all over the world, such as Foulsham's *Old Moore's Almanack* in England, have given the best planting and sowing times for the garden.

GARDEN PESTS

There are some plants that act as natural insecticides: Chives and parsley deter greenfly, onion fly, and carrot fly; marigolds repel the Colorado potato beetle; and nasturtiums discourage most aphids, beetles, and squash bugs. Garlic keeps aphids away. Hyssop repels blackfly; pyrethrum controls aphids and spider mites; *Euphorbia lathyrus* repels moles; and onions planted among lettuce repel rabbits.

Planting "plant decoys" is a smart move: Whitefly loves nicotiana and aphids love basil, so use them as sacrificial plants near other, more precious ones. And encourage predators: Create cover in your damp spots for toads and frogs because they eat pests, and encourage ladybugs by planting *Limnanthes*.

Slugs and Snails

Kate, my editor, remembers how her grandmother used to invert half-grapefruit shells with little "doors" cut into them, to entice slugs in. In they came, whereupon grandmother would pick them up and crush them between her fingers. According to Kate, she still uses this infallible technique. Kate's mother doesn't bother with the grapefruit, but simply dispatches slugs between her fingers while carrying on a conversation! If you prefer a less tactile method, kill slugs by sprinkling them with salt. You can protect

Invert half-grapefruit shells with little "doors" cut into them.

plants from slugs and snails with a ring of sharp gravel around the bottom. This "hurts their feet," according to the gardening expert Hugh Johnson. My gardener friend Barbara sprinkles crushed, toasted eggshells around the plants—but above all she encourages her toads to do the work for her!

A friend in the village sinks a bowl of beer into the ground: The slugs and snails fall in and drown—happy! They are repelled by a mulch of oak leaves or wood ash, and will also crawl under wooden boards where you can catch them unaware.

My mother's gardener used to strip the leaves from Brussels sprouts and lay them on the ground to distract slugs and snails from the plants. He also laid prickly thistles, bracken, or thorny evergreens near affected plants. He used to swear that if you put slices of turnip down for slugs and snails, they would die from overeating.

Ants

Ants are repelled by growing pennyroyal, spearmint, or tansy. Such pests travel up tree trunks, and you can stop them with a band of grease. Throw boiling water on the nest, says Barbara. A medieval gardener suggests throwing sawdust from oak planks onto the ant hill. According to *Le Ménagier de Paris* (1393), the ants will then die or leave when it next rains, because the sawdust retains the water. But a Chinese friend, whose father was a fruit farmer, told me that, since ants eat the larvae of fruit flies, he used to make little bamboo bridges for the ants to travel from tree to tree!

Flies (aphids, blackfly, whitefly, and so on)

Ladybird beetles, or ladybugs, are one of nature's most efficient predators of flies. Ladybugs particularly love *Artemesia* and *Limnanthes*, so if you grow some for them you will be well rewarded. Or, you can simply spray flies with soapy water. Flies dislike spearmint, stinging nettles, and nasturtiums, so these plants will act as deterrents.

An old gardener in Essex, England, told me of a natural—as opposed to chemical—way to get rid of the aphids that plague the garden during the summer months: An infusion of rhubarb leaves, used as a spray. (This remedy is known in Australia, too).

It works. Put 2 pounds rhubarb leaves in a large pan with enough water to cover. Bring to a boil and simmer for 2 minutes. The leaves disintegrate quickly. Leave to cool, then strain. Store the infusion in bottles, in a cool place, and use instead of chemical sprays. You can also make an effective spray by soaking stinging nettles in rainwater for three weeks; this spray kills lice and aphids too (see page 69).

The same gardener told me to spray cabbages with sea water to deter caterpillars, but I have found a more whimsical remedy:

> *Go into the garden at dawn on Sunday and on bare knees say three Ave Marias and three Paternosters in reverence to the Trinity, then take a cabbage or some other leaf eaten by caterpillars and put inside two or three of them, and say "Caterpillars come with me to Mass," then take the whole thing along to church, and before listening to the Mass let it fall. After this the caterpillars will disappear from the garden—this is not a joke, it has been proved to work and its practice is still in use.*
> Girolamo Firenzuola, sixteenth century

Deer

There's not a lot you can do to keep deer out of a garden, apart from erecting a very tall fence all the way around. However, a Norwegian friend had this solution: Go to the hairdresser and get a bag of human hair, fill small cheesecloth bags with it, and scatter them between your plants. Deer so dislike the smell of anything human that they will go elsewhere. The only trouble is that the hair must be fresh, and replaced frequently.

Mildew

My mother's gardener, Mr. Williams, used horsetail tea to combat mildew. Take two large handfuls of horsetail (*Equisetum* sp.), and put into a large pan with water to cover. Bring slowly to a boil and simmer very gently for 20 minutes with the lid on. Leave in a cool place for 24 hours and then strain. Dilute with two parts water and use as a spray. Liquid seaweed also gets rid of mildew, and chive tea is effective against mildew on gooseberry plants.

Birds, Spider Mites, and Blight

If you scatter powdered garlic on the ground, it stops birds from eating nearby plants. Try this near your fruit bushes. Simplest of all,

Mildew on garden plants can be eliminated with horsetail tea.

get a predator on the job: Have a cat patrol nearby, says Barbara. Garlic tea controls blight on potatoes and tomatoes, and spider mites can be easily detered with a spray of garlic and chili:

Chili Garlic Spray

3 hot green chilies
3 garlic cloves
3–4 teaspoons dishwashing liquid
3 cups water

Process the chilies and garlic finely in a small blender. Put into a bowl with the dishwashing liquid and add the water. Leave to stand for 24 hours, then strain. Add another 1/4 cup of water to dilute, then pour into a bottle with a spray nozzle.

Soil and Composting

A gardener friend with a propensity to poetry tells me that adding chemicals to the soil makes it deaf to the music of the spheres. She is convinced that chemicals are toxic and the effects detrimental. She inherited a famous garden in Hertfordshire, England, and has used totally organic methods to maintain—successfully—the stunning plantings. Paths meander through great mature trees, and beautiful shrubs make a backdrop for herbaceous flowering plants in spring and summer. As you wander you come across a pond, a summer house, a thicket, and everywhere is designed for a vista. Her mother-in-law told her how to get rid of weeds on the many paved areas: Sprinkle salt between the cracks. She also uses salt on the asparagus bed after it dies back, to keep the weeds down. Practical experience, hard work, and traditional country ways and wisdom have contributed to the creation of a work of art.

Soil needs nourishment, which it gets from compost or humus—organic matter from decomposing plant and animal remains. So allow stinging nettles in your garden, as they stimulate the formation of humus, the blackish-brown soil that you can see around a patch of nettles. You can also use seaweed extract as a soil conditioner.

Soil also needs trace elements to enable plants to absorb valuable minerals from the soil. Nitrogen is released into the soil by growing legumes, and clovers are the best fixers, along with blue lupin, alfalfa, peas, fenugreek, and beans. Tobacco plants and tansy both accumulate potassium.

Leaf litter protects the topsoil and is an invaluable soil food, providing minerals and by-products that feed the microlife of the soil and, indirectly, the plants themselves. Microlife enhancement means enrichment: Ancient wisdom says to keep the ground covered with weeds in winter and the worms will turn the soil for you underneath. In addition, growing yarrow and valerian encourages worms and other creatures. Add some soot to the soil to enrich it and break it up. If your soil is very alkaline, give it plenty of moisture and organic material.

Weeds are not necessarily always an evil. There are positive ways of looking at these much-maligned inhabitants of the garden, which have an advocate in the poet Ralph Waldo Emerson: "What is a weed?" he declaims. Answer: "A plant whose virtues have not yet been discovered." Some weeds are valuable mineral accumulators and thus can enrich the soil. By the law of return, they feed the soil population, which in its cycle builds up fertility. Insect remains are of special value because the chitin that forms the body armor is believed to improve plants' disease-resistance.

Other weeds aerate the soil and help with drainage—for example, dandelion and coltsfoot break up heavy clay. Some are capable of lessening the impact of heavy rain on the ground. They provide shelter and food for small animals whose excreta help fertilize the soil. Hoeing weeds and leaving them to rot helps to conserve moisture, as well as releasing nutrients into the soil as they decompose.

Liquid nettle manure poured onto the soil will promote plant growth and protect plants against unhealthy conditions. Cut the nettles, cover them with water, and allow to decompose for three weeks. This liquid can also be used as a spray for foliar feed. Or, as a gardener in Hertfordshire, England, told me, soak a sack of horse manure in water overnight, and use to enrich the soil.

Compost

The art of composting is also a science, one which my friend Barbara, both plantswoman and gardener, has perfected. A stream runs through her beautiful garden, which is bordered by a cowslip

Nettles stimulate the formation of humus and are an excellent companion plant for herbs. You can make a liquid manure from nettles.

Seaweed products release trace elements slowly back into the soil. They help resistance to disease and stimulate microlife in the soil.

meadow. The vegetable garden, edged with a young yew hedge, is next to a formal rose garden full of old-fashioned roses. Her knowledge and understanding of how plants and soil work are the foundations of this exceptional garden. Set behind a wild flower area in one corner is a row of compost bins, all neatly cared for and surrounded by comfrey plants to layer in with the garden and household waste. Composting is an art form here: She dismisses the over-use of artificial fertilizers since they do not give the soil the structure it needs, and she feels that you can over-feed with chemicals and upset the balance of nature. If you work with rotted

compost, nature does it for you, and she just forks it into the topsoil at the rate of one bucket per square yard. The Chinese use manure-based hot beds to warm the soil so that they can grow vegetables all year round, using both human and animal manure. They also make hot beds in greenhouses—using animal manure only.

Barbara separates herbaceous waste, weeds, and household waste from grass clippings and leaves, which are kept to rot separately, while tired topsoil, long grass, and other bits and pieces are mixed with farmyard manure to provide phosphates, potash, and nitrogen as well as humus.

Of her 14 compost bins, four are for household waste, four for grass clippings (in wire-mesh cages to allow air to circulate), two for leaves (best chopped by the mower or a shredder, rather than left whole), and four for miscellaneous bits and pieces. They are turned regularly with a long-handled hay fork to let in air, which activates the process of decomposition. There is nothing like compost, she declares; it is so rich in nutrients. Everything you take from the ground you have to put back. Everything natural can return to be recycled. She uses farmyard manure, more for its structure than for the nutrients—roots need air and moisture, so dig it in for an ideal growing medium. It makes a beautiful loam.

Compost Plants

Most annual weeds (except ones that have seeded) can go on to the compost heap—they contain valuable minerals, which return to the soil and replenish it. Exceptions are perennial weeds such as couch grass and bindweed, which will only multipy in the compost. And don't put on any weed seeds, as they will simply remain dormant until the compost is used. Some of the best compost plants include alfalfa, dandelion, bark of oak, chamomile, valerian, comfrey, spinach, sunflowers, yarrow, and as many herbs as possible (except wormwood). Yarrow is a fast activator of compost.

Stinging nettles (the leaves only, not the roots) make an excellent addition to the compost heap because they are so rich in minerals. They help fermentation and are an excellent soil conditioner. Barbara layers them in between other waste, including bonfire ash, which provides iron, and she recommends lots of thin layers in the bin. You can use the friable humus around nettle patches as straight compost.

Comfrey is rich in potash, nitrogen, and phosphates, so you can lay the wilted leaves on the soil as compost, particularly between rows of potatoes and around tomato plants in the greenhouse. Or put layers of comfrey between other compost: Barbara grows comfrey next to the bins so it is always handy. You can also make an excellent liquid manure from comfrey in the same way as nettles (see page 51).

Seaweed products release trace elements slowly back into the soil and make a gentle fertilizer. They help resistance to disease and stimulate microlife in the soil.

Don't put woody or thorny material onto the heap as it doesn't decompose—especially roses, which may harbor mildew or black spot. Conifers and other evergreens don't break down easily either. Don't put earthy roots on the compost heap: The earth will lower the temperature, and the roots of Brussels sprouts and greens may cause fungus problems. Potato tops may carry blight, so it is better to dispose of them.

Don't place your compost heap under conifers—their essential oils (used as a base for turpentine) retard fermentation. Never start compost on grass—remove the sod first since it also delays fermentation. Birch and elder trees seem to have a beneficial effect on compost bins nearby.

A gardener who opens her garden to the public told me that she digs in bits of old carpet and pillows, which rot away and enrich the soil. Even old shoes will do, she tells me: The protein in the leather decomposes to produce nitrogen. Her annual herbaceous display of flowers and shrubs is heavenly. She gives her onions a top-dressing of soot during the growing season, and her magnificent lilies are nourished with wood ash. Her delphiniums, hollyhocks, and sunflowers all benefit from liquid lunches of beer every two weeks, and her leeks love Guinness! Slightly milky water is also a good manure for herbaceous plants.

An Indian friend with a green thumb mulches her roses with all the tea leaves from the household, and sometimes crushed eggshells. Her mother swears by bananas: The skins are a rich source of magnesium, sulfur, silica, and sodium, trace elements that ensure a magnificent show of flowers. She layers them just under the surface of the soil. I know several gardeners who water their roses with tea, claiming that this increases their scent and encourages healthy growth.

It is no surprise, says Barbara, that inaccessible vegetable gardens are so fertile. She observes that they have no bathroom facilities nearby, so a certain amount of "recycled cider" returns to the soil. Slurry from sewage is a fine fertilizer for farmland, she says—the idea of throwing the slurry away into the sea or rivers is sacrilege to her. In her garden the walnut tree stands above their septic tank, and it is a huge, healthy tree with lustrous leaves and abundant fruit. The grass in the meadow, above the septic field from the house, is lush and verdant. "The answer lies in the soil" indeed.

COMPANION PLANTING

Some of the great successes of gardening lore are to be found in the realm of companion planting. In Bulgaria, where vast quantities of roses are grown commercially for attar and rose oil, they are planted alongside onion and garlic crops. It has been shown that inter-cropping roses with garlic produces a far stronger perfume in the rose, an effect you can also get by fertilizing your rose bush with compost made from garlic and onion refuse. All the alliums have fungicidal properties and attract beneficial insects. Aphids detest garlic.

Companion planting works in various ways. Some plants provide shelter from wind and sun, others give off root and leaf secretions that affect their neighbors, either beneficially or adversely. Some plants may improve the soil by accumulating minerals, or by providing green manure or humus. Some may repel harmful insects and other pests, or act as decoys, or they may support insect populations that are beneficial to neighboring plants. Or, they may attract birds that prey on these pests. Some plants are found to reduce the amount of fungal and other diseases in nearby plants, due to their chemical secretions.

Growing sweet peas up sunflowers is a good example of symbiosis: The sweet peas release nitrogen into the soil, while the sunflowers provide support and shelter. But there are examples of bad companions, too: Basil hates rue, tomatoes dislike fennel and kohlrabi, the crucifers and tomatoes don't grow well together. Garlic, onions, and shallots inhibit the growth of beans and peas, and pumpkins dislike potatoes. Never grow raspberries with blackberries, or radishes with hyssop. Tomatoes near potatoes can stunt growth, and the potato loses resistance to blight. Cabbage doesn't like the proximity of strawberries or early potatoes.

Herbs generally help plants growing around them, with the exception of fennel and wormwood, which need to be grown in isolation.

Good Companions

Alliums are strongly scented and discourage pests from attacking nearby plants. Since they also accumulate sulfur, they have a fungicidal effect. They are particularly beneficial for carrots, tomatoes, and lettuce.

Asparagus and tomatoes make excellent companions because root secretions from the asparagus kills *trichodorus*, a nematode that attacks tomato roots. In turn, the tomato guards against asparagus beetle. Parsley also protects against this beetle, so this trio thrives together.

Beans—especially fava beans—and potatoes grow well together, and potatoes repel the bean beetle. All leguminous species fix nitrogen in the soil, which helps not only potatoes but also carrots, cauliflower, beets, cucumber, and cabbage.

Cabbage thrives near aromatic herbs, whose leaf and root exudations deter pests. This is especially true of mint, which repels the white cabbage butterfly. Tomatoes and celery help cabbages in a similar way, by deterring the cabbage butterfly.

Cauliflower grows well with peas, onions, potatoes, and celery. Celery deters the cabbage butterfly, and celery and leeks grown together attract many beneficial insects, especially predatory wasps.

Chives keep fungal diseases down, and next to carrots help them grow healthy and exceptionally tasty. They discourage black spot on roses and scab on apple, and guard against aphids on tomatoes.

Chamomile grown next to peppermint makes both plants produce more essential oil. Chamomile accumulates potassium and sulfur and is a host to hoverflies and wasps, so grown next to cabbage and onions improves them in both yield and flavor. Chamomile's beneficial health-giving presence is well known to country folk, who have nicknamed it the "plant doctor," because planted near sick plants it helps them recover.

Aromatic herbs, in general, help plants grown around them, since their root and/or leaf exudations make them distasteful to pests.

You see few weeds around rosemary, rue, and wormwood because these plants inhibit the germination of seeds. The secretions of wormwood are so strong that nothing thrives nearby, so it needs to be grown in isolation.

Foxglove has a benign influence on most plants, stimulating their growth by accumulating potassium, iron and calcium, silica, and manganese to high levels in their leaves, which then drop and act as green manure to the soil around. It is especially good for pine trees.

Lettuce is a good companion for chervil and dill since the herbs act as a decoy to aphids and other predatory insects.

Limnanthes douglasii, a famous bee plant, is excellent next to shrubs and berries. It attracts pollinators as well as predators such as hoverflies. Insect remains and by-products add nutrients to the soil.

Mexican or African marigolds (*Tagetes* sp.) have a root secretion that kills minute parasitic worms known as nematodes. Grown near the greenhouse, they keep whitefly off tomato plants, since the odor of leaves and blossoms acts as an insect-repellent. They also attract predatory hoverflies. They are excellent for keeping pests off roses.

Nasturtiums secrete root and leaf exudations, which make them distasteful to pests. They help to keep whitefly from the greenhouse, aphids from broccoli, and woolly aphids from the apple tree. Radishes thrive near nasturtiums.

Onions repel carrot fly and carrots repel onion fly, so grown in alternate rows both thrive: The respective flies get confused! Onions go well with crucifers, tomatoes, and lettuce since the strong smell keeps off pests. Next to strawberries, they prevent mold on the fruit.

Peas, with their leguminous gift of fixing nitrogen in the soil, thrive next to radishes and all root crops, and radishes and chervil like each other. Nasturtiums nearby keeps pests away from radishes.

Radishes, planted near beans, eggplant, squash, and tomatoes, will discourage mites and beetles.

Scarlet runner beans and corn thrive together since the beans release nitrogen back into the soil, which the corn uses, and the beans use the corn to climb up. Corn, peas, and crucifers make a good trio; potatoes like the proximity of corn; and all squashes, including pumpkin, thrive with corn, an early discovery of Native Americans.

Salsify helps leeks and carrots, repelling the carrot root fly.

Spinach and strawberries love each other. Spinach adds saponins to the soil, which binds the humus together with coarser materials, helping it to retain moisture.

Yarrow helps all the aromatic herbs and is beneficial to all vegetables: A border of yarrow around the vegetable plot makes for a healthy harvest. It attracts worms and other creatures whose remains are of special value to soil life: Chitin from their body armor is believed to help the plants' resistance to disease.

BEES, LADYBUGS, AND BUTTERFLIES

Bees

There are five hundred bees for every human being on earth. We depend on them for crop pollination, so they are intrinsic to our survival on the planet. No wonder that bees have acquired such a special status in the eyes of country people who rear them, and who for centuries have found myriad uses for their honey and wax. They are welcome visitors to any garden, cross-pollinating as they collect nectar. One of the many staggering facts about bees is that it takes the nectar of one and a half million flowers to make a single jar of honey (see more about bees on page 146).

Beekeeping has been a part of rural economies worldwide for generations, and now thrives on a global commercial scale. Bees are held in awe for their industry and organization by all who work with them. Much garden lore has grown up around them, as beekeepers watched them at work and established a relationship with the colonies in their hives.

A committed beekeeper in our village, a lady in her eighties, told me that catching a swarm of bees is only any good at the beginning of the season, and that later swarms will not settle in and produce good amounts of honey:

> *A swarm in May is worth a load of hay*
> *A swarm in June is worth a silver spoon*
> *A swarm in July is not worth a fly*

"Telling the bees" is another widespread tradition, claimed by all who use it to have some mysterious truth to it: If you don't "tell" them, you lose them:

> *Marriage, birth and buryin'*
> *News across the seas,*
> *All you're sad and merry in*
> *You must tell the bees*

If you don't, they fly away to seek the departed, or die themselves. Furthermore, all hives must be turned or moved at the moment their dead owner's corpse leaves the house for burial.

Ladybugs

There are five thousand species of ladybird beetle, or ladybug, throughout the world. In any garden they are nature's best method of controlling aphids, scale insects, and mites. So efficient are these predators that when the California citrus industry was threatened with disaster in 1886 by an outbreak of cottony-cushion scale (*Icerya purchasi*), the Australian ladybug (*Vedalia*) was imported to deal with it. Within a year the scales had all but disappeared. So, always encourage ladybugs. They do a wonderful job on the aphids in my garden, and I encourage them in my conservatory, too.

Butterflies

Butterflies, beautiful as they are, are more of a mixed blessing. Although they are important pollinators, as they visit flowers for nectar, the larvae, or caterpillars, will chomp their way through vast amounts of foliage, stems, flowers, and even roots. There are over one hundred thousand species of *Lepidoptera* worldwide, and they occur on every continent except Antarctica. The largest family groups are found globally, and agriculture, forestry, food, fabrics, and fodder are all prone to the foraging of the various larvae. Yet, quite possibly, mankind also benefits from much unrecognized weed-eating by caterpillars. It is incontestable that we benefit in the garden, as with bees, from flower pollination by the adult butterflies. A few butterflies feed on overripe fruit, so if you wish to attract the Camberwell beauty (rare) or the red admiral (found virtually the world over), leave your windfalls on the ground.

You seldom see butterflies flying in dull weather, and this is because they use solar energy to energize their wings for flight. Hence the common sight of a butterfly "basking" in the sun before take-off.

Leave a corner full of nettles in the garden in which the red admiral can lay its eggs.

Plants for a Butterfly Garden

I talked to a butterfly gardener in his greenhouse, which was full of lantana, the prime butterfly plant, which produces so much nectar. Butterflies taste with their feet, he informed me! Around us flowered plumbago, bougainvillea, and heliotrope, pentas, cestrum, and jasmine. Hibiscus and morning glory intermingled, and a giant passion flower filled one corner of the greenhouse.

For the garden, he advised leaving a corner full of nettles for the red admiral to lay its eggs. His wild garden included scabious, plantain, foxglove, mallow, cornflower, and some giant thistles. There was ragged robin in abundance and valerian scrambling along the walls. A patch of origanum attracted hordes of meadow browns, peacocks and small tortoiseshells. The commas loved the rotting fruit under the apple tree, and his lavender was covered with cabbage butterflies in high summer.

Honeysuckle

Among other herbaceous butterfly plants he recommended aubretia, buddleia, honesty, sedum, Michaelmas daisy, sweet rocket, tobacco plant, yellow alyssum, goldenrod, pinks, hyssop, lilac, honeysuckle, forget-me-not, and violas.

Controlling Caterpillars

The most ecologically friendly way to control caterpillars is to hand-pick them off, rather than to use toxic sprays, which may well do unseen damage to plants and friendly insects. At worst, use a plant-based insecticide, such as the rhubarb spray on page 49. Some gardeners place a strip of foil around the root stem of cabbage seedlings to protect them from cabbage-fly larvae. Sprinkling crumbled mothballs over the soil around carrots and planting mothballs with potatoes does much to ward off both larvae of all kinds and other pests.

SOME GARDEN FLOWER LORE

More in the garden grows
Than the gardener sows
Spanish Proverb

The earliest known medicines and antiseptics came from herbs and flowering plants, and so before their properties were understood scientifically they were believed to be magic. Much fascinating country lore accumulated over the ages, some based on their practical virtues, some imbued with superstition. Flower and tree lore is an enchanting combination of the two and in its immensity fills many volumes. Most famous, white wild flowers bring bad luck if they are brought into the house, and there are omens associated with flowers blooming out of season. The doctrine of signatures dictated many folk cures, and divination with plants was widely practiced. Certain saints' days in the calendar have particular flowers associated with them, and rituals were enacted around the cultivation of many plants.

Here's flowers for you;
Hot lavender, mints, savory, marjoram;
The marigold, that goes to bed i' the sun;
And with him rises weeping.
William Shakespeare, *A Winter's Tale* (1610–11)

You can use the bright flowers of nasturtium to decorate a summer salad, and eat the peppery-tasting leaves.

Marigold Petal Salad

At the height of summer there are plenty of marigolds to spare for the table. Combine the petals with some nasturtium leaves and you have a deliciously unusual salad.

SERVES 2–3

1 head red leaf lettuce, washed and spun dry

1 handful nasturtium leaves, washed and shredded roughly

6–8 cherry tomatoes, halved

⅓ cup toasted sunflower seeds

1 handful marigold petals

DRESSING:

2 tablespoons olive oil

2 tablespoons raspberry vinegar

1 tablespoon soy sauce

Combine all the salad ingredients, reserving a scattering of marigold petals for the top. Mix the dressing ingredients together and toss thoroughly with the salad. Garnish with the remaining petals, and it is ready to serve.

Marigold

The marigold opens as the sun rises and closes at sunset. In Wales, they say that if the marigold does not open before seven, there will be thunder during the day. Some country people say that if you pick marigolds you will bring on a thunderstorm.

The marigold is a symbol of constancy in love. It was used in wedding bouquets and love potions, and has local names of "Summer's Bride" and "Husbandman's Dial." Used in love divination, marigolds were dried with summer herbs, powdered, and made into an ointment with honey and vinegar. A young woman would annoint herself before going to bed, with an invocation to Saint Luke to dream of her true love.

Marigolds were believed to reduce fevers and even to repel the plague if you carried them about with you in the streets. The petals have long been used to tint hair golden-red, and a conserve was recommended by some herbalists to alleviate depression.

The marigold is a symbol of constancy and love.

Aconite is highly poisonous. Arrows dipped in the juice were said to kill wolves, hence its alternative name of wolfsbane.

Broom has both sinister and beneficial qualities: A besom of blossoming broom would "sweep the head of the house away," whereas the plant was a symbol of good luck and plenty and made its appearance at country weddings, tied with ribbons.

Box sprigs were often placed at the door of a house at which there was a funeral. Each of the mourners would pick one up and later drop it into the open grave. Box was often used in well-dressing.

Carnations have been cultivated for over two thousand years, and their heavy scent was used in Elizabethan times to replace expensive cloves. To wear a carnation meant that the wearer was betrothed and other suitors might as well give up their pursuit.

Celandine was used as a cure for jaundice —by sympathetic magic because of its bright yellow color. I have a friend in Suffolk, England, who uses it on warts with success; a grandmother in Oxford has also done so for years. Just drop the fresh juice from the stem onto the wart and let it dry. Continue the treatment until the wart disappears.

Cherry: A good crop brings good fortune —"a cherry year a merry year." A friend of the family, who lived in Switzerland for many years says that traditionally a new mother eats the first cherries to ensure a good crop for the rest of the season.

Cornflowers were reputed to blunt the blade of a reaper's sickle, and were once used as an ingredient of ink. Watercolorists still use the juice from the flowers, mixed with alum (see page 66). A courting man could divine his love life: He put a cornflower in his pocket, and only if it lived would he marry his current girlfriend.

Daffodils: The Welsh say that whoever finds the first flower will have more gold than silver in the coming year. To point at a daffodil may stop it from flowering.

Forget-me-not was useful against dog and snake bites! Steel tempered with its juice was said to be hard enough to cut stone. Give a forget-me-not to someone starting a journey on February 29th.

Lilac is unlucky in the house, especially white lilac (as are many white flowers). It is associated with death. Also, it is unlucky to find a five-petaled lilac blossom.

Lily, symbol of virginity, purity, and innocence, is a favorite flower at weddings and funerals. The madonna lily will only grow for a good woman, or where the mistress is master. A ninety-year-old woman, who spent some years in the Belgian Congo in her youth and had some hair-raising experiences in the jungle, told me that the pygmies wore flame lilies in their belts to guard themselves against being eaten by a lion!

Marigold is a symbol of constancy in love, and a flower of the sun. A marigold conserve or tea will allay depression, and a flowerhead rubbed onto a wasp or bee sting is an instant cure. Thunder may follow if you pick marigolds. Boiling the flowers produces a yellow dye, and the petals can be used in salad (see page 59). The volatile oil is a wound-healer.

Mulberry: When the leaves appear there will be no more frosts. This was a sacred tree in ancient Rome—and Burma! In China, the mulberry is a symbol of industry.

Peach is a symbol of immortality throughout the Far East.

Pear is a slow-growing tree, so "plant pears for your heirs." It is considered a powerful charm against evil.

Periwinkle has long been thought to be a magical plant, and now the Madagascan periwinkle (*Vinca rosea*) is an important medicinal source of drugs used to treat leukemia.

Plum: "A plum year is a dumb year" my grandfather used to say. A Welsh woman tells me that if a plum tree blooms in December it foretells a death. But to dream of plums is a good omen.

Quince is a symbol of love. To dream of quinces means you will be cured of any sickness.

Snowdrops are a symbol of hope and purity, yet in some places they are thought to be unlucky in the house. A single snowdrop is an omen of death.

Strawberries: A Norwegian friend tells the story of Frigga, goddess of married love, who is said to have hidden the souls of dead children in strawberries, to smuggle them into paradise. Strawberries are dedicated to the Virgin Mary.

Violets: If they bloom early it means death or an epidemic, but to dream of violets brings good fortune. Worn around the neck, they prevent drunkenness. I found a "violet reviver" in a book of *Grandmothers' Recipes* of 1901, which claimed that boiling violet leaves in water and applying the liquid, on lint as a compress, was a cure for cancer (see page 119).

Yarrow is called *herbe aux charpentiers* because it was supposed to heal instantly wounds made by carpenters' tools. Achilles was said to have cured his warriors' wounds with its leaves, hence its botanical name, *Achillea millefolium*. It has local names of "woundwort" and "nosebleed."

Yew: Plant a tree at the southwest corner of the house for protection. Yew is the tree of immortality, being a long-lived evergreen that regenerates however much you prune it. The reason that it is planted in churchyards is because all parts of the tree are poisonous: The volatile oil taxine can cause immediate death to children, cattle, and sheep, and is therefore kept inaccessible to them. The alkaloid taxol is also an important constituent in an anti-cancer drug. In England you can offer your yew clippings as raw material for its processing to the companies that make the drug.

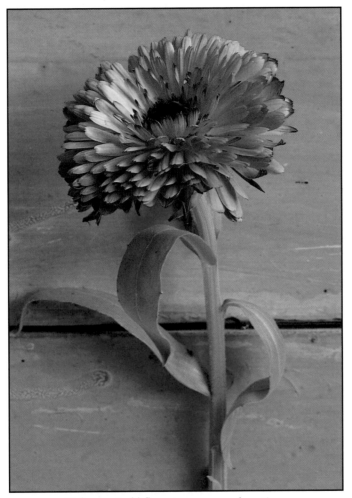

Rub a marigold flower on a wasp or bee sting.

NATURAL
BEAUTY

Natural beauty care is grounded in centuries of tradition: The legendary beauty of Helen of Troy was not based on industrial synthetics. Cleopatra bathed in milk. Egyptian women perfumed their hair with marjoram, rubbed pomegranate juice into their skins, and used rhubarb juice to counteract oily hair and highlight the color. Nature has always provided the human body with the oils, dyes, herbs, scents, and emollients needed to repair and beautify it. By means of steams and face packs, compresses and sweet baths, oil treatments and hair washes, the body is beautified the natural way. Scientific analysis today is showing "old wives' tales" to be true: The products work for reasons that we can now explain. The wisdom of our ancestors—usually female—is affirmed.

The advantage of making your own products is that you know exactly what has gone into them, and you can use pure substances that in the end are far cheaper than buying commercial products of similar quality. They are widely available throughout the world. Beeswax, cocoa butter, essential oils, and good-quality base oils, mixed with infusions of fresh herbs, will give your body a new look and feel. And it is all quite simple to do, as my friend Mary, an aromatherapist, confirmed. Mary's grandmother was Scottish, and her mother lived in Australia for many years before returning to England.

Mary was an only child and her mother paid great attention to her long blonde hair. As a child she would squirm and rebel as she had her hair "polished": Her mother would take a pure silk scarf and stroke the newly-washed hair with it until it shone like spun gold. She told her daughter that your hair should "squeak" when you run your fingers down it—meaning there was no residue of soap left after shampooing. This, she assures me, is the origin of "squeaky clean." And to get rid of split ends on this fair head of hair, her mother used to twist or braid it, and singe the ends with a candle to take them off and seal the ends. Her hair never caught fire.

Mary had a country childhood, on a farm surrounded by woods and streams, with a full kitchen garden and huge barns full of chicken and geese. She learned about natural products from her mother in her childhood, and then traveled the world at a young age, through Turkey to Thailand, ending up in the Bahamas for five years. She picked up tips and customs as she went, and has incorporated this knowledge into her professional practice. Her tips are practical and down to earth, yet infused with her love of the countryside and things natural. Her practical wisdom pervades all the recipes for natural beauty care—skin and hair, hands and teeth, eyes and body—and shows how we can look after our bodies in the natural way that women have used for centuries.

INGREDIENTS FOR HOME BEAUTY CARE

Many of the oils and other substances used in this chapter may not be familiar. Here is what they are, and where to find them.

Alum is a whitish transparent mineral salt that acts as an astringent. Available from pharmacies.

Ambergris is a grayish resin of waxy consistency secreted from the intestines of the sperm whale. It has been used in perfumery for centuries.

Borax is a salt (acid borate of sodium), used to remove grease and dirt. Available from pharmacies.

Benzoin, tincture of: Also known as "the frankincense of Sumatra," this is a balsamic resin obtained from the styrax tree, which grows in Indonesia and Vietnam. A tincture is a solution of the essential oil. Used as an antioxidant and fixative. Gum benjamin, as it is also known, crystallizes in shiny prisms and forms a brittle mass of whitish tears embedded in a translucent matrix. Available from pharmacies.

Almond oil is pressed from the seed of *Prunus amygdalus*, native of West Asia but extensively cultivated. Almond oil is a good emollient for all skin types and a useful base oil containing protein and many vitamins and minerals. Widely available from pharmacies and health-food stores.

Avocado oil is a heavy oil excellent for facial tissues and older skins. Its proteins, vitamins A and D, and lecithin are easily absorbed into the skin. Widely available from health-food stores or pharmacies.

Beeswax, in its pure form, is available in blocks from some furniture and antiques stores, and is very inexpensive for the quality ingredient that it is. It is an excellent moisturizer and enricher when used as a base for skin cream.

Castor oil comes from a shrub, *Ricinus communis*, native to India. Its prolific oval seeds are pressed for a viscid, colorless oil, which is an excellent skin emollient when mixed with other oils. Soothing for the skin and eyes.

Coconut oil is widely available. A rich oil pressed from the white meat of the coconut, it is often used to soothe sunburn.

Cocoa butter is a solidified oil (theobroma) used in many skin cream preparations. In its pure form it can be obtained from pharmacies, but it is fairly expensive.

Essential oils are the concentrated oils of flowers, leaves, seeds, bark, and roots of aromatic plants. They are very powerful and need to be used sparingly, usually in a carrier or a base oil such as almond. The quality can be good, bad, or indifferent, according to the country of origin, method of extraction, and manufacture. They are sometimes synthesized, and often adulterated. To be sure of purity and quality, buy authentic oils from accredited aromatherapists and health-food stores.

Glycerin is a colorless syrup obtained from animal and vegetable oils and fats by saponification. It is widely available from pharmacies.

Lanolin is oil washed from the wool of sheep after shearing. It acts as a protective lubricant and is an excellent softener and moisturizer. Use anhydrous lanolin, which is not mixed with extra water. Available from pharmacies.

Orange-flower water is prepared from orange blossoms. Available from specialty stores and pharmacies. You can make your own with dried blossoms (see page 94).

Pure alcohol is rectified spirits. Available from pharmacies.

Rose water is available from specialty stores and pharmacies, or you can make your own version—undistilled—from scented rose petals. It is an important ingredient of many cosmetics.

Wheat-germ oil comes from the germ of the wheat grain and is highly nutritious, containing vitamins B and E—the latter being *the* skin vitamin. It is also antioxidant and helps stabilize essential oils, making the preparation last longer. Widely available from health-food stores or from pharmacies.

Witch hazel helps to preserve lotions and creams, and is excellent for rough skin, pimples and blemishes, or minor skin irritations. It is extracted from the leaves and bark of *Hamamelis virginiana* and is available from pharmacies. Mix with rose water for an excellent skin tonic.

Natural Hair Care

Mary learned numerous tips from her mother, who cared for Mary's hair when Mary was a child, and she still applies this wisdom. She is emphatic about treating hair from the inside, by eating raw fresh fruit and vegetables to provide essential nutrients. She advises drinking plenty of fresh water, and making sure that you are getting enough protein and B vitamins, especially those found in wheat germ, soy, rice, and legumes.

Mary's mother always extolled the virtues of the old-fashioned "100 strokes" where you put your head down and brush the hair forward. This brings blood to the head, brings oils from the follicles into the hair, and gives it a marvelous sheen. To improve it further, my Indian girlfriend, who has long, glossy hair to die for, told me that if you cut your hair at the new moon it will grow thick as the moon waxes.

Hair Care

When she first left home, remembering that her mother had enriched her hair somehow with egg, Mary used whole egg by mistake, and the white began to cook in the hot water on her hair. It took forever to rinse out. So remember, add egg yolk only to your shampoo! It is especially good for fine or limp hair.

For oily hair, use ⅔ cup to 5 cups of cider vinegar or lemon juice in the rinse water. It removes all traces of soap and gives the hair luster.

For dry hair, she suggests taking wheat germ internally. Or warm 5 tablespoons of wheat-germ oil and pat onto the hair. Cover with a warm towel and leave for 30 minutes before shampooing. Be careful to protect your hair from sun and sea winds, which dry it out even more.

You can make a great difference to the sheen and body of your hair by treating it with herbal infusions, tonics, and rinses.

Herbal Hair Tonic

I tried this infusion in early summer, when fresh herbs are at their best in the garden, and it gave my hair a fabulous sheen.

Make an infusion (see next recipe) of equal proportions of chamomile flowers, rosemary, bay, sage, and southernwood. When cool, massage regularly into the scalp when rinsing—it strengthens and feeds the roots of the hair, and stimulates the scalp tissues. Use more chamomile for fair hair, more rosemary for dark.

Another time I added linden flowers, fennel, stinging nettle, horsetail, and yarrow, and the result was a thick, lustrous head of hair.

Master Infusion Recipe

Rosemary stimulates the hair follicles, and regular use can prevent early thinning. I made this simple infusion for my partner to rub into his scalp to make his hair grow healthy and strong, and it has been a huge success. He uses it as a rinse every time he washes his hair, and it gives it body and luster.

1 ounce dried rosemary, or a generous handful of fresh leaves
1 quart water

Add the rosemary to the water in a pan. Bring to a boil and simmer for 10–12 minutes, covered. Let cool for 1–2 hours, then strain. It is best used at once, but can be stored in the refrigerator for a week, or until it starts to ferment.

Use this as a master recipe, and double the quantities of herb for a strong infusion. For dry hair, use comfrey, elderflowers, quince blossom, or sage. For oily hair, use mint, horsetail, lemon balm, lavender, marigold, or yarrow.

Sage Infusion

This classic recipe stimulates the scalp and the hair, and consistent use darkens the hair. Make a strong infusion (see above). You can darken eyebrows by mixing it with several drops of olive oil and applying nightly using a clean mascara brush.

If you steep a slice of lemon peel in a small bottle of castor oil for several days, you have a mixture for longer, stronger lashes. At bedtime, brush the oil on your eyebrows and upper and lower lashes with a clean mascara brush.

Rosemary Oil

This is wonderful for my dry hair. Infuse 1 ounce fresh rosemary in 2½ cups olive oil and let it stand for a week on a sunny windowsill. Massage it into your scalp, then wrap your hair up in a hot towel for 10 minutes before you wash it.

You can also make a nettle oil in the same way, for luster and to stimulate growth.

Hot Oil Treatment

Mary's mother told her that to keep your hair in prime condition, gently heat ⅔ cup virgin olive oil in a double boiler and apply to layered sections of the hair. Wrap your head in a warm towel and keep the oil on for several hours before shampooing. My Indian friend uses sesame oil, and during Mary's time in the Bahamas she recalls that the locals used coconut oil. A friend of hers from Bali uses manuka (tea tree) oil.

Nettle Tonic

A local country girl gave me this recipe that her grandmother had passed down to her. She had beautifully soft and glossy hair, and told me that this tonic, which she often used, improves and brightens the natural color of hair. It also clears dandruff. Wear rubber gloves to gather the nettles!

½ pound young stinging nettle tops, washed
2½ cups water

Add the nettles to the water in a pan and heat slowly over a low flame. Simmer very gently for 3–4 minutes, keeping the lid on. Remove from the heat and let cool for 2 hours. Strain just before use, and use as for the chamomile rinse below.

Chamomile Flower Rinse

This comes from a beautician who lived in South Africa for many years. It puts brilliant highlights into blonde hair.

4 ounces dried chamomile flowers
3 cups water

Follow the recipe for Rosemary Infusion, substituting chamomile flowers for the rosemary. Warm gently to use. Rinse the hair several times, then leave on for 15–20 minutes before rinsing with cold water.

Beer Rinse

My cousin in the USA swears by this. Let a can of beer go flat and use as an after-shampoo rinse (see Chamomile Rinse, above). Stale beer is useful for setting hair because it gives it body.

Flat beer makes an excellent after-shampoo rinse.

HERBS FOR HAIR COLOR

Light hair: Chamomile, cowslips, great mullein flowers, nettles, turmeric.

Brown hair: Cinnamon, cloves, henna, marjoram, parsley.

Red hair: Ginger, henna, juniper berries, marigolds, sage.

Dark hair: Elder leaves, henna, lavender, raspberry leaves, rosemary, sage, black walnut (*Juglans nigra*).

Pre-Shampoo Conditioner

One of Mary's tips is to apply any conditioning treatment just before going into a sauna or steam bath: The pores of the scalp open and take in maximum nourishment. Give yourself a treat!

Egg yolk is an excellent enricher of hair, keeping it beautifully soft. Some people have even told me that they use homemade mayonnaise. Add 2 tablespoons cider vinegar to the rinse water to help remove all the traces.

You can use safflower, almond, or wheat-germ oil instead of the avocado used here. Coconut oil is an excellent pre-shampoo conditioner, especially in sunny countries, where hair can suffer from becoming dried out.

2 egg yolks

A few drops of glycerin

A few drops of cider vinegar

1 tablespoon avocado oil

Mix all the ingredients together and massage into the dry scalp half an hour before shampooing. Rinse very thoroughly after shampooing, with a little lemon juice or vinegar in the water.

Castor-Oil Conditioner

This strengthens hair and can be added to any combination of pre-shampoo conditioner. This mixture couldn't be easier to make.

2 tablespoons avocado oil (or oil of your choice)

1 beaten egg yolk

1 tablespoon castor oil

*1 tablespoon rosemary or sage (dark hair) or chamomile (light) infusion
 (see pages 68–9)*

Use as a pre-shampoo conditioner, as directed above.

Dandruff

My Indian friend's aunt had several Ayurvedic tips for dandruff. A paste made with young apple leaves used as a shampoo keeps hair silky-soft, and also prevents premature graying and hair loss. A paste of betel leaves and coconut oil prevents dandruff. Just washing your hair in cold water every morning without using a shampoo strengthens the roots of the hair and prevents dandruff.

Put 1 teaspoon cider vinegar into a glass of water and comb it through the hair morning and evening. Mary advises a lot of massaging of the scalp to stimulate the follicles—then the "100 strokes" to release oil into the hair. She gave me this recipe, which is used as a shampoo.

1 tablespoon chopped stinging nettles

⅔ cup boiling water

1 egg white

2 tablespoons mild liquid shampoo

Make an infusion of the nettles and water. Beat the egg white a little and add the shampoo. Strain the infusion into the mixture and use as a shampoo.

Mary recalled the silly days of the 1960s, when straight hair was all the rage. She, like many of her friends, would iron her hair under a damp cloth, contorting her neck to get her head on the ironing board. The lengths to which we will go for fashion.

CLOCKWISE FROM NEAR RIGHT: cinnamon, chamomile, juniper berries, sage, and turmeric can all be used to enhance hair color the natural way. Make an infusion (see page 68), rub into the hair, leave for several minutes, and then rinse out.

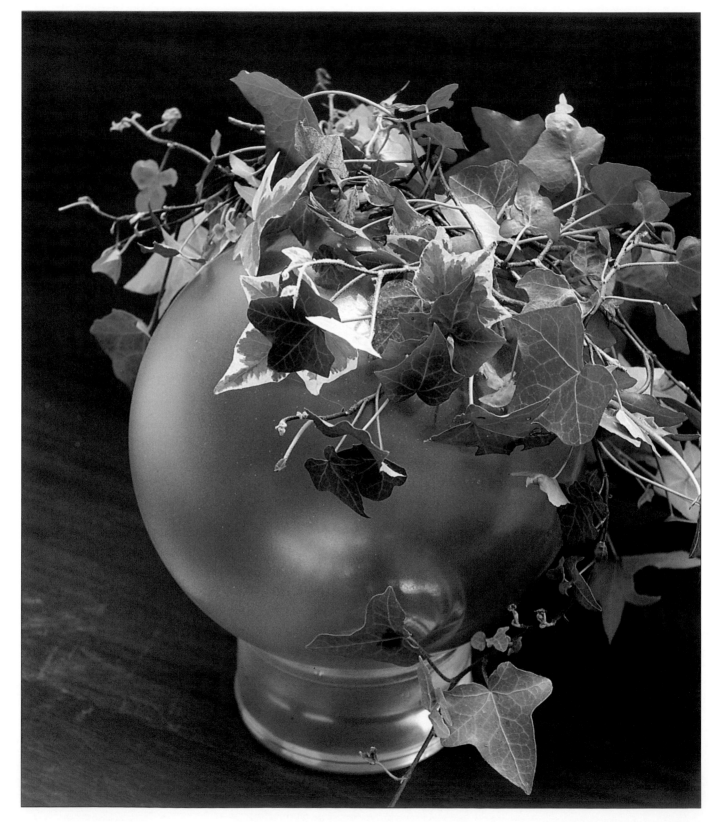

Baldness

Falling and thinning hair is often the result of stress, poor nutrition, prolonged illness, or poor circulation. Seeing to these factors may help to remedy the hair loss. However, over the centuries many wild and wonderful cures have been claimed for baldness. Here are some of them:

Stinging nettles have long been promoted as a cure for baldness. The Nettle Tonic on page 69 stimulates hair growth when rubbed well into the scalp every other night. Friends in New England sent me their family recipe:

> *1 part nettle leaves to 1 part onion to 100 parts alcohol (70°)*

Soak the leaves and the chopped onion in the alcohol for several days. Strain, and massage the liquid into the scalp daily.

A French friend told me that rubbing watercress juice into the hair does the trick. She was also keen on "treatment from within." Make up a cocktail in a juicer:

> *1 part lettuce juice (as many dark leaves as possible)*
> *1 part green bell pepper juice*
> *1 part carrot and alfalfa juice, mixed*

She also said that rosemary delays thinning by boosting the rate of hair growth. Rub a strong infusion (see page 68) into the scalp on a daily basis.

Yarrow steeped in oil is an old English remedy for preventing hair loss and growing a luxuriant beard. A Moroccan woman recommends her mother's version: Castor oil, walnut oil, and alum (see page 66). A balding comedian tells me that rum rubbed into the scalp promotes its growth more than anything else he has known.

Mary was skeptical about cures for baldness, but accepted the tonic effect of double-strength infusions of sage (see page 68), or a blend of any of the following:

artichoke leaves, lavender, linden blossom, maidenhair fern, marigold, nasturtium, nettle, quince blossom, rosemary, southernwood, thyme, grape leaves, watercress, willow leaves.

Use daily on the hair, and leave for 15 minutes before rinsing with cold water.

Some hints from Ayurvedic wisdom: Massage into the scalp coconut oil mixed with lime juice, or coconut oil in which fenugreek seeds have been steeped.

A wash to stop hair from falling out, from Virginia:

> *¼ ounce fresh tobacco leaves*
> *2 ounces rosemary leaves*
> *2 ounces box leaves*
> *5 cups water*

Mix all together in a saucepan. Bring to a boil and simmer very gently for 20 minutes. Cool, strain, and apply to the roots of the hair before shampooing.

Among the more wacky ideas: An old gardener from Herefordshire, England, told me his grandfather used to say that if you go to sleep wearing a cap of ivy leaves it would make your hair grow. "Apply a poultice of chicken manure," came from a French friend's grandmother. And, from an 18th-century *Commonplace Book*:

To Remedy Baldness

This is a hard thing to cure, yet the following things are very good. Rub the head or bald places every morning very hard with a coarse cloth till it be red, anointing immediately after with Bears grease; when fifteen days are past, rub every morning and evening with a braised Onion till the bald places be red, then anoint with honey well mixed with mustard seed, applying over all a plaister of Labdanum mixed with mice dung and powder of bees; do this for 30 days. William Salmon *(17th century)*

If that won't stimulate the hair follicles, nothing will.

An eccentric country tradition is that if you go to sleep wearing a cap of ivy leaves, your hair will grow back.

NATURAL SKIN CARE

Rafath's family lives in Hyderabad, and she and I traveled through India together some years ago. Her mother and grandmother had brought her up in a traditional Indian way, as part of a close family, with many traditions and customs passed down through the generations. Rafath has a mass of thick black hair that falls down to her knees, and a smooth, ageless skin. It is impossible to tell her age. One of the youth-and-beauty tonics passed down through her family was drinking the juice of a fresh lime in a glass of buttermilk every morning. Her hands are beautifully cared for, her teeth pure white. I was certain that she would have all kinds of unusual and inspiring tips for me. I was not mistaken.

Skin is an infallible indicator of general health: If the latter is good, your skin glows, it is clear and unblemished. If you are overtired, ill, or stressed, your skin will be sure to show it. Commonplace wisdom is that treatment starts from within: Give yourself lots of fresh fruit, vegetables, and salads for essential vitamins and minerals, plenty of water to flush the system, regular exercise, and the right amount of relaxation and sleep, and your skin will look and feel great. As Rafath comments, if you're not eating the right food, forget it.

She describes how Indian brides have a whole body massage prior to their marriage, with a paste of saffron or turmeric, thick cream, and Bengal chickpea flour. The brides are then bathed in sandalwood essence, after which their skin is silky-soft and glowing. A simpler recipe from traditional Ayurvedic wisdom is to mix the juice of a fresh lime into a glass of whole milk and add a teaspoon of glycerin. Leave it to infuse for half an hour, and then apply every night to the face, hands, and feet. Let it dry and go to bed without washing it off.

Freshly pressed juices do marvels, too. For fresh-looking skin, boil a bunch of watercress in 2 cups of water for 10 minutes, then strain. Add an equal amount of milk and a tablespoon of lime juice, and drink every morning.

Indian brides have a whole body massage with saffron, cream, and chickpea flour before their wedding

Mary's Recipes

Mary has been making homemade creams for years, and waxes lyrical about the beauty of the pure ingredients that go into them. But, she says, it is a bit like making bread: The creams never turn out the same way twice, and different people's turn out quite differently even when they are using the same recipe. It is delicate work to prevent them from separating as you stir—I used a small, slim wooden spatula as I worked. Always label creams—if you put a jar of cream in the refrigerator someone might think it's mayonnaise...

Cleansing Cream

This master recipe works wonders for a dry and sensitive skin. Apply gently but thoroughly, and leave for a minute or two before removing with a toner such as a flower water (see Sweet Waters, page 94).

¼ cup rose water
(see page 66)
¾ ounce beeswax
2 tablespoons wheat-germ oil

¼ cup avocado oil
3–6 drops essential oil of lemon verbena
A pinch of borax powder (optional)

Heat the rose water in a bowl set over hot water. Melt the beeswax in a bowl over gently simmering water. Add the oils, beating steadily with a small spatula. Trickle in the warm rose water slowly, stirring until smooth. Remove from the heat and stir until the mixture cools. Then add the essential oil. Stir well, and add a tiny pinch of borax if the cream separates or is too thick.

Cucumber and Yarrow Night Cream

A beautiful shade of palest green, this deeply moisturizing cream leaves the skin soft and enriched. It is the best night cream I have ever used.

¼ English cucumber, liquified in a blender
2 tablespoons double-strength infusion of yarrow (see page 68)

Put the cucumber in cheesecloth and squeeze to extract the juice. Mix with the yarrow infusion. Follow the Cleansing Cream recipe above, using this instead of the rose water, and essential oil of lavender or rose geranium in place of the lemon verbena.

Galen's Cold Cream

Mary gave me the precise quantities for this classic face cream, and it is the best I have ever used, softening and lightly fragrant. It has evidently stood the test of time. Galen, a Greek philosopher, lived in the second century A.D.

2 tablespoons rose water (see page 66)
½ ounce beeswax
¼ cup almond oil
6 drops essential oil of rose or lavender

Heat the rose water in a bowl by setting it over hot water. Melt the beeswax with the almond oil in another bowl over gently simmering water. Slowly trickle in the rose water, stirring well. Off the heat, add the essential oil and stir until cool. Place in a pot with a lid.

Yogurt

Yogurt, like buttermilk, contains lactic acid and helps oily skin because of its acidity. My Indian friend often adds 1 tablespoon yogurt to a facial treatment, or uses it as a splash. Yogurt bleaches the skin slightly, so it is useful for reddened skin or to bleach freckles.

Sour cream is good for dry skin. The lactic acid attacks bacteria and dirt, and keeps the skin elastic and young-looking. Use on its own as a face splash, or add to other facial treatments.

Oily Skin

Lemon is an excellent cleanser, restoring natural acidity to the skin. It bleaches freckles and, used with beaten egg white, helps oily skin. Add to rose water (page 66), brandy, or white wine as a blackhead and acne treatment.

Dry Skin

Dry skin needs regular moisturizing, and benefits from herbal and flower waters (see page 66). A few drops of cider vinegar are beneficial added to every skin treatment. Vinegar tones the skin, cures flakiness, and counteracts excess dryness with its restorative acidity. Add water to cider vinegar in a ratio of 8 parts water to 1 part vinegar, and finish with a few drops of essential oil of rose.

SCRUBS

Cornmeal can be used as a scrub to remove rough skin and dead cells. Mixed with milk it will remove dirt and grime from the skin. Rafath's mother told me that *soogi*, the Indian cornmeal, is excellent because it is fine and not too abrasive.

Honey and Oatmeal Scrub

Oatmeal can be used in the same way, raw or cooked. You can use rolled oats, or mill them in the blender to refine them a little. Oatmeal is nourishing: It dislodges dirt and draws out impurities, and it heals rough skin. Try this:

1 egg yolk　　　　　　　*1 tablespoon honey*
2 tablespoons medium-ground oats　　*5 drops cider vinegar*
1 tablespoon olive oil

Mix all the ingredients together. Apply to a clean face and leave for 20–30 minutes. Rinse off with warm water and finish with a flower water (see page 94)

Chamomile Oatmeal Scrub

A classic from Mary's collection.

2 tablespoons strong chamomile infusion (see page 68)
3–4 tablespoons fine-ground oats (process rolled oats in a small blender)
3 tablespoons warm milk

Mix to a thickish paste. Leave to soak for 2–3 minutes, then gently rub onto the face, avoiding the eyes. Leave for 10 minutes, then rinse off with warm water.

Blemishes and Pimples

A very simple, old country recipe for a facial wash to remove skin blemishes is: Peel an onion, put it into a glass of water, cover with clean cloth and let soak in the refrigerator for 1 hour before use.

You can dry up blemishes with white wine, cider vinegar, or lemon juice. Or, rub watercress into the skin to remove a rash. In Bahamian folk medicine, skin problems are dealt with by slicing aloe vera, rubbing it into the affected area, and then sticking the plant to the skin. Healing takes place within twenty-four hours.

Bread Poultice

Mary swears by a bread poultice, which she has used ever since her childhood. Wrap a slice of bread in cheesecloth, dip into very hot water and apply as hot as possible to the skin. Leave on until cool. Her mother used to used a poultice of cooked carrots in the same way.

Calendula Oil

This can be used on scarred or damaged skin, and is useful for treating diaper rash, bedsores, and bruises.

2 ounces marigold petals, crushed with a mortar and pestle
1 cup virgin olive oil

Put the petals into a glass jar and add the oil. Cover tightly and leave on a sunny windowsill or in the greenhouse for 4–5 weeks. After 2 weeks, strain the oil through cheesecloth, pressing out every drop. Add fresh petals, and repeat the process. Shake the jar thoroughly daily. Finally, strain through cheesecloth into clean bottles and seal.

From Rafath's aunt, who is an expert in Ayurvedic applications: Rub fresh lime peel over pimples. It cures them permanently.

A bread poultice draws out spots and even splinters.

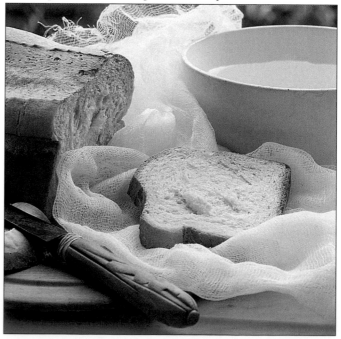

Skin Care for Men

Herbal After-Shave

This is a superb astringent, with a woody, slightly spicy fragrance. My partner now uses it all the time in preference to any other. It soothes the skin and heals blemishes.

4 teaspoons tincture of benzoin, or vodka
12 drops essential oil of bay leaves
3–4 drops each essential oil of rosemary and rose
  geranium
¼ cup rose water (see page 66)
½ cup witch hazel

Pour the benzoin (or vodka), which acts as a preservative, into a large bottle and add the essential oils. Shake well. Add the rose water and witch hazel.

After-Shave for Oily Skin or Acne

I gave this to a young man who had suffered from acne for years, and he reported that it worked wonders.

2 drops each essential oil of lavender, geranium,
  and bergamot
5 teaspoons vodka
7 fluid ounces orange-flower water (page 94)
3½ fluid ounces witch hazel

Add the oils to the vodka and shake well. Add the orange-flower water and witch hazel and shake again.

From my gardener: If you cut yourself while shaving, try rubbing on a handful of fresh yarrow leaves to stem the flow of blood. Or use witch hazel, which doesn't sting nearly as badly as alcohol-based after-shaves from over the counter.

COMPLEXION

Gathering dew on May Day morning is a long-established country tradition for those who wish to have a fair complexion. Young girls would rise early and bathe their faces and necks in the pristine dew from grass, aromatic herbs, lady's mantle (*Alchemilla mollis*), or may blossom (hawthorn—*Crataegus* sp.) for a beautiful skin. A distillation of tansy was also renowned for promoting a clear complexion.

A cottage remedy from the north of England suggests fava bean pods soaked in wine and vinegar, then mixed with very fine cornmeal and milk, to make the complexion smooth and soft. Country folk say that if you eat watercress regularly it will give you a clear complexion. Dandelion leaves have the same effect.

European ladies in the seventeenth century used lemon on their skin to give them a fashionably pale appearance, and lemons have always been used to improve the delicate color of the skin. So if your color is redder than you would like, rub a cut lemon over your face.

Mary told me that if you have broken veins and capillaries on your face, rub on chamomile herbal oil (chamomile flowers macerated in oil). Dab on regularly until they diminish.

Buttercup Lotion

A woman in the village, who has lived in the country all her life, gave me this delightful recipe. She tells me that you can substitute elderflowers and add a few drops of lavender water—both of these will ensure a radiant complexion.

> *8 ounces petroleum jelly*
> *4 large handfuls of buttercup flowers (not the stems)*

Melt the petroleum jelly over a gentle heat in a pan. Put in the buttercup flowers so that the jelly just covers them, and simmer

very gently for 45 minutes. Strain, and place in a pot with a lid. Rafath's aunt has this recipe from Ayurvedic texts: Spread grated apple over your face and leave for an hour, for a beautiful complexion and to banish any blemishes on the skin.

The Moroccan maid of a French friend gave me her mother's recipe for improving the complexion: Make a paste with yeast, flour, and almonds and cover the face with it at bedtime. Wash off in the morning with rose water. Or, she said, make a paste of egg yolk, muddy clay, cloves, benzoin, and coriander with orange juice to mix. Apply as a face mask and leave on for 24 hours. A simpler idea was to macerate cloves in olive oil and use as a lotion on your face every evening.

Lady's Mantle Lotion

A stunning complexion cream that I have made many times. It is softening and non-greasy.

> *1 ounce lady's mantle infused in 2½ cups water for 30 minutes*
> *1 ounce lanolin*
> *6 tablespoons almond oil*
> *4 teaspoons wheat-germ oil*
> *3–6 drops essential oil of violet or geranium*

Measure 2 tablespoons of the infusion, then follow the Master Infusion recipe on page 68.

This advice from a *Handy Hints* book of the late nineteenth century echoed a lotion that the Moroccan girl Rajina told me about, into which she had mixed ground eggshell.

To Render the Complexion Fair

Bruise some sweet almonds in a mortar, and add water very gradually, a pint to 20 or 30 almonds; add sugar to prevent the separation of the oil from the water. Mix immediately, strain through a fine cloth, and perfume the mixture with orange-flower water.

Complexion Herbs

Certain herbs have specific effects, so you can make infusions of these herbs (see page 68) to add to the Cleansing Cream on page 75 to suit your skin.

Linden flower: Improves circulation, smooths wrinkles, slightly bleaching.

Chamomile: Soothing, astringent, healing.

Peppermint: Stimulates circulation and is disinfectant.

Fennel: Smooths wrinkles, good for the eyes.

Rosemary: Warming, improves blood supply, stimulating. Good for skin and hair. Used for centuries.

Elderflower: Cures sunburn, removes freckles and wrinkles, softens and cleanses the skin. Used since ancient times.

Yarrow: For oily skins, and good for chapped hands.

Stinging nettle: Improves both skin and hair.

Marigold petals: Healing for acne, scar tissue, and rough skin.

Sage: Cooling and astringent, good for skin and hair.

Lady's mantle: Used by the Arabs in cosmetics. Astringent and restorative for the skin. Helps inflammation and acne and can be used to lighten freckles.

Washing in the May Day dew is said to give you a beautiful complexion.

Left to right: almond oil, olive oil, Rosemary Astringent Lotion, peanut oil, Lettuce Milk Lotion, and (front) lanolin

LOTIONS AND OILS

There is no need to rely on industrial synthetics—nature supplies us with numerous oils and lotions.

Hot Oil Treatments

You will get to know which oils suit your skin type. Mary, with her light skin, swears by almond; Rafath, with her Indian skin, uses sesame and also recommends peanut oil highly. Olive oil works wonders on my dry skin. Whichever you use, hot oil treatments are a treat.

Olive Oil is excellent to soften the skin. Simply warm the oil and apply with absorbent cotton pads. Allow to soak into the skin for anything up to 30 minutes, then wash off with warm water and finish with a flower water (see page 94). The very first face creams of two thousand years ago were based on olive oil.

Peanut Oil is particularly good for the dry skin on the neck. First draw your hair up from the hairline. Heat 5 tablespoons of peanut oil. Dip a large piece of absorbent cotton into the oil, squeeze out the excess, and wrap around the neck. Lie down on a towel and leave until cool, then apply a second wrap.

Almond Oil has been used since the days of the ancient Greek, to restore the skin's natural oils that dry up under the Mediterranean sun. Almond oil keeps the skin lubricated, and makes an excellent base for creams and lotions for all skin types, being rich in vitamins and minerals.

Buttermilk, on its own, is an excellent facial skin conditioner, used as a simple face splash. *The Art of Simpling,* of 1656, suggests soaking tansy in buttermilk for nine days, then using it as a face lotion. Apply with absorbent cotton pads.

Coconut Oil, a tropical oil with a scrumptious scent, does wonders for aging skin, as well as giving shine to hair. It is a wonderful oil for after-sun care, too.

Lanolin (see page 66) is a sensitive copy of your own skin's oil, and can be mixed into oils and lotions for extra effect.

Honey and Almond Softener

Honey acts as a moisturizer and softener, and heals blemishes. This lotion is wonderful for daily face care.

2 ounces lanolin	*1 ounce almond oil*
1 ounce honey	

Melt the lanolin in a bowl set over simmering water. Add the honey and whip with a wooden spatula. Slowly beat in the almond oil. Remove from the heat, stir until cool, and then bottle.

Lemon Lotion for Oily Skins

This makes the skin pearly and clear. It is cleansing and purifying, and restores natural acidity to the skin.

1 egg white	*Juice of ½ lemon*

Whip the egg white to a froth and add the strained lemon juice. Heat gently over hot water until the mixture thickens. Bottle and label. Store in the refrigerator for up to a week.

Hand Lotion

This is surprisingly effective for something so simple. The recipe comes from Mary's Scottish grandmother. Glycerin is a natural

moisturizer that helps tissues to retain water, and is a good softener. It can be obtained from pharmacies.

Juice of 1 lemon
6 tablespoons rose water
¼ cup glycerin

Mix the three ingredients together. Rub evenly into dry or chapped hands.

Lettuce Milk Lotion

Lettuce has been used in beauty treatments for centuries. Mary introduced me to this lotion, which is sensationally good as a conditioner for all skin types.

1 head of lettuce
Water just to cover

Place the lettuce and water in a pan and bring to a boil. Simmer gently for about 45 minutes. Cool a little, then strain. Add a few drops of tincture of benzoin as a preservative. Store in a labeled jar.

Rosemary Astringent Lotion

A refresher for all skin types.

7 tablespoons rosemary infusion	*5 tablespoons orange-flower water*
(see page 68)	*1 tablespoon witch hazel*
½ teaspoon borax powder	

Mix the rosemary infusion with the borax in a bowl and stir until the borax has dissolved. Add the orange-flower water and witch hazel, pour into a screw-top bottle, and cap tightly.

Lady's Mantle Lotion for Spotty Skin

An elderly lady gave this recipe to Mary, who has made it up frequently for her clients. It opens the pores, clears excess oiliness, and does wonders for spotty skins.

2 tablespoons lady's mantle (Alchemilla	*5 tablespoons boiling water*
Vulgaris) leaves	*5 tablespoons buttermilk*

Make an infusion of the leaves and water (see page 78). Cool, then strain. Add the infusion to the buttermilk and use as a lotion.

EYES

According to country wisdom, garden dew is good for the sight, as well as giving a fair complexion. Thinly sliced cucumber reduces puffiness and eye strain. The Egyptians call lapis lazuli "Stone of Heaven," and believe that it improves the eyesight, along with emerald and quartz. A traveler friend, who had just returned from Australia, told me that an Aboriginal cure for blindness or poor sight was to place a grain of sugar in each eye.

Mary considers the herb eyebright (*Euphrasia officinalis*), available in decoction or tincture form from herbalists, the best of all for eyes. The French call eyebright *casse-lunette*—because you can throw away your spectacles after using it! To the Germans it is "consolation to the eyes," and to the Italians *luminella*.

Cornflower Compress for Tired or Weak Eyes

A French friend tells me that the women in her village use cornflower for gritty eyes or irritated skin around the eyes:

Add 1 heaped teaspoon dried cornflowers (or 1 tablespoon fresh) to 1 cup boiling water. Steep for 5 minutes, then strain. Soak several layers of lint, cut into rounds, in the lukewarm infusion and place over each eyelid. Lie down and relax for 5–10 minutes.

A cold tea poultice is good for sore or tired eyes—especially Earl Grey, because the bergamot in it is uplifting and soothing. For weak eyes, bathe them in cold water with a few drops of cider vinegar added. A witch-hazel compress is effective, too; first apply a thin layer of wheat-germ oil to reduce the stinging effect. Rue flowers steeped in white wine were said to sharpen the eyesight.

Some Gems of Ayurvedic Wisdom
(via Rafath's aunt)

• Eat a cardamom seed daily with a tablespoon of honey, to improve the eyesight.
• Use fresh onion juice with honey for eye disorders.
• Use drops of fresh pomegranate juice for eye strain or conjunctivitis.
• Placing the pulp of a baked apple over your eyes for 1 hour before retiring to bed cures eye strain.

For a Sty

Rub it with a gold wedding ring or with the hair of a black cat's tail.

The Arabs of North Africa use the juice of cotton lavender (*Santolina*), sometimes mixed with milk, to soothe and protect the eyes from the wind and grit of the desert.

You can make an infusion of dried cornflowers to soothe irritated eyes.

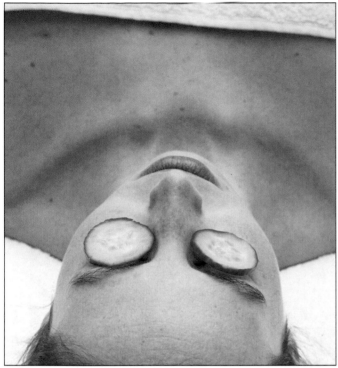
Cucumber has a cooling and restorative effect on the eyes.

TEETH

"A diamond is not as precious as a tooth," writes Cervantes in *Don Quixote*. Teeth that fall out during the seventh year of age should be preserved: In later years they have the power of relieving toothache. "Hen's teeth" is an expletive to express the same sentiment as "pigs might fly." And a correspondent from Michigan sent me this proverb:

> *If your teeth lie one on the other*
> *You will always live with your mother.*

On a visit to North Africa, our Moroccan maid, Rajina, told me that her grandmother used to brush her teeth with a mixture of charcoal and rock salt. In Britain, a charcoal tooth powder used to be on sale, and people also used to rub their teeth with the ashes of burned bread, or burned ground hazelnuts—said to be the best of all. This all tied in with my Indian friend Rafath telling me to use charcoal to clean my teeth—the rough bits that get in between the teeth act as floss. She told me that in India they chew betel

leaves to protect the teeth from decay and to freshen the breath. Mary told me that when she was in Thailand they would chew betel nut, because the fibers had a brushing action. Burned eggplant is another of her tips. For sweet breath, chew mint leaves, or a cinnamon stick.

You can also clean teeth effectively with salt: Moisten the salt and rub on with a soft brush—it is good for the gums, too. Ayurvedic wisdom suggests adding some pepper. My mother used to use baking soda. To whiten teeth, rub with sage leaves, my old gardener told me. Or, chew lemon peel instead of using toothpaste. Chewing a slice of lemon is good for toothache.

Strawberries are good tooth cleaners—just squash a strawberry through the mouth to leave it feeling fresh and to prevent tooth discoloration. Leave on the teeth for 5 minutes, then rinse off with a weak solution of baking soda.

Cures for Toothache

Austria: Wash the mouth with a blackberry-leaf infusion. **Cambridge, England:** Chew an elder twig. **Herefordshire, England:** Carry a gall from a wild rose in your pocket. **India:** Rub with a pinch of powdered pepper mixed with clove oil, or chew mango leaves. **Russia:** Chew fresh ginger, or bite on a cube of sugar soaked with essence of leaf buds of birch—a sure cure. **Suffolk, England:** Carry a hazelnut with two kernels; chew yarrow leaves. **Traditional:** Rub with oil of cloves, or with onion juice; rest your face on a pillow of warm hops.

My mother used baking soda to clean her teeth

FRECKLES

In Victorian times, ladies seeking the fashionably pale look used three parts fresh lemon juice to one part rum to treat their freckles. Although freckles are no longer considered unsightly, my daughter, who complains of too many, has been the guinea pig for these potions, and they work!

Anti-Freckle Lotion

A simple remedy, easy to make and highly effective.

> 2 tablespoons lemon juice
> ¼ teaspoon borax powder
> 1½ teaspoons essential oil of rosemary
> 2 tablespoons tincture of benzoin

Rub a cut strawberry onto freckles to make them fade.

Mix all the ingredients together and leave to stand for a few days before using. Rubbed on the hands and face, it will lighten the skin and eventually make the freckles disappear. Apply where required morning and night, gently dabbing the affected area with absorbent cotton or a soft cloth.

Buttermilk

This is a mild bleach and an effective treatment for freckles: Marie Antoinette used a compress of buttermilk to remove hers. Here is a country recipe given to me from Germany. If you have a very oily skin you can use yogurt instead of buttermilk.

> 6 tablespoons buttermilk   1 teaspoon grated horseradish

Mix the milk and horseradish together. Lightly oil the face with olive or almond oil. Apply the horseradish mixture to unwanted freckles and allow to dry for 20 minutes. Wash off with tepid water. Rinse, and oil the face lightly.

Culpeper recommends rubbing bruised watercress leaves into freckles to remove them. A late-nineteenth-century book of household hints suggests mixing the juice of a lemon with 1 tablespoon borax powder and 1 tablespoon confectioners' sugar. Apply it to the freckles, leave on for 20 minutes, then wash off with warm water. Cream the face after rinsing.

Strawberries can be used cosmetically to improve the complexion and lighten freckles. Use them in any facial (see page 90), or just rub the cut surface of a strawberry onto the skin. They bleach it mildly, making freckles less apparent.

The adverse effects of over-exposure to the sun are well known, and most people are aware of the dangers of developing skin cancer. Suntanning became fashionable only in the twentieth century. Weathered-looking skin was once regarded as a sign of hard outdoor labor.

Too much sun dries the skin, and the natural oils need to be replaced. Burns need to be soothed. Certain oils and flowers—including lavender and elderflower—are highly effective in these treatments, and the ones you make are a good deal cheaper than the ones you can buy.

Elderflowers

Elderflowers are renowned as a skin herb. A friend in the next village gave me this excellent and effective lotion to refresh the skin after sunburn, which also counteracts the drying effects of swimming in salt water. It is best kept in the refrigerator and applied cold.

> *Several handfuls of elderflowers*
> *Boiling water*
> *¼ cup pure alcohol*

Press the elderflowers into a large jar and fill it up with boiling water. Add the alcohol, cover with a dish towel, and leave to stand in a warm place for 2 hours. Cool, strain, and bottle, then cork well. Rub into the skin where required, or put some into the bath.

Elderflower Water

You should apply this when the moon is waning!

Pack as many elderflowers into a large pitcher as will fit, and pour over them at least 2½ quarts boiling water. Cover with a cloth so that none of the steam can escape. Leave to stand for 24 hours, then strain and bottle.

Honeysuckle Ointment

Mary's long-term standby for burned skin is this lovely scented ointment that can bring soothing relief to sunburn and other minor burns. Lavender works really well too, in place of the honeysuckle, and marigold petals extend the healing properties of this remedy.

> *3 ounces petroleum jelly, available from pharmacies*
> *3 heaped tablespoons honeysuckle flowers*

Bring the petroleum jelly to a boil with the flowers and simmer for 20 minutes, stirring from time to time. Strain into warm jars and leave to cool before covering and labeling.

Sunburn

As we all know, it is not good to expose our skin to too much sun, but if we do overdo it, it is wise to find mild relief in some of the following cures.

Sunburn Cures

From an American friend of my daughter's: Rub two strawberries over your face and leave the juice on for about half an hour. Wash off with tepid water, with a few drops of tincture of benzoin added to the rinse.

She also suggested making a face pack of crushed wild strawberries for a bad case of sunburn.

A Greek once told me that a good way to relieve sunburn is to wash the face with sage tea. Strong tea, cooled and applied on a soft cloth, soothes sunburn, as does live plain yogurt. Cider vinegar stings, but relieves the burning.

HANDS

Softening lotions for "household hands" can be made from a range of everyday products, including potatoes, lemons, and bananas. Rafath, my Indian friend, told me that if you cut up an eggplant and soak it in water, then use the water on your hands and face, it has a refining effect on the skin. Tamarind pulp has the same effect. Her grandmother's recipe was even simpler.

Grandmother's Lotion

5 parts glycerin to 15 parts rose water

Simply rub into roughened hands. You can add a pinch of borax if the hands are stained.

This variation is fragrant:

¼ cup glycerin   *Squeeze of lemon*
12 drops lavender oil   *6 tablespoons elderflower water*

Mix together and rub into the hands.

Glycerin and rose water make a simple hand lotion.

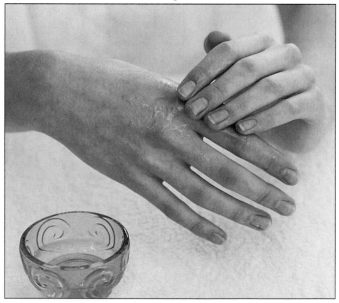

Lemons

• Rub lemon halves over roughened elbows to soften them.
• Whiten reddened housework hands with lemon juice.
• Massage a mixture of lemon juice and honey into rough, dry hands to make them soft and white.
• Rub lemon into nails to make them really clean.
• Use cider vinegar and water (1:8 parts) for softening the hands.
• From Mary: The essential oil of benzoin added to a base cream with lemon juice is wonderful for cracked hands (and feet).

An Indonesian friend declares that this makes a wonderful hand cream: Mix 1 tablespoon mashed banana with 1 tablespoon sunflower margarine. She also told me to mix coconut milk and glycerin, and rub it into hands and feet to soften them. This I have found to be incredibly softening.

Nails

Soft or brittle nails can be a real problem. Several country friends have told me that parsnips are an excellent internal help for brittle nails—eat as many as you can. If you have a juicer, juice the parsnips and drink regularly, or make soup. Likewise, drinking cucumber juice helps to prevent splitting nails and also falling hair.

Mary advises eating masses of parsley, and soaking the nails in almond oil regularly—10 minutes daily for several weeks if they are bad. Rub cocoa butter into the cuticles. I treat myself to a manicure where my hands are covered in hot paraffin wax and left to soak under plastic wrap. Beeswax does a wonderful job, too.

Horsetail and mugwort are both herbs that improve nail condition. Make a double-strength infusion (see page 68) and soak the nails in it for 10 minutes daily.

An Indian superstition: Never cut your nails after sunset, and never let the parings fall onto the floor, let alone step on them, for that will bring bad luck.

The water left after soaking a chopped eggplant has a refining effect on the skin, according to Ayurvedic wisdom.

WRINKLES

A French woman with beautiful skin told me that she always sprays her face lightly with a mineral-water atomizer before putting on her make-up, and that this moisturizing process helps prevent wrinkles. In general, keep the face well lubricated with oil, since dry skin wrinkles more easily: Anhydrous lanolin, coconut oil, and almond oil are all good. They are even more effective mixed with egg yolk or honey. Homemade mayonnaise is a good anti-wrinkle device, too.

A young woman from New Zealand, with a good sense of humor, told me that the Maori answer to wrinkles was to get tattooed—and this was their answer for balding as well. My Indian friend Rafath has always used mustard oil to soften her face, and she has no wrinkles! Rajina, the Moroccan woman, gave me her grandmother's recipe *pour ne pas vieillir*. Mix honey, ginger, cloves, and nutmeg; take 2 spoonfuls midday and evening. Another tip was adding ground melon seeds to egg yolk and applying it to the face at night, then washing it off in the morning with one of the world's most wonderful rose waters, from the Dades valley in the Atlas Mountains.

My tip for a quick fix for wrinkles: Pierce a vitamin E capsule and mix the contents with a little lanolin. Dab on and allow to soak in. Wipe off with a flower water (see page 94). Simpler still is to use pure wheat-germ oil, which contains vitamin E, a prime skin conditioner. Dab it on the face with absorbent cotton pads, leave to soak in for an hour, then clean off with rose water.

Coconut oil used in the same way prevents dryness around the eyes and prevents heavy wrinkles. Rafath swears by it, and recommended that I sleep with a mask of warm oil on the face (see page 80). She also described how a pulp of ripe banana mixed with a teaspoon of rose water, allowed to soak in for an hour, prevents premature wrinkling. Above all, she recommended the special brides' bath (see page 93), used regularly in wealthy families with a special maid to attend to it, a treatment that she had until she was twenty-one.

Cocoa-Butter Ointment

Mary recommends rubbing a cocoa-butter stick from the pharmacy into the bags under the eyes. Or, make this simple ointment.

1 ounce cocoa butter

1 ounce lanolin

1 teaspoon rose water

Melt the cocoa butter and lanolin together in a bowl set over hot water. Stir in the rose water, remove from the heat and stir until cool. Use two or three times a day under the eyes.

Mary also extolled the virtues of *Rosa rubiginosa* oil for dry and aging skin. It helps smooth out wrinkles, and is also excellent for scarred skin, and those brown spots that come with age.

A woman born in Shropshire, England, told me that her grandmother used to drink chamomile tea (see page 123) regularly, and she had hardly any wrinkles. Nettle tea had the same effect, she claimed. A face pack of pulped apples keeps the skin firm and helps prevent wrinkles.

Anti-Wrinkle Cream

A softening, aromatic cream that, using the Cleansing Cream as a base, enriches the skin and leaves it smooth. It sets hard, but softens on contact with the skin.

¼ ounce beeswax

½ ounce cocoa butter

1 teaspoon honey

2 tablespoons almond oil

2 teaspoons wheat-germ oil

1 tablespoon infusion (see page 68) of your chosen anti-wrinkle herb (see below)

3 drops essential oil of honeysuckle or other

Follow the directions for the master recipe on page 75.

Anti-Wrinkle Herbs

Make infusions (see page 68) with any of the following: Comfrey, elderflowers, fennel, honeysuckle, houseleek, lady's mantle, linden blossom, marsh mallow.

Anti-Wrinkle Wash

Make a strong infusion (see page 68) of poppy flowers. Spray onto the face liberally with a fine atomizer before applying the Anti-Wrinkle Cream above.

FACIALS

In some parts of the world, face masks serve a double purpose. For example, women in Mozambique wear herbal face paint that also protects their skin. Facials are nourishing for the skin. They literally "feed your face," drawing out impurities and improving the circulation. They contain either egg (yolk for dry skin, white for oily), banana, or honey as binders. A few drops of cider vinegar help the acid balance of the skin. Facials are also relaxing since you have to lie down quietly for 20 minutes!

Two useful tips from Mary, based on long experience: First, always take out contact lenses or false teeth before you start a facial treatment; second, if you apply the facial through a layer of fine gauze it makes the process neater and cleaner—you simply peel it off at the end of the treatment, instead of having a mess to deal with. Buy fine gauze from a pharmacy, cut out an oval quite a bit larger than your face, and cut small holes for the eyes and nostrils.

You need 1–2 tablespoons of any mixture below for a face pack. Store leftovers in the refrigerator and use up within a week.

To Apply a Facial

Pull the hair back from the face. Clean the skin with cold water or a cold cream. Lay the gauze over the face and pat the prepared facial onto it with your fingertips or with absorbent cotton pads. Lie down and relax for 20 minutes to let it soak in and take effect. Don't bother to answer the phone or the door. Peel off the gauze, and refresh the skin with your favorite flower water (see page 94).

Cucumber

Cucumber has the same acid-alkaline balance as the skin, and has a positive but neutral effect on the skin. Peeled cucumber is an excellent addition to facials. Or, just rub a piece of peeled cucumber over the face to cool it. Rinse off with tepid water 10 minutes later. Drink a tumbler of cucumber juice every day, made in a juicer, to clear the skin. Or, just lay slices of peeled cucumber over the face while lying down, and relax for 10 minutes— deliciously cool.

Buttermilk

This is good for oily skins. It is rich in calcium and protein, and added to a few mashed strawberries, makes a healthy drink.

buttermilk   *1 cucumber, peeled*

Wash your face in cold water and dry thoroughly. Apply a thin layer of buttermilk and allow to dry for 15-20 minutes. Slice the cucumber, layer over the face, and relax for 10 more minutes.

You can also try buttermilk followed by strawberries, which is very good for oily skins. Apply in the same way. Strawberries have a mildly bleaching effect and help remove discoloration and blemishes from the skin.

Brewer's Yeast

Brewer's yeast moistened with rose water is an excellent addition to any facial for oily skin.

Carrot Facial

Mary remembers her mother making this mixture. The large amounts of vitamin A in carrots are healing for the skin. Either juice two large carrots in a juicer, or soak 2 tablespoons of grated carrot in 1 tablespoon safflower oil. Add a few drops of cider vinegar or lemon juice. To bind, add 1 tablespoon crushed banana or honey, or a beaten egg yolk.

Grapes

This facial helps restore the natural acidity of the skin, especially when the skin has been dried out by too much sun. Grape juice is a good flush for the system and improves skin tone generally. This recipe comes from a friend of mine who lived in Italy for many years.

4 ounces seedless grapes, mashed
1 tablespoon honey
1 egg yolk, beaten (or egg white for oily skin)

Mix all together and apply as a mask.

Take time out for a facial and relax. Find a quiet place, close the door—and recuperate.

Avocado

Avocado is rich in fats and vitamins, and Mary recommends it highly for a mature skin. The make-up of avocado oil is the nearest in nature to that of our human skin, and avocado's buttery richness replaces the natural oils lost in washing and weathering. It leaves the skin feeling smooth and velvety. You can also use this as a body rub before a warm bath.

2 tablespoons mashed avocado

1 teaspoon honey

3 drops cider vinegar

Mix all together well and add some sesame oil, if you wish. Apply as a facial (see opposite page).

Coconut

Rafath traditionally uses coconut "milk" to moisturize and enrich her skin.

Pour ⅔ cup boiling water over ½ cup dried shredded coconut and leave to stand until it reaches room temperature. Strain and use as a thin mask, washing it off after it has dried. Or, add 1 teaspoon to a facial made of honey, ground almonds, egg yolk, and cider vinegar.

Tahini

This makes a brilliant face mask: It feeds the skin, tightens the face, and brings vitality to the skin. Its protein nourishes and its oil lubricates.

Mix some tahini with a few drops of cider vinegar, and leave on the skin for 10 minutes. Rinse off with warm water mixed with a few more drops of cider vinegar or lemon juice.

Oatmeal

This acts as a cleansing scrub to remove dead and dry skin, and nourishes the pores. Mary suggests soaking the oatmeal in orange-flower water first.

1 egg yolk   *1 tablespoon honey*

1 tablespoon fine-ground oats   *1 tablespoon sesame or almond oil*

Mix together and apply to a clean face. Allow to dry for 20 minutes, then rinse off with warm water. Wipe the face with a flower water to finish.

Alternatively, beat up an egg white, mix with a little fine oatmeal, and apply to a clean face.

Apricot

This is a favorite of mine, more like cooking than beauty care. I use unsulfured apricots (and eat one or two as I go along, to increase the effect of the treatment!).

Mash or blend fresh or dried, soaked apricots and mix with olive oil to form a paste. Apply and leave for 20 minutes. Great for dry skin, and a source of vitamin A.

Almond

A woman I met in San Francisco got this recipe from her Mexican maid. I tried it, and my skin loved it. Almonds soften the skin, cleanse it with their abrasive action, and nourish it with protein.

¼ cup ground almonds

2 tablespoons rose water

3 tablespoons almond or olive oil

1 egg white for oily skin, 1 egg yolk for dry skin

Mix the ingredients together and apply.

An old-fashioned mustard footbath is a great reviver.

BATHS AND BODY RUBS

Soaking in a warm bath is a great restorer. I love to add herbs for special effects. The beauty of herbal baths is that they cost very little and they stimulate the pores of the skin, yet are soothing, rejuvenating, and pleasurable.

Herbs for the Bath

The most practical way to make an herb bath is to put the herbs into a cheesecloth bag and tie it around the faucet so that the water runs through it. Add a little ground oats to soften the water, and give smoothness to the skin. Squeeze thoroughly once the bath is run, to get the ultimate extraction.

You can also infuse about 4 ounces fresh leaves or flowers in 1 quart boiling water. Pour the water onto the herb and leave to steep for 10 minutes. Then strain and add 2 cups of the infusion to the bath water.

Rosemary: To bathe in rosemary makes the old young again, so they say. Either use a bag, as above, or steep 2 ounces rosemary leaves in 2 cups boiling water for 10 minutes; add to the bath water and soak in it. Or, simmer a handful of dried rosemary leaves in 2 cups of wine for 20 minutes; cool, strain, and add to the bath.

Balm leaves relieve nervous tension and insomnia.

English walnut leaves are excellent for rheumatism, gout—and sweaty feet! This is according to an American friend.

Chamomile flowers are extremely good for skin problems, varicose veins, and sores.

Elderflowers cool sunburned skin.

Blackberry (young leaves and shoots) makes a superb tonic after a long winter.

Other Recommended Mixtures:

• Chamomile, rosemary, and lavender.

• Sage, fennel, and yarrow.

• Peppermint, rosemary, and horsetail.

• Thyme and lavender.

• Stinging nettle and dandelion.

Baths to Restore Energy

An Australian friend swears by pouring a cup of cider vinegar into a tepid bath. This will also soften rough skin. Mary advises Epsom salts in the bath to relieve aches and pains—or Dead Sea salts, if you can get them.

Footbaths

Footbaths are surprisingly revitalizing and have the effect of restoring a tired body. Soak your feet in a warm herbal footbath, then massage them with 1 teaspoon of wheat-germ oil mixed with 3 drops of essential oil of rosemary or lavender. Mary suggests rubbing coarse salt onto the feet to remove the dead skin first.

The best herbs to infuse (see page 68) for the feet are: elderberries, stinging nettles, peppermint, pine needles, rosemary, sage, and yarrow. Soak the feet for 10 minutes.

Old-Fashioned Mustard Footbath

Mary's Scottish grandmother passed down this recipe. Put 8 ounces mustard powder in a cloth bag. Place in a pan with enough water to cover and bring to a boil. Boil for 10 minutes. Add to a hot footbath for colds, flu, and so on.

For Tired and Aching Feet

An old English country remedy:

2 ounces fresh marigold leaves
5 cups boiling water

Pour the boiling water onto the leaves. Cover and leave to cool. Strain into the footbath. An infusion of lavender is equally good.

Horsetail Infusion for Tired and Aching Limbs

One of the best-known footbaths is made from this common weed (*Equisetum* sp.).

5 cups water
2 ounces dried horsetail

Pour the water onto the horsetail and leave to soak for 2 hours. Then bring to a boil and simmer for 15 minutes. Strain into the warm footbath.

Bath Oils

I add 10–12 drops of a favorite essential oil to my bath once it has been run. You can add sandalwood oil to ½ cup base oil—almond is good—to give the bath an exotic fragrance. Rub the oiliness into the skin as you wash. Using treated (sulfonated) castor oil, instead of almond, leaves no ring around the bathtub.

Lavender Essence for the Bath

From a household hints book of the early 1900s. The name lavender comes from the Latin *lavare*, to wash.

Infuse 3 handfuls of lavender flowers in 1¼ cups rectified spirits (pure alcohol, see page 66) for 3 days, then strain. To the liquid add a few drops of oil of lavender, 2 tablespoons orange-flower water, and ¼ cup distilled water. Shake thoroughly, and pour into a narrow-necked bottle. Use sparingly.

Body Rubs

Body rubs cleanse the pores, getting rid of dead cells, while at the same time nourishing and moisturizing the skin. Indian brides go through days of ritual massaging with coconut or mustard oil before their wedding, plus treatments with cream and saffron or turmeric to make the skin radiant. They are rubbed with chickpea flour mixed with cream to take away any hard or dead skin, and then they have a complete bath in olive oil. These two rubs are less exotic, but still bliss.

Take a cup of coarse sea salt and moisten it with a little cider vinegar. Prepare a cup of almond oil (or you can use safflower, olive, soy, or sesame). Run the bath, and, when it is ready, rub your body all over with the oil. Put some salt onto a washcloth and rub it over the oil layer. Massage well to remove dead or rough skin. Then soak in your bath.

Mix ½ cup avocado oil with 1 tablespoon each of honey, egg yolk, and mashed banana to bind, plus a few drops of cider vinegar. Add some coarse-ground oats for a rough and stimulating rub, or fine-ground for a softer effect. If you only have rolled oats in the house, process them in a blender. Rub into the body, massaging well, and let it soak in for 10 minutes at least, to moisturize the skin. Wash off in a deep, warm bath.

If you suffer from cellulite, massage the areas with rosemary and geranium essential oils, or infusions, after the bath.

SWEET WATERS

Use flower waters as skin toners. If you apply them to the face before a moisturizer, this will contain the flower water and increase its effect. My grandmother used to use a mixture of witch hazel and rose water with a little glycerin added. Flower waters used to be put into finger bowls at the table, for dipping fingers into between courses.

Distilled flower waters, used in cosmetic care and for fragrance around the home, are best bought ready-made: Lavender water, rose water, and witch hazel are readily available from pharmacies and deserve a place in the bathroom cupboard. You can make your own elderflower water, but it is perishable and needs to be kept in the refrigerator. It tones and refines the skin.

Elderflower Water

1 handful fresh elderflowers   2 cups boiling water

Put the flowers into a bowl, crush them gently, and pour the boiling water over them. Cover and leave to steep overnight. Strain through a paper coffee filter into a bottle, and store in the refrigerator. Add a tablespoon of vodka to make it last longer, or a teaspoon of tincture of benzoin to preserve it.

You can use this method to make any flower water.

Jasmine makes the most exquisite flower water—excellent for a dry, sensitive skin—and the scent is wonderful.
Quince blossom is wonderful, too, refining the pores of the skin and whitening it.

Orange-Flower Water

This was highly esteemed by Marie Antoinette, who found that it refined and lightened her sallow skin.

1 heaped tablespoon dried orange   6 tablespoons boiling water
blossom, available from herbalists
and good pharmacies

Place the orange blossom in a small bowl and pour on the water. Cover and leave for 15 minutes. Strain off the water, pressing the flowers well. Bottle, and keep in the refrigerator. Add a little vodka to make it keep longer.

Lavender Water

Lavender is wonderfully soothing and calming for inflamed skin, and an excellent toner for normal skin. This recipe comes from a *Commonplace Book*, dated 1813.

5 cups pure alcohol   1½ teaspoons essence of ambergris
1 tablespoon essential oil of lavender   5–6 drops musk
1 tablespoon essence of bergamot

Put all the ingredients into a bottle and shake well. Store for 3 months before use.

A simpler version is to mix 2 tablespoons essential oil of lavender with 3¼ cups pure alcohol. Shake well.

Hungary Water

Used by Queen Elizabeth of Hungary, who was renowned for her great beauty even at the age of eighty.

1½ cups pure alcohol   1½ teaspoons essence of ambergris
2 tablespoons essential oil of   Finely grated zest of 1 orange and
rosemary   1 lemon

Place all the ingredients in a bottle and shake well. Seal and leave for 24 hours. Shake daily for a month before using.

A Sweet Water

This wonderful water tones a lackluster skin, and you can also use it as an after-shave. Or, just inhale it—its perfume lifts the spirits!

Take Damask Roses at discretion, Basil, Sweet marjoram, Lavender, Walnut Leafs, of each two handfuls, Rosemary one handful, a little Balm, Cloves, Cinnamon, one ounce, Bay Leaf, Rosemary tops, Limon and Orange Pills*, of each a few; pour upon these as much white wine as will conveniently wet them, and let them infuse for ten or twelve days; then distil it off.   Sir Kenelm Digby, Receipts, 1668

*Use 2 tablespoons of finely grated orange and lemon zest

"Hungary Water" was invented for the legendary Hungarian beauty, Queen Elizabeth, who continued to attract lovers well into her old age.

Facial Steams

Gently fragrant, facial steams cleanse the pores deeply, and soften and moisturize the skin. Mary recommends these as being particularly good for blemished and oily skins. Don't use them on very dry, sensitive skins, and avoid them if you are asthmatic. Cover your hair and clean the face. Place 2 tablespoons of your chosen herb in a bowl and pour on 2 cups of boiling water. Hold your face 8–12 inches above the water, with a towel over your head so that the rising steam can penetrate the pores. Stay there for 8–10 minutes. Allow your face to cool, then wipe with a cold washcloth dipped in a flower water of your choice.

The Herbs

Choose from linden, sage, peppermint, chamomile, yarrow and lady's mantle (for acne), basil, sweet pea, elderflower, marigold flower, nasturtium, cornflower, lavender flower, or fennel.

HEALING HERBS

The art of using herbs to cure all manner of ailments goes back to the beginnings of civilization, when man was intricately connected to the natural world in his everyday life, and in tune with the cycles and rhythms of the turning year. He would observe how animals would select certain leaves to cure themselves, and how sick people would instinctively eat particular plant foods. A Bedouin mother would wash her newborn child in camel's urine: Today's biologists have found this to be a protection against several sorts of infection. In the days before penicillin, the Canadian lumberjack knew that the mold of had bread was the best thing for an axe wound. And people used herbs to cure ills and maintain health. Over the centuries a vast body of wisdom has accumulated, both oral and written, some of which still survives in rural parts of the world, and a great deal of which has been authenticated by scientists.

The earliest roots of herbalism come from country people, often women, living in simple rural communities, and passing on their wisdom informally down the generations. It was only later that scholars picked up on and disseminated this knowledge by means of the written word, at about the time that "physic" gardens came into their own. There is fragmentary evidence of ancient Egyptian "medicinal" gardens, which were further developed in Greece under the influence of Aristotle and Hippocrates, but they virtually disappeared until the Middle Ages in Europe, when herbal medicine was almost entirely practiced by monks. They were the first great practicing herbalists, growing "physic herbs" in their infirmary gardens to supply the poor and the sick with medicines in monastery hospitals. Herbs were regarded as holy because they were given by God to cure our ills. An infirmary garden was small, enclosed, and sheltered, and typically would include the planting of many foreign herbs brought back by the Crusaders from Egypt and Syria. It was a peaceful place, enclosed by thick hedges or high walls, sweet-smelling and tranquil, restorative to the soul as well as the body.

The first formal physic gardens were what we now know as botanical gardens. The first one in western Europe—and in the world—was set up in Pisa (1543), followed by Padua and Florence in 1545. Bologna, Leiden, Montpelier, Strasbourg, Uppsala, Paris, Amsterdam, Oxford, and Edinburgh followed over the next 100 years. They were given various names: "Hortus medicus," "Jardin des Plantes," and "Physick garden." Here grew plants for medicinal, educational, and scientific purposes, for students of medicine and apothecaries to use like a library.

One of the world's most famous physic gardens, although not the oldest, is in Chelsea, London, planted by the Apothecaries Company in 1683. Linnaeus, the great eighteenth-century Swedish botanist and explorer, who created a uniform system for the botanical naming of plants, walked there. Another of its many claims to fame was that it had the first hothouse in England. Its four acres are still there, to be used for the ongoing purposes of education and science: The learning gleaned from this research can be found in herbals and pharmacopoeia, both ancient and modern.

Culpeper assigned certain flowers and herbs to each sun sign.

HERBAL WISDOM AND ASTROLOGY

Those men and women skilled in applying the healing qualities of plants have always held an honored place in their societies: Many were also priests or priestesses acting as mediums for the gods as they dispensed their mysterious and magic medicines the world over. It is thought that a Chinese emperor composed an herbal around 2700 B.C., but Chinese herbals have only relatively recently been translated for Western use. Indian herbal wisdom dates back to the Vedas, written around 1500–1200 B.C., and the practice of Ayurvedic medicine has continued to this day in India and elsewhere. The development of medical studies in ancient Egypt and Mesopotamia spread to the countries of the eastern Mediterranean, to Persia and Armenia, and thence to ancient Greece. They took root in Europe and from there traveled to the

New World, where the native peoples had already independently evolved their own herbal practices. These they claimed came through dreams and intuitions, and the word of the "little people." Russia had had "wolf-men" who dispensed herbal medicine, the Celts had Druids. An Aztec herbal, translated in 1522, shows quite independent evidence of herbal medicine in South America from very early days.

In Europe, the systems of Aristotle and Theophrastus laid the foundations for the great herbal of the first true medical botanist, Dioscorides, in the first century A.D. His Materia Medica became the model for the herbals of the Anglo-Saxons and the medieval monks. Saint Hildegard of Bingen, the German visionary, wrote an herbal in the eleventh century based on local folk-cures, as well as on the received word of God. At about this time, Arabic medicine, with its proximity to medicinal plants from the East, culminated in the work of Avicenna. Out of sixteenth-century Germany came the herbals of Brunfels, Bock, and Fuchs; from Holland those of Dodoens, L'Ecluse, and L'Obel; and Mattioli's from Italy. The Renaissance had a profound effect on medical knowledge, producing the famous herbals of Turner and John Gerard in England. The most famous herbalist of them all, Nicholas Culpeper, was also an astrologer.

Astrology

From Babylonian times, men and animals, vegetables, and minerals were thought to be under the dominion of the planets. The oldest astrologers taught that the seven known planets (Sun, Moon, Mercury, Venus, Mars, Saturn, and Jupiter) all had influence over plant life and that they had their own herbs, trees, and flowers. Both

Hippocrates and Galen advised physicians to be instructed in astronomy, and in primitive cultures the moon in particular is acknowledged as an influence in certain diseases. Many of the great herbalists have combined the profession of herbalist with astrologer. "He must know the mathematical sciences, and especially astrologie," wrote Culpeper's contemporary, the seventeenth-century Italian herbalist, Giambattista della Porta.

Above all things next to grammar a physician must surely have his Astronomye, to know how, when and at what time every medicine ought to be administered. Sixteenth-century physician

Culpeper assigned to each herb its ruling planet. The attribution of plants to the signs of the Zodiac is one of the lighter sides of astrology. The theory goes that the vibrations or force fields emitted by particular plants are compatible with, and can have beneficial effects on, the health of people born under the ruling of that planet.

Aries (Mars): thistles, nettles, brambles, mustard, onion, peppers, geranium, honeysuckle, witch hazel, rosemary, marjoram, garlic, horseradish, cowslip.

Taurus (Venus): damask roses, violets, primroses, vine, rose, poppy, foxglove, mint, thyme, tansy, coltsfoot, lovage.

Gemini (Mercury): lily of the valley, speedwell, lavender, mild aromatic herbs (parsley, dill, fennel, caraway, marjoram).

Cancer (Moon): waterlilies and all water plants, forget-me-nots, saxifrages, white poppy, mouse-ear, acanthus, wild flowers, agrimony, balm, daisies, lettuce, cucumber.

Leo (Sun): sunflowers, dahlias, St. John's wort, saffron, rue, marigold, rosemary, borage, chamomile.

Virgo (Mercury): lily of the valley, speedwell, lavender, mild aromatic herbs (as Gemini), small brightly colored flowers, southernwood, savory, fennel, valerian or heliotrope.

Libra (Venus): large damask roses, violets, primroses, vine, blue flowers, dandelion, yarrow, pennyroyal.

Scorpio (Mars): thistles, nettles, brambles, onion, mustard, peppers, dark red flowers such as rhododendrons, basil, tarragon, barberry.

Sagittarius (Jupiter): red roses (not damask), meadowsweet, jasmine, houseleek, asparagus, pinks, dandelion, sage, chervil.

Capricorn (Saturn): pansy, poisonous plants (henbane, hemlock, deadly nightshade), onions, ivy, comfrey, red beets, sorrel, Solomon's seal.

Aquarius (Uranus): orchid, golden rain, elderberry, fumitory, mullein, barley.

Pisces (Jupiter and Neptune): red roses (not damask), meadowsweet, jasmine, houseleek, waterlily, fig, bilberry, rose hip, lungwort.

APOTHECARIES AND STILL-ROOMS

The late Middle Ages saw the emergence of the apothecary as somewhat more than a quack (he was originally a simple shopkeeper who sold drugs and herbs) and above the ranking of "grocer" with which he was associated in the trade companies. Apothecaries all over Europe began to establish their own physic gardens, to serve as a link between horticulture and medicine, where they grew their own medicinal herbs. They also purchased herbs and roots collected from the countryside by "green men and women," and imported drugs and spices from abroad. English apothecaries succeeded in setting up the Worshipful Company of Apothecaries in 1617, which allowed them to prescribe and diagnose without consulting a physician, a practice that remained legal until 1886.

A typical seventeeth-century apothecary's shop had walls lined with wooden chests of drawers in miniature, the shelves lined with bottles and jars of all colors and descriptions, weighing scales, pots and pans, boxes and burners. In such a place, between the fifteenth and seventeenth centuries, the apothecary would diagnose his patients, then make up and sell the required herbal remedies.

Distillation

The practice of distillation was refined in Arabia in the fourth century with the Hermetic science of alchemy, and these practitioners eventually became expert in the distillation of aromatic waters and alcohol. The legend goes that a doctor was called away to a patient in the middle of a meal. When he returned, the plate that had covered his food was beaded with moisture. He pondered on this, and did the first experiments in distillation.

A still consists of a retort, in which substances are heated, a condenser, in which the vapors are condensed, and a receiver, in which the condensed vapors are collected. "It is to be understood that distilling is nothing else but a purifying of the gross from the subtle, the subtle from the gross, each separately from the other to the intent that the corruptible shall be made incorruptible and to make the material immaterial." So begins the first great treatise on distillation, written in 1500 by Brunschwig, a physician of Strasbourg. A seventeenth-century recipe describes a water

distilled from the flowers of jasmine, honeysuckle, violet, and lily "to retain the smell of their flowers." Distillation today is chiefly from leaves, barks, and woods; lavender, rosemary, and mint oils and rose water and orange-flower water are distilled from the flowers.

The Still-Room

In Europe, while the peasant had to make do with simple preparations from a homemade still, using herbs from the hedgerows and flowers from his cottage garden, the rich man in his castle would as often as not have a still-room where the still-room maid had dominion. She ruled over the herb garden and orchard, ensuring that both were harvested at the right time, in tune with the phases of the moon and with the correct charms, rites, and ceremonies. Her knowledge of medicinal herbs was sufficient to provide the household with simple remedies, and her skills extended to aromatic vinegars, syrups, and conserves, aromatic candles and perfumes. Her pot-pourri would scent the rooms, and her oil of roses would soothe the baby's skin after bathing. Her beauty lotions from "the toilet of Flora" as the Elizabethans called it, beautified the skin of the lady of the house; her homemade wines furnished the servants' table. Her job it was to strew bedchambers and privies with aromatic herbs and flowers, and to make posies of herbs and flowers for the lord and lady to carry in the street, protecting them from frightful smells and infectious diseases. Posies were even carried to church, to ward off any noxious smells from the common people and to refresh the brain during the service.

The still-room maid would undoubtedly have had an herbal on the shelf, alongside jars of spring water, pots and funnels, mortar and pestle, and a stag's horn for mixing. The still-room was a fascinating, fragrant place, with bunches of herbs and flowers hanging to dry, and rose petals spread out to make scented bags, like this one from an eighteenth-century commonplace book:

A Bagge to Smelle unto for Melancholie or to Cause One to Sleep

Take drie rose leves keep them close in a glasse which will keep them sweet and then take pouder of mynte, powder of cloves in a grosse pouder, and putte the same to the Rose leves thanne putte all these togyther in a bagge and take that to bedde with you and it wyll cause you to sleepe and it is goode to smelle unto at other tymes.

NATURAL FRAGRANCES FOR THE HOME

Part of my childhood was spent in a beautiful house at Cambridge University in England. My mother had a keen eye for the elegant, and extended her skills to homemade aromatics, made from the flowers the college gardeners grew for us in the herbaceous walled garden. I used to help her dry the petals and herbs, and loved the days spent mixing the fragrances to make what seemed like magical combinations to scent the house. These are some of the recipes we made together.

Pomanders

These were originally threaded on a cord and carried about to ward off infection, or to protect the bearer from the evil smells of the street. Sometimes carried in a perforated box of ivory, silver, or even gold, pomanders were worn as a fashion accessory.

Pomanders are a lovely way to scent a room, or to perfume a closet, and are also good for keeping moths away from cupboards where clothes and fabrics are stored.

> *1 orange*
> *Good quality cloves, with the heads intact*
> *Orris root (Iris germanica) powder*
> *Ground cinnamon*

Stick the orange full of cloves, leaving a small space between each one since the orange will shrink as it dries. Use a fine knitting needle to make the holes.

Mix orris root and cinnamon, and roll the finished pomander in the mixture, rubbing it in well. Place in a warm, dry place for 2 weeks, then tie with a ribbon and hang up.

Sweet Bags

My mother used to perfume the linen cupboard with these bags, which also keep moths away. You can also hang these over a chair,

A pomander

Potpourri

thyme, lemon thyme, tarragon, woodruff, rose geranium, angelica, rosemary, lemon verbena, or bergamot.

Dry the leaves of hops. Make small pillows 8 inches square, using a porous natural fabric such as fine linen or cotton, and stuff with the mixture.

Flower Potpourri

Bowls of pot-pourri add elegance as well as fragrance to a room. You can use scented petals, leaves, flowers, and herbs: Orange blossom, lemon verbena, honeysuckle, lily of the valley, stocks, lavender, clove pinks, rose petals, sweet geranium, bergamot, violets, jasmine, lemon peel, rosemary, and bay leaves are all excellent. Dry them on newspaper or cheesecloth in a warm place until they are brittle—about a week to 10 days.

5 cups dried flowers

1 ounce orris root or benzoin powder (fixative)

1 teaspoon ground spice, such as nutmeg, mace, cloves, cinnamon

1 tablespoon whole spices, such as cloves, cinnamon, mace, cumin, allspice

10–12 drops essential oils of your choice, such as lavender, rosemary, geranium, lemon, and so on

Put the dried flowers into a bowl layering with fixative. Add the ground and whole spices and, finally, drop in the essential oils. Turn by hand once or twice each week. The mixture will last for up to two years.

Incense

Not really incense, but it fills the room with a memorable and exotic scent—flowery and spicy, with all the mystery of the East.

½ ounce each dried lavender flowers, rose petals, and lemon verbena

½ ounce each whole cloves and stick cinnamon, pounded in a mortar

1 ounce orris root powder

½ ounce gum benzoin

8–10 drops each essential oils of sweet orange, clove, bergamot, and rose

Combine the dry ingredients and mix well. Sprinkle the oils over and mix again. Store in a dark place for 2 weeks, covered, for the scents to combine. Then place the mixture in a metal container on top of a radiator. As it heats gently it will perfume the room.

or loop them onto clothes hangers. Use any combination of flowers or herbs (see Potpourri below), plus a few drops of essential oil. My mother's favorite was dried lemon verbena leaves. Make up small bags with cheesecloth or fine linen, attaching a length of ribbon to hang them by.

Plain lavender bags are hard to beat, too. I make them with little squares of raw silk and tie them with ribbons. They keep their scent for a year. Once you have stripped the stems, pack the flowers into old stockings and use to scent the linen cupboard.

Herb Potpourri

Use a mixture of peppermint, sweet cicely, sage, basil, rosemary, angelica, lemon thyme, lemon balm, red bergamot, lovage, tarragon, marjoram, or rose geranium leaves, all dried. Add ground coriander and nutmeg for a highly aromatic mixture, and proceed as above.

Herb Cushions

Hop pillows are famous for helping insomniacs—King George III couldn't sleep without one. Lavender is excellent, too, and rosemary, they say, keeps bad dreams away. You can also use peppermint, sage, or lemon balm, plus a choice of dill, marjoram,

CURES FROM THE KITCHEN

"You are what you eat," a popular aphorism in many cultures, is ascribed to Chinese wisdom, and there are numerous foods that can double as medicines. The obvious connection between what you put into your body and how your health is affected is the basis of Indian Ayurvedic medicine, but this philosophy appears independently in other cultures, too. Magdalena, a teacher from the Nahuatl tribe in northeast Mexico, was highly respected in her community as a powerful healer. Her three "pillars of health" were onions, lemons, and garlic—for prevention as well as for cure. She used onions to purify the blood; their sulfur compounds stimulate the digestive system and their natural antibiotics maintain healthy gut flora, increasing

the body's resistance against disease. The antioxidant properties of lemons have a similar effect. They help digestion, are antiseptic and detoxifying, and improve the circulation. Garlic, famous throughout history for its beneficial effects, is powerfully antibiotic and antiseptic. It has been found to reduce cholesterol levels, is expectorant and decongestant, and it improves the digestion. Magdalena's personal panacea was

to eat several cloves of garlic, raw, before breakfast on an empty stomach!

My Indian friend Rafath's aunt lent me her Ayurvedic "bible," well marked with all her favorite remedies, some of which are included here. There is a wealth of everyday wisdom from the Ayurvedic tradition, which is grounded in herbs, spices, and food plants. So comprehensive is it that it took the author sixteen years to complete the book. In his introduction he quotes Socrates: "Diet is health and diet is medicine," and informs his readers that the Greek word for diet means "way of living."

This tradition is rich in everyday remedies: Among the simplest are using vinegar for shingles and impetigo, and washing sores in warm tea. For nerves, eat an apple with honey and milk daily; for cramps in the calf muscles, drink half a teaspoon of salt in a glass of water three times daily. If you want to lose weight, drink the juice of a fresh lime mixed with a glass of cold water and sweetened with honey every morning on an empty stomach for two months—and eat a low-calorie diet. Alternatively, eat two tomatoes every morning on an empty stomach. Eating a clove a day increases longevity—and sitting regularly under the shade of a nutmeg tree cures obesity!

Headaches: Rafath's mother would make a tea with cardamom, fennel, and lemon grass, put a mask over her eyes, and lie down in a quiet room. Alternatively, make this ginger poultice, which will relieve muscle tension, as well as soothe and cure: Make a paste with 2 tablespoons ground ginger and a little water, and warm it gently in a saucepan. Spread this on a pad made with lint and absorbent cotton, and apply to the forehead, before lying down in a quiet place.

Coughs and Colds: Rafath's family cure was weak tea with ginger and honey, and lemon added if there was a chesty cough. Ginger is antispasmodic and so relieves the urge to cough, and it is a warming spice much used in colds. For the early stages of a cold or bronchitis, take 1 teaspoon onion juice with 1 tablespoon honey three times daily. You can chew a clove (they are antispasmodic and antiseptic) with a crystal of salt to relieve throat irritation.

Hippocrates recommends vinegar as a decongestant to

treat coughs: Try a couple of teaspoons in hot water. No germs can survive the high acid content of vinegar. Alternatively, make this garlic juice: Cut several cloves of garlic into thin slices, cover with honey, and leave for 2–3 hours. Take the resulting juice by the teaspoon at intervals during the day. Or you may combine the honey with chopped raw onion.

Sore Throats:

For a chesty cough, my old nanny used to administer vinegar, honey, and brown sugar heated together. Sometimes she would add cloves, other times garlic. The commonest remedy of all for coughs and colds is a simple mixture of lemon and honey, 1 tablespoon of each, in a cup of warm water. For the grown-ups, add Scotch whisky.

Dominic's great-aunt Beryl, who lives in Greenwich, England, prescribed frozen grapes for a sore throat. He reported that they were delicious, and also had the desired anesthetic effect.

A gargle of salt water is an ancient home cure for a sore throat.

Flu:

From Ayurvedic wisdom, for flu and rhinitis add a pinch of pepper and honey to powdered cinnamon, add hot water, and sip. Pepper is expectorant, and cinnamon a "warming" spice that has long been used for chills and colds. A remedy from Wales for bronchitis is to rub goose fat into the chest and cover it with a red flannel.

Chilblains:

A Russian friend told me that her family had always put cayenne pepper into their socks during the terrible Russian winters. A Chinese woman uses ginger. Cayenne has long been used in the Americas, Southeast Asia, India, and Europe for its warming, stimulating effect. A simple ointment of base oil with cayenne or chili powder stimulates the blood flow and is excellent for chilblains as well as for lumbago and muscular pain.

Arthritis:

Rafath's aunt rubbed mustard oil into her arthritic hands. This cure is also used on horses, both in India and the West. Mustard is extremely effective at stimulating the circulation. Also from her aunt's canon: To reduce pain and stiffness in painful joints, use equal measures of lime juice and castor oil, and drink 1 teaspoon of this in warm water with honey. The purging effects of castor oil clear the body of toxins.

One of the best-known cures for arthritis is the cider vinegar and honey recipe on page 111.

Earache:

Rafath's mother would warm some olive oil, prick a clove of garlic with a pin, soak it in the oil, place it in the ear, and plug with absorbent cotton. A woman from the Fens in East Anglia, England, a complete stranger to Ayurvedic medicine, recommended an almost identical remedy, but made with a baked onion. Or, Rafath continued, use onion sprinkled with turmeric and heated on a flat griddle.

Stomach Problems:

A friend in her nineties, who lived in South Africa for many years, tells that when she was sick as a child she was given vinegar and salt to make her vomit, to clear up infection and clear the system of toxins. One teaspoon of mustard powder in a cup of hot water is emetic, and useful in cases of food poisoning. Likewise a solution of salt. Ayurvedic wisdom offers drinking coconut water (the clear liquid from inside the shell) for biliousness. And drink lemon or lime juice in water with salt and pepper for stomachache.

Oats are soothing to the digestive tract and help gastritis, constipation, diverticulitis, and irritable bowel syndrome. Ginger, with its soothing effect on the digestive system, is ideal for motion sickness, and has proved exceptionally useful in morning sickness. Drink ginger tea, or chew a little of the root—or, if all else fails, ginger snaps or ginger ale go a long way to helping.

The simplest of all relief for regular stomachache is a cup of tea.

Hangovers: Hot red chili peppers encourage the body to release its natural painkillers, the endomorphins. A California remedy is 3 chilies blended with 2 cups tomato juice and a squirt of soy sauce.

The natural sugars and complex carbohydrates of this remedy from an African doctor help increase the calming brain chemical serotonin: Blend a banana with 2 cups soy milk and 2 tablespoons of fruit concentrate. Chill for 30 minutes and drink up.

Jaundice: Mr. Leeroy, now in his eighties, lives on Harbour Island in the Bahamas. "Everything that grows on Mother Earth is healing to the nation," he declares. Diagnosed as being dangerously ill with jaundice, he defied death by treating himself with a mixture of watermelon seeds, sweet cicely, yellow limes, baking powder, and water. He drank a mugful every three hours, and was cured in three days.

Urinary Tract Infections: Cranberry juice is a scientifically proven remedy in the prevention and treatment of urinary tract infections. For generations, North Americans have used it for cystitis and kidney complaints. Research suggests that cranberries contain a substance that stops the infectious bacteria from clinging to the cells that line the urinary tract and bladder, preventing them from multiplying. Recent Israeli research has found that blueberry juice has a similar effect.

Blend cranberries in a food processor and add a little water to bring to a liquid consistency. Stir well, and drink three times a day.

Arteriosclerosis: Russians recommend that everyone over forty should eat a grated raw potato before breakfast, to delay arteriosclerosis.

Onions are thought to bring down blood pressure. They contain an antiseptic oil that substantially lowers blood cholesterol, and this reduces the risk of coronary heart disease. One tablespoon of chopped onion per day will suffice, raw or cooked—the oil is not destroyed on cooking.

Oats reduce cholesterol by means of the soluble fiber binding to the cholesterol and causing it to be excreted rather than reabsorbed. So eat lots of oatmeal porridge!

Small Wounds and Cuts: Garlic is highly antibiotic and combats infections of all kinds. Eat a lot of it, raw or cooked. The ancient Egyptians gave it to the workers who were building the great pyramids, to make them strong. So powerful is garlic that doctors used it in World War I against TB, dysentery, and typhus. Onions, too, are intensely antibacterial, and were used as an antiseptic for soldiers' wounds in World War II. There was a well-known tradition of leaving a cut onion in the sickroom to cleanse the atmosphere, because onions absorb bacteria. Vinegar is antiseptic—but it stings. Lavender oil on a cut or burn heals it and prevents scarring.

"Make food your medicine and your medicine your food," said Hippocrates. Oats are soothing to the digestive system.

HONEY

Honey was always included in old herbals and still is a universal cure in folk medicine. From earliest times honey was found to be an excellent decongestant, to remove phlegm, and to be antiseptic, especially healing on burns and lacerations. So highly esteemed was it that Zeus, King of the Gods, was fed on a diet of milk and honey. Roman soldiers carried honey in their packs for treating wounds. The ancient Egyptians used it for embalming, since sugar acts as a preservative. Honey was used by the ancient Greeks to rub the gums in cases of toothache—a remedy still used today by country folk. The vitamin K in honey prevents the acid bacteria that causes decay from forming in the mouth. The Koran recommends honey for those who are weak and sick: Honey is easily absorbed because it is formed of simple carbohydrates, fructose and glucose, not complex ones that need to be broken down before they are assimilated.

Hay Fever and Other Cures

A neighbor, whose bees used to visit my sage and hollyhocks every summer, told me that pollen can be used for the treatment of hay fever. Chew honeycomb daily for a month before the hay fever season begins, and the pollen that is present in the wax will immunize the system and work like an inoculation.

Honey is a well-known folk cure for acne. Nobody knows why, but whatever antibacterial properties it contains, the condition is greatly helped by regular applications of honey.

A Scottish medical herbalist told me that if you take 2 tablespoons of honey every 20 minutes, repeated as necessary, a hangover will be cured. Honey is a good source of potassium, and counteracts the craving that is evidence of potassium deficiency, let alone the craving for sugar. For bruises, apply honey and glycerin in equal parts.

Honey and Cider Vinegar

One of the oldest folk cures in the world for arthritis.

2 teaspoons honey   *2 teaspoons apple cider vinegar*

Mix in a medium-sized mug and fill with hot water. Stir, and drink twice daily.

An old-fashioned bee skep

OLD WIVES' TALES

A Bahamian grandmother, Elsie, has always used folk medicine to cure family ailments: White sage for measles, the juice of young coconuts for jaundice, okra for an easy birth. Such old wives' tales occur worldwide, sometimes overlapping in cultures that have no contact with each other. They touch on many levels, uniting common sense and fantasy. They have a wide appeal, and mostly can be taken with a large pinch of salt. It is impossible to resist mentioning some non-herbal eccentricities that beg to be included here.

Bee stings: An Aboriginal remedy is to take a small palmful of earth and spit in it. Mix it up into mud and spread over the sting with your finger. Keep moistening it with saliva.

Bone-setting: Third-generation blacksmiths are said to have special powers of healing and, especially, of setting bones.

Burns: An Italian friend told me to smear a burn with toothpaste—it relieves the pain immediately and heals the skin without a scar.

Colds: From Mineke's childhood in Holland: Cut an onion in half, put it cut side up on a saucer by your bedside, and your cold will go away.

Corns: A Californian recommends putting a slice of garlic on a corn or wart. Wrap loosely, and it will be gone in 10 days.

Cramp: Eat honey. Or, dip a towel in hot water and apply to the part affected for immediate relief. Several older people have told me to place a wine cork in the pillowcase to prevent night cramps. One said to put your shoes and stockings in the shape of a cross at bedtime, or to place a bowl of cold water under the bed, to "draw" the cramp away. A traditional cure in certain parts of the UK is to carry a "cramp-bone" from a sheep or hare to protect you.

Colic: In Sicily, they save a piece of the umbilical cord and then rub it over the abdomen of the sick child.

Cuts: A retired farm-worker in East Anglia, England, remembers that when they cut themselves working in the barn they applied a handful of cobwebs to stop the bleeding.

Conjunctivitis: A Scotswoman recommends fresh garden dew rubbed over the eyes.

Epilepsy: Pliny suggested drinking spring water, at night, from the skull of a murdered man.

Goiter: Make a braid from the hair of a stallion's tail and wear around the neck.

Headache: An ancient and long-lasting superstition, from Pliny through to modern European folklore, is to take a rope that has been used to hang a man and tie it around the head. The Irish version suggests doing the same with the shroud of a recently dead person.

Hangover: Vomit over a frog and then throw it as far away as possible. Or, rub a snail or slug into the forehead and then throw.

Insomnia: My Indian friend's mother told her always to eat an onion in the evening meal.

Jaundice: Scandinavian folklore recommends roasting and eating a yellow-hammer. An ancient tale recommends drinking your medicine from a gold goblet.

Lameness: Carry a live shrew in a box around your neck until it dies.

Memory: From Greece—for a bad memory, drink sage tea sweetened with honey.

Muscle sprain: From a Chinese woman in Singapore—soak the area in vinegar for a few minutes.

Nosebleed: A woman from North Carolina passed on this old wives' tale from her mother: Place a drop of vinegar in the ear on the same side as the nosebleed. An English version is to place a cold key down the back of the sufferer. My neighbor suggested nettle juice on lint, up the nostrils.

Pregnancy: A friend who lived in South Africa in the 1940s was told that papaya seeds act as a night-after contraceptive pill.

Paralysis: Carry a live mouse in a box around the neck until it dies; this cures the effects of a stroke.

Rabies: Fry the liver of the mad dog and eat it.

Rheumatism: Several tales come from various places, including France and Holland. Wear a chamois-leather over rheumatic joints, or wear a garter of eel-skin, or carry a stolen potato in your pocket, or wear a copper bracelet, or always carry a chestnut in your pocket.

Stammering: Eat a roasted nightingale.

Sunburn: Rub a cut potato over sunburn for immediate relief, a Brazilian woman told me.

Sore throat: Wrap a red rag around the neck. My neighbor would tie a black stocking around her neck at night, and the sore throat was gone in the morning.

Toothache: Wear the foot of a mole, cut off while still alive, as an amulet. The eccentric aunt of my Dutch friend, who lived in a quiet farming village near Maastricht, always used to put a rolled-up geranium leaf in her ear when she had a bad toothache, and keep it there all day. *Geranium robertianum*, a common wild geranium, has sedative and anti-inflammatory properties.

Dutch wisdom holds that a cut onion by your bed cures a cold.

TRADITIONAL HERBAL REMEDIES

The home medicine cabinet was an important element of country households worldwide, and still is where transport is slow and communities isolated, far from professional medical help. The ancient wisdom of using herbs to heal everyday disorders was and is practiced by the wise man or woman of the community, who pass their knowledge down through the generations. There is usually great wisdom behind the correct use of the right plants: Poultices of periwinkle (*Vinca* sp.) were recommended for breast cancer in Suffolk, England, two hundred years ago; now alkaloids from the Madagascan periwinkle (*Vinca rosea*) are an important medicinal source of anti-leukaemia drugs. Algae was used by the Mayans and Aztecs as a medicinal tonic, and now a much-hyped multi-mineral-and-vitamin elixir, based on this same algae, is a multi-million-dollar industry. The Native Americans used hot chili peppers to cure and prevent tumors: Capsaicin, a substance found in the seeds, is now used to help recovery after chemotherapy.

They also used a wild mushroom, *Grifola frondosa*, "hen of the woods," in food and medicine. This is now marketed under the name of *maitake* and extensively traded by the Japanese on the international market. Scientists claim that it is the most powerful immune-enhancer in the world, and are using it in the treatment of HIV and AIDS.

The world of herbalism is such a vast one that the rigors of selection have forced enormous sins of omission. Only the commonest of plants around the world can be included, and in the briefest synopsis. If you are tempted to make your own traditional cures, be careful: Be sure that you pick the correct plant, and that you wash it well before you use it. If in any doubt about the remedy, check with a good herbal encyclopedia, or ask your local herbalist to advise you on the preparation. Herbs contain powerful substances and must be treated with respect. Many have contraindications and should be used with caution.

Bay (*Laurus nobilis*): Best known for its culinary uses, the stimulating effect of bay can be helpful for a weak digestion, and the oil is antiseptic. Externally it is used as a rub for rheumatism, sprains, and bruising.

Chamomile (*Anthemis nobilis*): Chamomile, the "plant physician," contains muscle relaxants that calm the stomach, soothe sore eyes, and that are effective in menstrual disorders. Chamomile oil relieves sciatica and arthritis, and can be administered for headaches, migraine, and neuralgia.

Coltsfoot (*Tussilago farfara*): The flowers and leaves of coltsfoot have for centuries been smoked to ease a bronchial cough. Pliny recommended this cure as far back as the second century A.D., and the Greeks called it "cough plant." The leaves were dried, and rolled into handmade cigarettes, and are today to be found in herbal tobaccos, although nowadays it is more usual to take coltsfoot in the form of an infusion. It is expectorant and anti-inflammatory, and relieves bronchitis, catarrh, asthma, a heavy cough, and laryngitis. Although a native of Europe, northern and western Asia, and North Africa, coltsfoot (named after the shape of its leaf) has been introduced and naturalized in North America.

Left: violet; below: chamomile

Coltsfoot

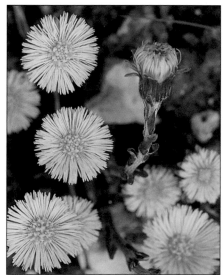

Comfrey (*Symphytum officinale*): The alternative names of knitbone, boneset, and bruisewort aptly describe the uses of comfrey over the centuries. It is, however, undergoing a lapse in popularity—the alkaloids in comfrey were found to damage liver cells in rats who were administered the herb in vast quantities (with nothing else to eat). It is argued by the opposition that these alkaloids are destroyed on processing the herb and are not absorbed by the human digestive system. Be that as it may, comfrey has a high protein content (35 percent) and is an important animal food crop in Africa. It contains vitamin B12, unlike any other plant. Above all, comfrey heals damaged tissues: It contains allantoin, a substance that stimulates the production of connective tissue which forms bone and cartilage. Used for centuries to mend fractures and relieve sprains, comfrey is efficacious for horses, too: The leaves wrapped around cracked heels heal them fast. Comfrey is native to Europe and Asia, but grows all over the world.

Dandelion (*Taraxacum officinale*): Dandelion is a powerful diuretic, and dandelion tea (see page 123) is excellent for cellulite, water retention, and urinary infections. It detoxifies the system, and is beneficial for liver problems and gall-bladder infections. You can eat the young leaves in salad—their diuretic action, which eliminates uric acid from the body, is helpful for rheumatism and arthritis. For warts, apply the milky sap from the stem for a few weeks. Originating from central Asia, the dandelion is a very valuable medicinal plant.

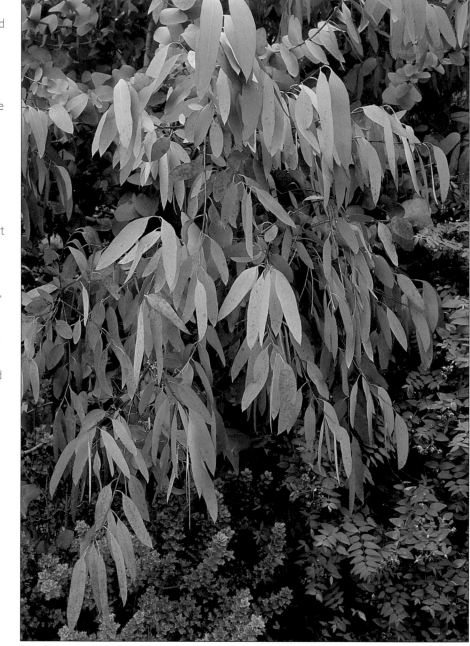

Eucalyptus

Dock (*Rumex crispus*): Dock, a native of Eurasia, is now widely distributed in temperate and subtropical countries as a weed. Its long taproot extracts iron from the soil, thus making it an excellent remedy for anemia. Crushed dock leaves are well known to relieve nettle stings and scalds, and Native Americans applied them to boils. People have used them on ringworm and scabies, too, with success. Less well known are dock's detoxifying effects: Since the ancient Greeks, a decoction of dock has been used to clear up skin complaints and cure digestive problems. The Chinese use dock to bring down fever, and dock seeds were a traditional remedy for dysentery and diarrhea in European folk medicine. Bitter glycosides in the root stimulate the liver and are revitalizing.

Elder (*Sambucus* sp.): The elder has been in long and continuous use ever since the days of ancient Egypt. Native to Europe, North Africa, and western Asia, it was the country medicine chest, since all its parts could be used: Flowers, leaves, berries, bark, and root. The flowers are highly anti-catarrhal, and elderflower tea (see page 123), sometimes mixed with yarrow, is often used in the treatment of colds and flu, or as a gargle for sore throats. Native Americans used it for colic as well as for headaches. The berries have a high vitamin C content and are a prophylactic against colds and infections. They have a laxative action (you can add them to other stewed fruits).

This recipe for Elderberry Rob is a relief for chest troubles, and brings on a sweat to rid the body of toxins.

5 pounds ripe elderberries
a few whole cloves
2¼ cups sugar
Scotch whisky (optional)

Simmer the berries and cloves with the sugar until the mixture is the consistency of honey. Strain and bottle. Take 1–2 tablespoons at bedtime in very hot water, adding a tablespoon of whisky, if desired.

Eucalyptus (*Eucalyptus globulus*): Indigenous to Australia and Tasmania, infusions of eucalyptus were an Aboriginal remedy for bringing down a fever, for dysentery, and for sores. A woman who lived in Zimbabwe used a decoction of eucalyptus leaves for colds, coughs, and flu, and as a gargle for a sore throat.

Traditional Chinese medicine recommends rubbing diluted eucalyptus oil into inflamed joints to relieve arthritis. It can also be used as a compress for wounds and burns—and athlete's foot! Rub it into the temples when you have a headache, or mix it with tea-tree oil, diluted in a base oil, and rub it into hands and feet as a general tonic to boost the immune system.

Eyebright (*Euphrasia officinalis*): Throughout its native Europe, eyebright is still the best known herb to treat eye conditions and has been so since the days of ancient Greece. It sharpens the sight and combats infection. The dried flowering plant is used in infusion and decoction as an anti-inflammatory and astringent, and as a mild lotion it has been used in traditional country medicine to treat conjunctivitis. You can also use this as a nasal spray for catarrh and sinusitis. When applied as a poultice, eyebright aids the healing of minor wounds.

Feverfew (*Tanacetum parthenium*): Today, feverfew is one of the most popular herbs for treating migraine, and is undergoing extensive scientific scrutiny: Trials to date report that 70 percent of migraine sufferers feel an improvement in their condition after taking feverfew. Native to southeastern Europe, and introduced

elsewhere around the world, feverfew grows easily in the garden, with its feathery leaves and daisy-like flowers. Try chewing one or two leaves a day as a prophylactic for headaches and migraines, or make a feverfew sandwich. Do this judiciously: The leaves are very bitter and can cause canker sores or skin irritation.

Lavender (*Lavandula angustifolia*): The famous fragrance of lavender is loved for its own sake, but the aromatic oil has powerful remedial values, too. It is strongly sedative, so a few drops in a nighttime bath will facilitate restful sleep. Some hospitals are now burning lavender oil in their wards instead of administering sleeping pills. Lavender oil is anti-depressant and can be

Lavender

used to lessen emotional tension. Rub lavender oil into the neck and temples for a headache, or drink lavender tea made from the flowers. Used in massage oil, lavender eases muscular aches and strains and can help rheumatism.

Marjoram (*Origanum sp.*): A tea of *Origanum marjorana* or *Origanum vulgare* (oregano) can be taken for colds and digestive upsets. The essential oil of marjoram is used by aromatherapists to ease digestive spasms and period pains, and rubbed into rheumatic joints. Recent research shows that it can prevent premature aging of cells, and may combat free radicals that damage healthy cells.

Marigold (*Calendula officinalis*): A native of the Mediterranean, the marigold is a versatile plant. Both medicinal and culinary (see pages 59–60), it also yields a yellow dye and is used in cosmetic preparations. In traditional remedies it has been used for its

Rosemary

astringent, antiseptic, anti-fungal, and anti-inflammatory properties. Taken internally for menstrual disorders and digestion—Saint Hildegard recommended it for intestinal and liver problems—it is also used externally for thrush, minor cuts and grazes, chilblains, and sores. Rub a marigold flower into a bee sting. Marigold tea can help with the hot flashes of the menopause. Since Roman times it has been used to bring down fevers and was taken seriously as a wound herb during the Civil War and World War I: The eminent English gardener, Gertrude Jekyll, sent crates of marigolds from her garden to the field hospitals in France, where they were made up into ointment and applied to the soldiers' wounds.

Meadowsweet (*Filipendula Ulmaria*): Classified by the eighteenth-century Swedish botanist Linnaeus as *Spiraea*, meadowsweet gave rise to the brand name "aspirin" because it was from the flowerbuds that salicylic acid was first discovered in 1839, and from which aspirin was later synthesized in the 1890s. Known to herbalists as the herbal aspirin, meadowsweet is used as a relaxant, to promote a good night's sleep. An infusion of the leaves and flowers is good for colds and flu and fevers. It soothes gastritis and indigestion, and is the most effective plant remedy for hyperacidity. It has been successful in the easing of arthritic and rheumatic pain. Also known as "queen of the prairies," this beautifully fragrant plant, once used to flavor mead (see page 170), is native to Europe and Asia, and has been naturalized in North America.

Sage

This Meadowsweet Compress is excellent for treating headaches.

1¼ cups boiled water
½ ounce fresh meadowsweet flowers

Pour the hot water over the flowers, cover, and leave for 10 minutes. Soak a pad of absorbent cotton covered with a strip of lint in the warm liquid, then squeeze out excess liquid. Lie down in a quiet place and apply to the forehead.

Note that white willow also contains salicin: Country people used to chew the bark for a headache or a hangover, and also to relieve arthritis. An infusion of willow leaves can be taken for a fever.

Stinging nettles (*Urtica dioica*): Nettles are so useful that in spite of being a ubiquitous weed, they were once cultivated in Scotland, Denmark, and Norway for medicinal use and as a commercial source of chlorophyll. In World War II, they were used to dress infected wounds and speed their healing. Famous in country wisdom for being a spring tonic, you can make a delicious soup or drink nettle tea. Nettles stimulate the liver and kidneys and help the body detoxify itself. Their diuretic properties help arthritis and gout; they also stimulate the digestive system and are helpful in respiratory infections. The nettle is a remedy for menstrual irregularity and heavy bleeding. A tincture stops the bleeding from cuts and wounds. The powdered dried leaf can be used like snuff, and will stop nose-bleeds.

My French friend Françoise insists that if you hold your breath while walking through stinging nettles, you won't get stung. It works every time, she says.

Rosemary (*Rosmarinus officinalis*): Rosemary is antiseptic and antibacterial, and is also said to be anti-aging and a memory-enhancer. It does, in fact, increase the flow of the blood to the brain, and has been used for a host of ailments, ranging from nervousness, exhaustion, and hangovers to period pains, fevers, and chest infections. A drop or two of rosemary oil rubbed into the temples dispels a headache.

Sage (*Salvia officinalis*): "Sage the Savior" was one of the most valued herbs of antiquity. It is a rejuvenating tonic and a memory-herb, while its antiseptic and astringent properties make it an excellent remedy for tonsillitis, asthma, catarrh, and sinusitis. It is expectorant and used for coughs; it boosts the immune system; and it settles the stomach and liver. It is diuretic,

and its astringency reduces menstual cramps and heavy bleeding. It is first-rate on cuts and wounds. Use sage tea as a gargle for a sore throat.

Thyme (*Thymus vulgaris*): Thyme is a powerful antiseptic. Suffering from an extremely sore throat in Morocco, I bought a large bunch from the market, made an infusion, and gargled with it; I also drank it as tea, and the pain disappeared. Thyme is a panacea in folk medicine: for digestion, for intestinal upsets, for any fungal infections such as thrush. It is also good for anxiety and insomnia, urinary tract infections, and gout.

Thyme

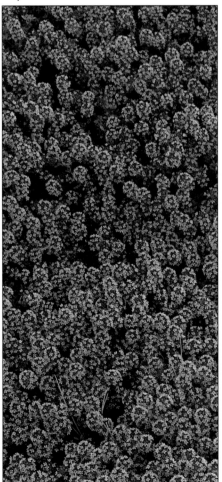

Violet (*Viola odorata*): Violet leaves are suggested in various European herbals for chronic catarrh and bronchitis, and occasionally in the treatment of rheumatism. *The British Pharmacopoeia*, of 1983, records that sweet violet (*Viola odorata*) has been used both internally and externally for treating cancers. A commonplace book of 1901 suggests pouring 2 cups of boiling water over a handful of fresh green violet leaves, covering them, and letting them stand for 12 hours. Strain, dip lint into the liquid, and apply as a compress. Replace when dry or cold. In London, I unearthed a newspaper clipping from *The Times* (c. 1900) telling the story of Lady M. who had serious throat cancer and was on the verge of death, when a friend suggested this remedy. Within a week the external swelling had gone and the pain had ceased. Another week later the cancer had disappeared.

Yarrow (*Achillea millefolium*): For centuries this herb has been used to heal wounds and stem the flow of blood. During World War I soldiers carried yarrow ointment for use as a first-aid dressing on wounds and burns. It can reduce high blood pressure and is used to cool a fever. A diuretic, it is used in urinary tract problems, and mixed in an infusion with elderflower and peppermint, it is excellent for colds. Don't use yarrow in pregnancy, however, as it stimulates the uterus, although it can regulate menstrual periods. Chew a fresh leaf to alleviate toothache. Native Americans used yarrow to soothe the nerves and lift the spirits, as well as to cure fevers and colds.

The calming, sedative effect of lavender has been utilized for centuries by country people.

HERBS TO HELP SLEEP

The ancient Greeks recommended drinking wine to make you sleep—obviously in the right dosage! The soporific qualities of the hop are legendary, so beer will have a similar effect. The dried leaves of beautiful lady's mantle, used to fill a pillow, also induce sleep. Country wisdom suggests sleeping on a mattress filled with oat husks, since oats are a well-known nerve tonic. Cider vinegar with honey was recommended on retiring to bed, and medieval folk found that hawthorn tea worked wonders. Principally, however, there are six major herbs that have been used in cures for insomnia for centuries:

Chamomile (*Anthemis nobilis* and *Matricaria chamomilla*): Chamomile has been a well-established sleep herb since the time of the ancient Egyptians. Indigenous to Europe and northern Asia, it has naturalized in the USA. Culpeper wrote that "the bathing with a decoction of chamomile taketh away the weariness, and easeth pain." He recommended the "flowers boiled in a posset drink" (see page 171). Chamomile is a relaxant for the nervous system, soothing, calming, and tranquilizing for restless or over-

sensitive people. Its volatile oil, with its delicious scent, has the effect of relaxing muscles and aiding the digestion.

Chamomile Tea
Make an infusion of 2 tablespoons chamomile flowers to 2 cups boiling water. Let stand, covered, for 15 minutes, then strain and sweeten with honey.

Hop (*Humulus lupulus*): Hops grow vigorously in northern temperate zones and are cultivated in Europe, the USA, and Chile. Dried hop flowers, the female "cones" of the hop, which are so strongly scented, have been used to make "hop pillows" for the sleepless for generations. They help to soothe the highly strung and to relax twitching or restless muscles, and are a mild sedative. Make a cup of hop tea at bedtime, using the same method as for chamomile tea (above), for a good restful night's sleep.

Lavender (*Lavandula angustifolia*): This best-loved of aromatics, this native of the Mediterranean, introduced widely elsewhere, can be used to make a pillow in the same way as the hop pillow above, adding, if you wish, a few hops, some chamomile flowers, and linden blossoms. Sprinkle a few drops of lavender essential oil over the flowers before you sew up the pillow.

John Parkinson, herbalist and apothecary to King James I, describes in his *Paradisus in Sole* the fragrance of lavender as "piercing the senses":

> *Boil a good handful of lavender flowers in enough water to cover for 10 minutes. Strain into the bath and have a long soak.*
>
> *Sprinkle a few drops of lavender essential oil or a little good quality lavender water on to your pillow to enhance the effect—and you will be asleep in no time.*

Lettuce (*Lactuca sativa*): Lettuce has a very old reputation as a harmless herb to help and encourage sleep. Its country names include sleep-wort. In the eighteenth century, lettuce was cultivated for the white sap in the stems, which contains lactucanum, used as a sedative up to the end of the nineteenth century. This substance was introduced into medical practice in 1771, and called lettuce opium. It was even used to adulterate true opium, being a mild sedative.

My Chinese friend Frank told me that their "sleeping milk," or *Ku-chin-kan* was made from the white juice of the lettuce plant. Wild lettuce juice was used in other parts of the world, too, before the days of anesthetics, to give relief from pain.

So the best advice is to eat a good salad at night so you can partake of this natural sedative, soothing restlessness and muscle tension. The tale of the Flopsy Bunnies falling asleep after ravaging Mr. McGregor's lettuce was based on science!

Linden Blossom (*Tilia americana, T. vulgaris*): In ancient times the linden tree was sacred to the Indo-Germanic peoples. The almost overpowering scent of a linden tree in flower comes from the yellowish flowers, which bees love, that are used to make the world-famous herbal tea, *tilleul*. Also called lime-flower tea in Europe, this mildly honey-scented drink is deliciously soothing to the stomach. It is a nerve tonic, and helps sleeplessness. It is antispasmodic, sedative, and diuretic, and is used in eastern European folk medicine to reduce blood pressure.

Either make a cup of linden-blossom tea before retiring to bed, or make an infusion for a soothing bath (see rosemary bath, page 92).

Valerian (*Valeriana officinalis*): Valerian has an ancient reputation as a powerful medicinal herb and was promoted by Arab physicians in early times. It still has a place in pharmocopeias worldwide as a non-addictive tranquilizer, and has found its way into numerous over-the-counter preparations. It reduces blood pressure, is useful in stress and insomnia, and is good for menopausal symptoms. Valerianic acids are found in many sedatives. All-heal, Self-heal, and Blessed Herb are among its country names. "Phu" was another—undoubtedly because of the stink of the crushed roots, which cats love in the same way as they are attracted to catnip, happily rolling in it!

Valerian should only be used by prescription since large doses are inadvisable and it does not mix well with orthodox drugs. But it is powerfully sleep-inducing and soothes the over-sensitive, the tremulous, and the irritable, and it has been used to effect in nervous exhaustion and anxiety states. Tincture of valerian was used to treat shell shock in World War I.

A small homemade pillow filled with hop flowers induces deep sleep.

HERBAL TEAS AND TISANES

Making infusions of fresh or dried herbs is one of the best methods of extracting their qualities.

Making Herbal Teas

Always use good-quality herbs. Some packaged dried herbs are almost entirely without aroma or flavor.

Using dried herbs

One teaspoon for each cup is the general rule. Put it into a teapot, cover with boiling water, put on the lid, and let steep for 5–8 minutes. Do not over-brew, as this will ruin the delicacy of the herb. For the most delicately flavored herbs, it is better to add more of the herb to the infusion, and brew for a shorter time.

Using fresh herbs

Bruise 1 tablespoon of leaves by crushing them in a clean cloth. Place in the bottom of a small china teapot. Cover with boiling water, put on the lid, and let infuse.

Using seeds (e.g. fennel, dill, caraway)

Crush them in a clean cloth first, and make the tea with 1 tablespoon per 2½ cups of water. Put into a saucepan and simmer gently for 5–8 minutes. Strain, and sweeten with a little honey, if desired.

For iced herbal teas, make as above, strain, and chill in the refrigerator. These are wonderfully cooling and refreshing in summer. You can serve them with some cold milk and ice for a shake-style drink.

Blackberry leaf (*Rubus* spp.): Gather the young leaves in spring. This tea is excellent for pimples and sore throats; it can even be used as a gargle once it has cooled. You can also mix it with other spring leaves—for example, try three parts each of blackberry leaves, wild strawberry leaves, and woodruff. Add a pinch of thyme to make a delicious combination that is thirst-quenching and slightly diuretic.

Bergamot (*Monarda* spp.): Red bergamot (*M. didyma*) makes the most fragrant of teas, which is soothing and relaxing, excellent taken at bedtime. It has been called bee balm, and Oswego tea, after the Oswego Indians who made it regularly. American colonists took to it when they boycotted British tea before the War of Independence. Bergamot leaves add their inimitable fragrance to China tea, as well as to wine cups and lemonade.

For a nightcap, pour 1 cup hot milk over 1 tablespoon shredded bergamot leaves and let steep for 5 minutes or longer. Sweeten with honey and drink warm.

Chamomile (*Anthemis nobilis* and *Matricaria chamomilla*): This *tisane*, one of the most famous of them all, is often drunk as a digestive after a meal because it has a soothing action on the gastrointestinal tract, chamomile being sedative and anti-inflammatory. It has been found to be

very good for aging skin. Sweeten the *tisane* with honey, if desired.

Dandelion (*Taraxacum officinale*): Dandelion tea is strongly diuretic, and improves liver and gall-bladder functions, as well as being said to help rheumatism (see page 116). Use fresh leaves. Dandelion is safe in large amounts.

Elderflower (*Sambucus* spp.): An old lady in the village uses elderflower tea for a cold, as an alternative to aspirin. Sometimes her grandmother mixed it with linden flowers to help sweat out a chill or flu. Elderflower's volatile oil promotes sweating. You can also add elderflowers to ordinary tea, to flavor it and give it a delicate muscatel aroma.

Juniper berry (*Juniperus* spp.): Juniper grows from the Mediterranean to the Arctic, in the Himalayas, and in North America. Its antiseptic properties are useful in cystitis; it is diuretic and relieves gastric discomfort. It is not to be used in pregnancy or where kidneys are inflamed.

Use about 12–18 berries for each cup, cover with boiling water, and let steep for 10 minutes. It is palatable sweetened with a little honey, if desired.

Lady's mantle (*Alchemilla vulgaris*): This tea has been used throughout Europe, its native habitat, for gynecological disorders. "Woman's best friend" it has been called by country people, as its

regular use relieves menstrual pain and excessive bleeding. It is astringent and anti-inflammatory and is highly recommended for menopause.

Lemon balm (*Melissa officinalis*): I make this tea in early summer with a large bunch of the young leaves, infusing them in hot water for 10 minutes, and drinking it in the sun. It is sensational: Light, refreshing, and aromatic. The ancient Greeks called it a cure-all—it is a sedative and a gentle herb for upset stomachs. It has long been used for depression or over-tiredness, and for anxiety and tension headaches.

Mint (*Mentha* spp.): Made with fresh leaves, this peppermint tea is one of the most attractive of them all. Its antispasmodic properties calm the stomach, and it is good for nervous headaches, as well as for colds. Use whole leaves for a more subtle flavor, or shred them if you want to make it stronger. A delicious drink can be made by infusing a tablespoon of peppermint leaves in 1 cup boiling milk for 7–10 minutes, then straining. Serve hot.

Similar teas can be made with rose geranium (*Pelargonium graveolens*), rose hip (*Rosa canina*), sage (*Salvia officinalis*), thyme (*Thymus vulgaris*), and lemon verbena (*Aloysia triphylla*). You can also make delightful combination teas such as balm with lavender, hawthorn with sage, sage with honeysuckle, and yarrow with elderflower.

Herbal Lore and Legend

The lore and legends of herbs have filled many books from antique times, but certain anecdotes and associations have found their way into popular culture via long-standing traditions, or been made famous by literature and poetry.

Balm (*Melissa officinalis*): Balm is the "scholars" herb, given to students to clear their heads and sharpen both their memory and their understanding. In the Language of Flowers, balm stands for joking because it makes people cheerful and merry, and composes even the most agitated. It has a "cordial and exhilarating effect," according to John Evelyn, the seventeenth-century English diarist. Wearing a sachet of balm leaves next to your heart will make you attractive, happy, and healthy. The farmer's wife would give balm leaves to her cows to increase the flow of milk, and balm is "good against a surfeit of mushrooms."

Basil (*Ocimum basilicum*): Every good Hindu goes to his final rest with a basil leaf on his breast—his passport to Paradise. Hindus believe that good fortune awaits those who build their houses on a spot where basil has grown freely, and there is no forgiveness in this world, or the next, for anyone who uproots it.

In Italy, leaves of basil are love tokens, and a pot of basil in the window is a sign that a girl is expecting her lover; in Crete, basil is also sown in pots as a love plant. In France, however, *semer le basilic* means to slander someone. To dream of basil means grief and misfortune.

Dill (*Anethum graveolens*): Dill is a powerful herb in the armory of witches, who used it in their spells and charms. Yet dill was also powerful against witches, hung over doors or windows as a protection from the Evil Eye. It is generally a plant of good omen: English country brides used to wear a sprig of dill on their wedding day.

Fennel (*Foeniculum vulgare*): Prometheus concealed the fire of the sun in a hollow stem of fennel to bring it from heaven to earth for the human race, according to ancient Greek legend. Knowledge came to man from the gods of Olympus in the form of a fiery coal contained in a fennel stem. It is a powerfully protective plant against witchcraft, and sprigs of fennel hung in the rafters would drive evil spirits away. In classical times, fennel was strewn across the pathway of a newly married couple.

Lavender (*Lavandula angustifolia*): Lavender is dedicated to Hecate, the goddess of the moon revered by witches and sorcerers. Yet, ambiguously, it was one of the herbs used to avert the Evil Eye. In the Language of Flowers, lavender represents "mistrust," and it was believed that the viper made lavender its habitat. Legend goes that lions and tigers become docile with the scent of lavender.

Rosemary (*Rosmarinus officinalis*): Rosemary has more folklore attached to it than any other herb. The blue flowers are said to have taken their color from the Virgin Mary's blue cloak, when, during the flight into Egypt, she threw it over a rosemary bush to dry. Until then the flowers had been white. Rosemary grows to the height of Christ and no higher, and for no longer than his 33 years of age. Rosemary grows in the gardens of the righteous, and where it grows "mistress is master." At country weddings, sprigs of rosemary were dipped into the wine before the newlyweds drank, to ensure their continued love and happiness. Rosemary stands for remembrance.

Sage (*Salvia officinalis*): "Sage the Savior" was believed to prolong life:

> *He that would live for aye*
> *Must eat sage in May.*

A thriving sage bush indicates thriving family fortunes, and it flourishes or withers according to the prosperity of the master of the house. But:

> *If the sage tree thrives and grows*
> *The master's not master and he knows!*

In the Language of Flowers it stands for esteem: Sage plants were valued so highly that they needed protection from the Devils' familiar, the toad. So rue was often planted nearby in order to attract toads away from this valuable plant.

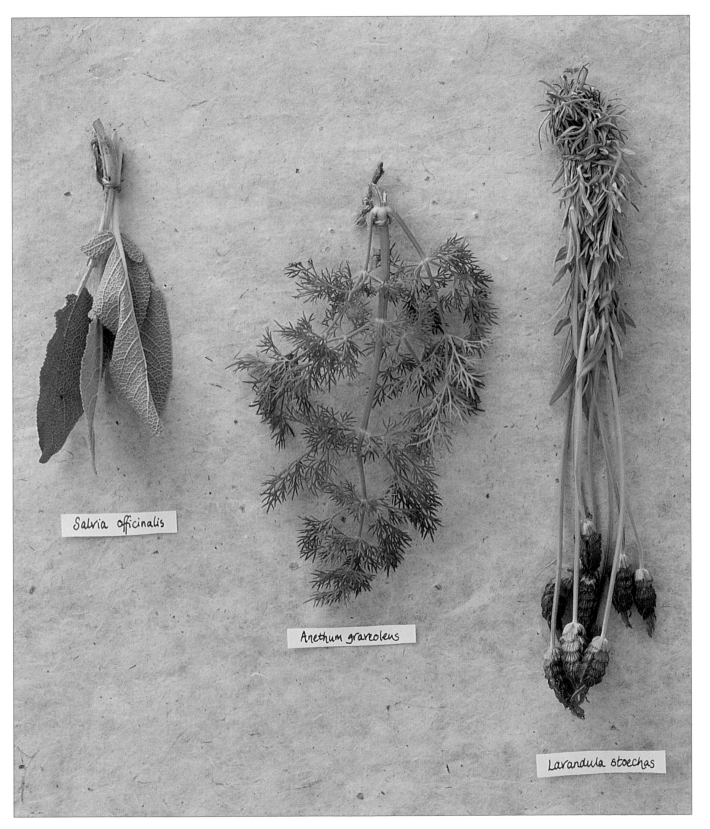

Salvia officinalis

Anethum graveolens

Lavandula stoechas

THE COUNTRY HARVEST

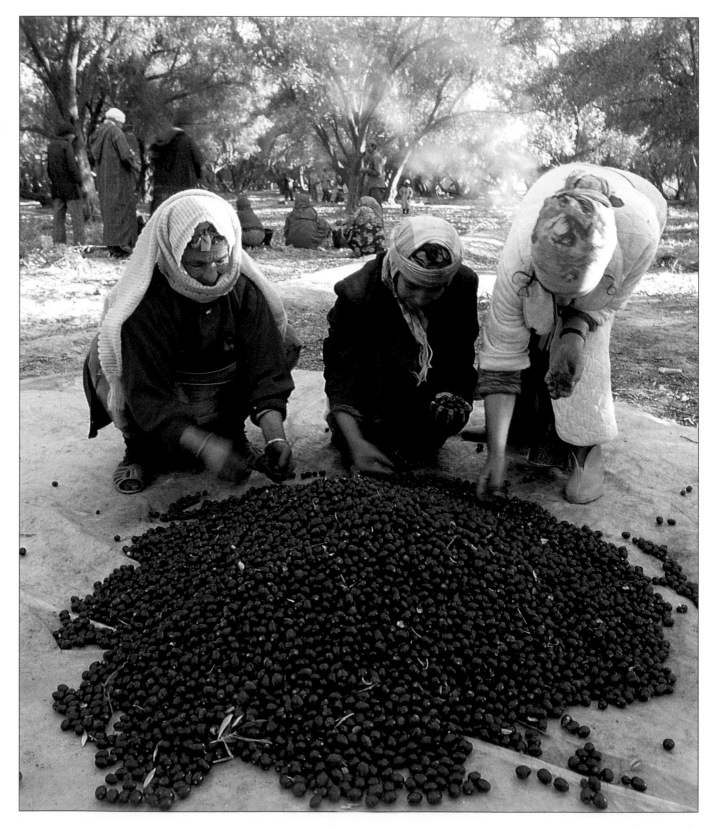

The celebration of plenty happens all over the world, and in many forms. The rice harvest in Japan is celebrated with traditional festivities dedicated to Inari, the rice goddess. In India, Vishnu and Lakshmi are offered a dish of rice or *idli* (steamed rice cakes), or newly harvested grain cooked with cashew nuts and jaggery (raw lump cane sugar). The olive harvest is marked in the South of France, at Nyons, with the pageantry of Les Olivades, where the Knights of the Olive Trees parade through the town, and *pan bagna*—bread soaked in olive oil—is eaten. In parts of the world where fish is plentiful, the fish harvest is celebrated: On the Volga in southern Russia, Maslenitsa in mid-June celebrates their "living silver," the catch of bream and sturgeon. In Taranto, Italy, in September, a feast is dedicated to Stella Maris—Star of the Sea—who protects fishermen at sea, and special fish grills are set up along the beaches. In New Mexico, an annual chili festival is held to celebrate the state's biggest cash crop, and California celebrates its "silver pearl" in a famous event in Gilroy, where thousands turn out to pay homage to garlic. There are Chestnut Fairs in southern France around All Souls' Day, November 1st, and honey fairs the world over. The mushroom harvest in Russia is a national pastime, immortalized by Tolstoy, and at the annual Apple Tree festival in Finistère, Brittany, a grand fair and fireworks mark the celebrations amid much cider-making.

Before the mechanization of farming, the end of the grain harvest, with its "Harvest Home" feast, was the crowning point of the farm-worker's year, celebrating the filling of the granaries with the year's crop. Wilf, my neighbor in the village, told me how the Last Sheaf was brought home in triumph, the harvest wain decorated with flowers and boughs of oak and ash. It was drawn by four or six great working horses, decked out with garlands of wild flowers. That evening a harvest supper—the "Horkey"—was held in the big barn for all the farm-workers, a traditional roast meat meal followed by apple pie and plum pudding, all washed down with generous amounts of ale or cider. They danced and sang, and toasted the farmer and his family. An American lad, who worked on his father's farm in South Dakota, remembers the obligatory church service before a similar harvest supper, with a rousing sermon to send them on their way. The Harvest Festival service held in many churches is a remnant of this custom.

This wild harvest can be converted into preserves of many kinds—pickles, chutneys, jams and jellies, and even unusual marmalades to stock the pantry for the winter months. The annual mushroom feast provides you not only with the delights of gathering them from the damp woods, but also with many delicious meals while they are in season. And the honey harvest from your local beekeeper may well furnish your kitchen shelf with enough to make some delectable sweet treats. Pies and soufflés, cakes and puddings, cookies and ice creams can all find their way to the table from the hedgerows, fields, and woods.

GRANDMOTHER'S DAIRY

Fresh eggs and new milk were a major part of the meals in Hallington Hall, the summer home of the distinguished British historian G. M. Trevelyan, where as children we spent regular holidays. Still warm from the adjoining farm, the eggs and milk were brought solemnly to table in the formal dining room in elegant china pitchers or silver dishes. The fruit used to come from the walled kitchen garden, with its long greenhouses, espaliered trees, and huge fruit cages, collected daily for the kitchens by Sidney, the gardener. My mother got on well with the cook, Mrs. Thomas, and I remember her jotting down recipe tips. After she died I found these written in a little note book, and some of the dairy and egg recipes here come from that source. The cook made delicious country pies and puddings, too, which I have never seen anywhere else.

Lemon cream

Lemon Cream

This is pure bliss—cool and delicious for hot summer days. You can make it with wine instead of sherry for a lighter effect. Eat with large spoons—it's like a sweet soup.

SERVES 6

2½ cups crème fraîche

⅔ cup ground almonds

3 glasses cream sherry

Grated zest and juice of
   1 lemon

3–4 tablespoons granulated
   sugar, to taste

2 tablespoons golden syrup or
   honey, to decorate

Lemon zest, to decorate

Mix the crème fraîche with the ground almonds in a pitcher. In another pitcher, combine the sherry, lemon zest and juice, and sugar to taste. Pour rapidly from one pitcher to the other until the mixture is frothy, then pour into wineglasses. Chill. To decorate, heat the golden syrup or honey with shreds of lemon zest for 1–2 minutes, then pour on top of the individual servings.

Baked Apple Custard

Apples are a symbol of fruitfulness and plenty, and friends in Normandy, France, say you must always leave the last apple on the tree for good luck. This apple dessert is a lovely and unusual pudding. It has a marbled effect, as the apple and the custard separate. Serve chilled, with cream.

SERVES 4

6 large apples, peeled and
   chopped

A little cold water

Brown sugar, to taste

Grated zest of ½ lemon

1 teaspoon ground cinnamon

1¼ cups milk

4 eggs

½ cup granulated sugar

1 small sweet apple

2 tablespoons butter

Preheat the oven to 350°F. Heat the chopped apples in a pan with the water; as they begin to soften, mash them to a pulp. Sweeten with brown sugar. Add the lemon zest and cinnamon and leave to cool. (A tip to soften hardened brown sugar: Add a slice of bread or apple to the container and leave for a couple of days.)
Put the apple sauce into the bottom of a baking dish. Heat the

milk to just below the boiling point. Beat the eggs with the granulated sugar until thick, then gradually pour on the hot milk. Pour this over the applesauce. Place the dish in the oven and bake for 25–35 minutes. Decorate with slices of apple sautéed in butter.

Elderflower Floating Islands

I have always loved the muscatel scent of elderflowers, and use them often in jams and soft drinks. I have based this on a classic recipe from France, *Iles flottantes*.

SERVES 4

2 clusters elderflowers
5 cups milk
2 tablespoons semolina or farina

½ cup superfine sugar
Pinch of salt
4 eggs, separated
Ground cinnamon

Snip the blossoms off the stems and infuse them in the milk over a low heat for 10 minutes. (An old-fashioned tip to prevent milk from boiling over is to place a clean marble in the bottom of the pan.) Strain the milk and stir in the semolina, half of the sugar, and the salt. Beat the egg yolks in a bowl, then pour in the milk and semolina mixture. Set the bowl over a pan of hot (not boiling) water, and heat gently, stirring, until the custard thickens. Pour into a glass dish and let cool.

Just before serving, beat the egg whites until stiff. Add the remaining sugar and beat again until the mixture will hold a stiff peak. Scoop up tablespoons of the egg white and float on top of the custard. Decorate with a sprinkling of cinnamon.

Hazelnut Ice Cream

Hazelnuts, cobnuts, and filberts are all names for the same wild nut, dedicated to Saint Phillibert, whose saint's day falls at the end of August, at about the time of the hazelnut harvest. Their crunchiness contrasts with the smooth creaminess of the ice cream and is mouthwatering.

SERVES 6

1½ cups ground hazelnuts
2½ cups milk

1 tablespoon butter
6 tablespoons granulated sugar
4 eggs, separated

Simmer the nuts with the milk in a heavy pan for 20 minutes. Put the butter, sugar, and egg yolks into a bowl, set over hot—not boiling—water, and beat together. Gradually add the milk and nuts

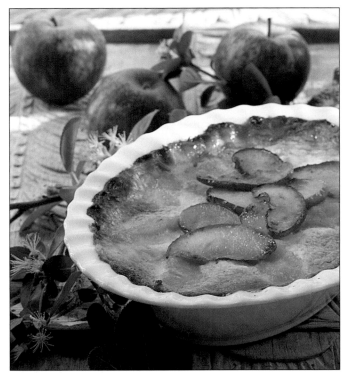

Baked apple custard

to the mixture, beating until thick. Do not let it reach boiling point or it will separate. Pour into a container, and when cool, put into the freezer. Freeze for 1 hour until well chilled. Beat the egg whites until stiff and fold into the ice cream. Return to the freezer.

English Custard Sauce

As children we used to beg our Northumbrian cook, Mrs. Thomas, to make this for us most nights. Sometimes she made it with duck eggs for richness, and occasionally she even used cream for a superlatively rich custard.

SERVES 8

2½ cups milk
6 tablespoons granulated sugar

Grated zest of ½ lemon
A few drops vanilla extract
5 eggs

Put the milk into a pan with the sugar, lemon zest, and vanilla, and leave to infuse over a low heat for 30 minutes. Bring to the boiling point, then strain into a bowl. Beat the eggs and stir into the cooling milk. Strain into a bowl and set it over a pan of hot water. Stir until the mixture thickens. Do not allow it to boil, or it will curdle. Serve with pies and other desserts.

EGGS

Some of my earliest memories of childhood are of my mother rounding up the chickens into the hen house every evening, and of one inevitably escaping and causing havoc in a neighbor's garden. The flavor of those eggs, and the rich color of the yolks, were sensational. There was also, unknown to me, a rich and varied harvest out there somewhere, of gull eggs, goose eggs, the eggs of plovers, moorhens, ostriches, partridges, pheasants, pigeons, quail, turkeys, and guinea fowl. Even penguins. Eggs for the specialists.

Chicken eggs, however, are both eaten and celebrated the world over, from China, with its thousand-year-old eggs (preserved in salt, wood ash, and lime), to a tiny village in the French Alps where the reappearance of the sun from behind the mountains after one hundred days of deepest winter is celebrated with a cook-in of omelets. The obvious symbolism of eggs as life-force, of the unending cycle of creativity, ensures their place in Easter festivities throughout the Christian world—boiled, painted, blown, or imitated in chocolate.

Apple Snow

My mother used to make this for the family, and we all loved it. I still use her recipe, which she had inherited from Mrs. Thomas in her Northumberland kitchen.

SERVES 4	
5 large apples, peeled, cored, and cut into quarters	Finely grated zest of ½ lemon
	4 egg whites
	½ cup superfine sugar

Put the apples into a pan with the lemon zest and a little water, just enough to prevent burning. Cook until tender, about 20 minutes, then mash the apples to a pulp and let cool.

Beat the egg whites, add the sugar, and continue beating until the mixture is stiff. Gently fold into the apples, and heap in a large glass dish. This is lovely with a custard sauce (see page 131).

Elderflower Fritters

For me, midsummer means elderflowers. I use this plentiful harvest to flavor gooseberry jams and pies, and every year I make my own elderflower cordial. These fritters are exceptionally delicious, served simply with a sprinkling of fine sugar and a touch of ground cinnamon.

SERVES 4	Batter:
8 stems of elderflowers, flowerheads separated	¼ cup all-purpose flour
	A pinch of salt
Vegetable oil for deep-frying	3 tablespoons vegetable oil
Sugar and a little ground cinnamon	⅔ cup warm water
	1 egg white, stiffly beaten

To make the batter, sift the flour with the salt, and stir in the oil. Gradually add the water, stirring until smooth and creamy. Leave to stand for 2 hours. Just before using, fold in the beaten egg white.

Dip the flowerheads in the prepared batter and deep-fry in very hot oil for about 1 minute until golden and crisp. Drain on paper towels, dust with sugar and cinnamon, and serve immediately.

Hazelnut and White Chocolate Meringue

Hazelnuts grow thickly in the hedges near a village in northern France where a friend rents out her cottage. Inspired by a meal at the local restaurant, I tried my hand at this wonderful dessert, light and nutty yet with a hint of chocolate. The layers are put together with whipped cream making it fit for a special occasion.

SERVES 6–8

¼ cup hazelnuts

5 egg whites

1 cup, plus 2 tablespoons
   superfine sugar

3 ounces each semisweet and

white chocolate, roughly chopped

1 teaspoon ground cinnamon or
   apple-pie spice

1¼ cups heavy cream

Confectioners' sugar, for dusting

A few raspberries (optional)

Line two large baking sheets with parchment paper. Preheat the oven to 275°F.

Toast the nuts and chop them fine. Beat the egg whites until stiff, then beat in the superfine sugar until stiff and shiny. Fold in the nuts and the chocolate. Spoon the mixture into two large rounds on the prepared baking sheets and bake for 2–2½ hours. Turn off the oven and leave the meringue layers inside to cool.

Whip the cream until fairly thick, and spread it over the top of one of the layers. Cover with the second. Dust with confectioners' sugar, decorate with a few raspberries, if desired, and serve.

A tip for using up eggshells: Add them to cloudy stock to clear it, then strain (they absorb impurities).

Pickled red cabbage

VINEGARS AND PICKLES

The pungent smell of pickles cooking with vinegar is highly evocative of autumn, reminiscent of those first chilly, misty mornings as summer fades and you feel a warning of winter in the fields and lanes. You can pickle a huge variety of vegetables: The range extends from cauliflower, shallot, artichoke, and beet to melon, peach, and pear, as well as to many Asian vegetables.

The Russians have a time-honored tradition of pickling mushrooms, and the Chinese pickle a variety of vegetables for winter use. Sichuan preserved vegetables are pickled in salt and chili, and eaten alone or added to stir-fries. The pickled vegetables, or *tsukemono*, of Japanese cuisine have a crisp texture and tangy flavor; they are often eaten with rice for lunch. They are traditionally pressed and pickled in rice bran and salt.

When you are making pickles, do use good vinegar: It is a false economy to buy it cheaply because nasty vinegar will affect the flavor of whatever you are cooking. Check that the vinegar has an acetic acid content of at least 5 percent, and use white vinegar because it shows off the color of a pickle better than dark vinegar. Store your pickles in glass jars with two-piece screw-on lids. Process pickles in a hot-water bath, at 180°–190°F, for 10–15 minutes before storage.

Spiced Pickling Vinegar

1 quart vinegar
½ ounce each whole cloves, allspice berries, fresh ginger, cinnamon
*   sticks, and whole peppercorns*

Warm the vinegar in an enameled or stainless steel pot. Add the spices, cover, and infuse over a low heat for 2 hours. Let cool. When cool, strain the vinegar into clean bottles and seal.

Pickled Red Cabbage

A great stand-by for the pantry shelf, this particular recipe comes from Ireland.

MAKES ABOUT 4   *¼ cup salt*
1-PINT JARS   *1 quart hot spiced*
1 medium head red cabbage   *pickling vinegar (see left)*

Remove the outer cabbage leaves, and divide the head into 6 segments. Remove the core, and shred the segments very fine. Put the cabbage into a large bowl and sprinkle with salt. Cover and leave in a cold place for 1–2 days.

Drain the cabbage, but do not rinse. Pack into clean jars and fill with the boiling spiced vinegar. Cover and process. Store in a cool, dry place for at least 3 weeks before using. Eat within 3 months—after that the cabbage loses its crispness.

Old-Fashioned Gooseberry Vinegar

This vinegar is at its best if you allow it to mature for a year. Then it will make the most superb vinaigrette, a deliciously different change from the more usual raspberry vinegar. You can use as many gooseberries as you wish, as long as you use the right proportion of water and sugar. I tend to use about 3 pounds fruit and enough water to cover.

Ripe gooseberries,
*   ends trimmed*
Lukewarm water
Light brown sugar

Work the gooseberries in a blender until they are roughly mashed, but not puréed. Place in a bowl with enough lukewarm water to cover, and leave to soak for 24 hours. Strain and measure the liquid. For every 2½ cups add ¾ cup sugar. Stir well, then pour into a large cask and cover. Stir 2–3 times a day until the sugar dissolves completely, then secure a linen cloth over the bunghole. Leave to stand for 9 months in a warm place in the kitchen, then decant into bottles. Store for at least 12 months before using.

Pickled Blackberries

These are an inspired addition to the pantry shelf, delicious with bread and cheese. I also love them with cream cheese and sugar as a dessert. Beware, however, of picking blackberries after October 12th. Legend goes that this is the anniversary of the Fall, and that Satan, cast out of heaven, fell into a blackberry bush and cursed it in his anger. From that date on blackberries taste sour, so they say.

MAKES 4 POUNDS

1 pound (2¼ cups) granulated sugar

1¼ cups white wine vinegar

1 teaspoon allspice berries

1 teaspoon whole cloves

2 (3-inch) cinnamon sticks

2 pounds blackberries

Put the sugar into a pan with the vinegar and dissolve slowly over a low heat. Tie the spices in a cheesecloth bag and place in the simmering mixture. Cook for 5 minutes. Add the blackberries and simmer gently for another 10–15 minutes. Remove the spices, and drain the blackberries in a nylon strainer, reserving the liquid. Pack the berries into warm jars, filling by about two-thirds. Return the liquid to the pan and boil hard until it reduces to a thick syrup. Pour the syrup over the blackberries to fill the jars, and seal. Process for 10 minutes.

Pickled blackberries can be eaten with ice cream and shortbread as an unusual but delicious dessert.

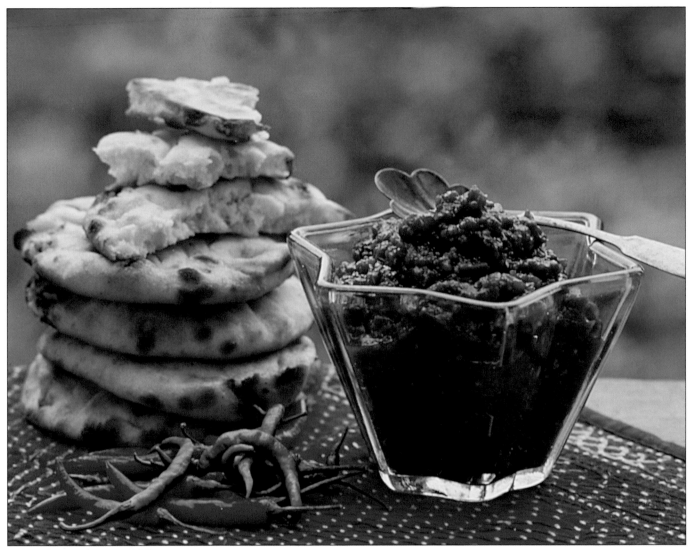

Indian chutney (see page 139)

CHUTNEYS

In traditional European country cooking, chutneys are made principally from apples, onions, and tomatoes, with dried fruit such as raisins and dates added. Garlic and shallots can also be added, and frequently chutneys are laced with chilies, peppercorns, or mustard seed to give a zing.

Chutneys are first cousins to pickles. The main difference is that the vegetables and/or fruit for pickles are left whole or cut into large pieces, whereas those for chutneys are cooked until soft and mushy. Also, dark malt vinegar is generally used.

The word "chutney" actually originates from the Hindi *chatni*, meaning a relish of sweet fruit or vegetables cooked with vinegar and hot spices. Some Indian chutneys, however, are made up uncooked and served alongside the meal rather like condiments.

In Britain, chutneys have always been served with the famous plowman's lunch: bread and cheese. This is one of the best of simple meals when all the ingredients are top quality. Chutneys are also delicious with curries and rice dishes, and make a pleasant change with roast chicken. A selection of chutneys greatly

Old-fashioned tomato and apple chutney

enhances a buffet table, adding character and flavor to cold cuts and other cold dishes.

Use jars with two-piece screw-on lids. Process chutneys in a hot-water bath at 180°–185°F for 10–15 minutes.

Old-Fashioned Tomato and Apple Chutney

If you grow your own tomatoes, you may, in a good year, be overwhelmed by your harvest. So use up either ripe or green tomatoes in this chutney—an admirable way of dealing with a late summer glut.

MAKES 12 POUNDS

6 pounds tomatoes, sliced
1 pound apples, cored
1 pound onions, peeled
2 ounces coriander seeds
½ ounce dried hot chilies
1½ tablespoons salt
1 ounce ground ginger
1 pound (2¼ cups) raw brown sugar
1 pound (3 cups) golden raisins
Juice of 1 lemon
¼ cup light corn syrup
3 cups malt vinegar

Place the sliced tomatoes, apples, and onions in a preserving kettle. Tie the coriander seeds and chilies in a cheesecloth bag and add to the kettle. Sprinkle with the salt and leave overnight.

Add the remaining ingredients the next day and bring to a boil. Lower the heat to medium and cook for 2 hours until thick. Pack into hot, clean jars, cover, and process.

Indian Chutney

From chutney's country of origin, this was given to me by an excellent Indian cook. This is not for timid taste buds.

MAKES 8 POUNDS	
15 large baking apples	1 pound (2¼ cups) raw brown
1½ cups chopped onions	sugar
1 cup chopped garlic	7½ cups malt vinegar
2 fresh hot chilies, sliced	2 ounces mustard seeds
8 ounces (1½ cups) raisins	2 ounces ground ginger

Bake the apples at 350°F for 25–30 minutes, until soft. Scoop out the flesh from the skins and remove the seeds.

While the apples are baking, put the chopped onion into a pan with the garlic and cover with water. Simmer for 20 minutes until soft, then drain. Discard the cooking liquid.

Put the apples and onions into a preserving kettle with the remaining ingredients. Bring to a boil and simmer for 20–30 minutes until well amalgamated and most of the liquid has evaporated.

Pack into hot, clean jars, cover and process.

Autumn Chutney

I first came across this at an annual fund-raising market in the village hall, made by a woman who has become a great recipe-swapping friend. This chutney makes the most of the autumn harvest and is wonderful to have on the pantry shelf through the winter.

MAKES 7 POUNDS	
1 pound plums, halved and pitted	1 pound (3 cups) golden raisins
1 pound apples, peeled and cored	2½ cups malt vinegar
1 pound tomatoes, chopped	¼ teaspoon ground mace
1 pound onions, sliced	¼ teaspoon apple-pie spice
1 large garlic clove, chopped	½ ounce ground ginger
	1 pound (2¼ cups) raw brown sugar

Mix the fruit and vegetables together and put into a preserving kettle with all the other ingredients except the sugar. Simmer for 30–40 minutes until tender. Add the sugar and stir until dissolved.

Simmer gently, stirring frequently, until thick. Cool, then pack into hot, clean jars. Cover and process. Store in a cool, dark, dry place.

Smooth Gooseberry Chutney

One of my greatest favorites. This is almost like a purée in texture, full of interesting flavors, and excellent served with hot or cold meats. It is lovely with cheese, too, and does a lot to spice up a simple side salad.

1 pound gooseberries	light brown sugar
1½ cups chopped onions	½ ounce salt
1¼ cups chili or herb vinegar	1 tablespoon ground ginger
(available from most	½ teaspoon cayenne
supermarkets)	1¼ cups white vinegar
1 pound (2¼ cups) packed	1¼ cups water

Poach the gooseberries in water to cover for 5 minutes, then drain. Liquefy with the chopped onions and spiced vinegar. Add the remaining ingredients and bring to a boil. Simmer for 15–20 minutes until it is the consistency of a thick sauce. Pack into hot, clean jars, cover and process.

Plum Chutney

There is a damson plum tree along one of the lanes near my cottage. When it fruits abundantly I make jellies, jams, and cheeses—and this inimitable chutney. It is the best thing ever with a plowman's lunch.

MAKES 2 ½ POUNDS	
1 pound damson plums,	2 cups malt vinegar
stems removed	¼ ounce each whole cloves and
1 large cooking apple, peeled,	fresh ginger
cored, and chopped	½ dried hot red chili
1 large onion, chopped	1 teaspoon salt
½ cup golden raisins	Pinch of dry mustard powder
	1¼ cups white sugar

Cook the plums gently in a little water until soft, but not breaking up. Drain. Remove the pits with a slotted spoon. Put the fruit into a preserving kettle with all the other ingredients, except the sugar, tying up the spices in a cheesecloth bag. Simmer gently for 20–30 minutes. Add the sugar, then boil hard until thick, stirring from time to time to prevent the mixture from sticking to the bottom of the pan. Pour into clean, hot jars. Cover and process.

PRESERVES, JAMS, AND JELLIES

Making preserves, jams, and jellies was a matter of course for our grandmothers. These women were highly creative, preserving whatever grew around them and often in inspired and unusual combinations of ingredients. I have collected numerous old recipe books, and over the years have shared many recipes with other cooks. The country markets are a great source, not only of ideas, but also of quality products, and this informal research has furnished me with a fabulous selection of gleaming jars for the pantry shelf as well as hundreds of useful tips—not least among my favorites is that of adding chopped nuts to jam.

Making jam is synonymous with homemaking, and much traditional wisdom has accrued from it over the years: Always pick your fruit on a dry day to reduce the chances of jams going moldy. Always use ripe or just under-ripe, and never damaged, fruit, for similar reasons. Use refined white sugar. You will need a large, heavy-bottomed enameled or stainless steel preserving kettle, so that the jam can boil rapidly without boiling over; a long-handled wooden spoon; a slotted spoon; a jelly thermometer; and a jelly bag for jellies. Always store jams and jellies in a cool, dark, dry place to minimize the chances of mold forming.

It is best to pick fruit in dry weather, in the morning with the sun on them if possible, when their flavor is fullest. Damp weather dilutes the flavor and encourages mold at a later stage. For jams and preserves, the general rule is to discard over-ripe or unripe fruit, and use as soon as possible after gathering it. For jellies and chutneys you can use damaged and windfall fruit, as long as it is under-ripe and the damaged parts are cut away. In this way, you can make full use of food from the garden as well as from the wild—plums, blackberries or quinces, apples or crabapples—all the fruit that has long played its part in the rich harvest of the autumn countryside.

Testing for Doneness

Making jams and jellies is an incredibly simple operation, but the crucial part comes when testing for doneness. Some jams take longer than others to gel, depending on the water content of the fruit, and altitude can affect timing. The time taken can vary 10–20 minutes. It is when the mixture becomes thick and syrupy that it is approaching the gel point. You need to have an infallible method of testing. The most reliable is a thermometer—jams and jellies are done when they reach 220°F (at 1000 feet above sea level). The "refrigerator test" is an alternative: Spoon a little of the mixture onto a cold saucer and refrigerate for a few minutes. If the jam or jelly wrinkles a little and does not run when you push it with your fingertip, it is done. If it is still liquid, continue boiling and test again a little later. The "sheet test" can be used for jellies: Dip a cold metal spoon into the boiling jelly, lift it out, and turn it so the jelly runs off the side. If the jelly runs off in a sheet, it is done. Process preserves, conserves, jams, and marmalades in a boiling-water bath at 212°F for 5 minutes.

Pumpkin Preserves

I have been making these highly unusual preserves for years. They are excellent on toast for breakfast, and I also use them as a filling for sponge cakes. They look stunning—a pale gold color, clear and translucent—and have a mouthwatering texture. I love the spike of the ginger!

MAKES 10 POUNDS	2½ cups lemon juice
6 pounds pumpkin, peeled,	2½ cups water
seeded, and cut into small cubes	About 4 ounces candied
6 pounds granulated sugar	stem ginger, to taste (optional)

Layer the pumpkin in a deep dish with the sugar. Pour the lemon juice over the top and leave overnight. Place the pumpkin in a preserving kettle with the water and cook until tender, about 30–40 minutes. Allow to stand overnight again. Drain off the liquid, boil it until it is quite thick, and skim. Pour the boiling syrup over the pumpkin. Add the ginger, cut into small cubes, if using. Spoon into jars, seal, and process.

Old-Fashioned Gooseberry Jam

A lovely summer jam from an old lady in the village, this is delicious on scones. The recipe uses currant juice instead of water to cook the fruit. You can reduce any scum on top by stirring in a lump of butter just as the jam begins to gel, or rub the inside of

Golden pumpkin preserves, spiked with ginger

the pan with butter before you start. Another precaution is to add 2 tablespoons of vinegar to the final rinse water for the jars.

MAKES 6 POUNDS

1 pound red currants or
  black currants
2½ cups water

6 pounds red gooseberries,
  ends trimmed
3 pounds granulated sugar

Put the currants into a pan with the water and simmer for 10 minutes. Leave to cool, then strain the juice.

Place the gooseberries in a preserving kettle with 2½ cups of the currant juice. Bring to a boil and simmer fast until the gooseberries begin to break up. Add the sugar and simmer slowly until done (see opposite). Pack in warm jars, seal, and process.

Lemon and Rhubarb Preserves

A useful rule of thumb is never to fill your preserving kettle more than halfway, since jams and preserves are liable to boil over and make a terrible sticky mess on the range. These are stunning early summer preserves, with the slight crunchiness of a few chopped almonds. Delectable.

MAKES 3 POUNDS

3 pounds rhubarb, cut into chunks
2 pounds (4½ cups)

granulated sugar
Finely grated zest of 2 lemons
¼ cup minced blanched almonds

Put the rhubarb into a kettle with the sugar. Boil very gently, stirring constantly, for 30 minutes. Add the lemon zest and almonds, and boil until done. Pack into jars, seal, and process.

Great-Grandmother's Strawberry Preserves

The secret of success with strawberry preserves is not to cook too long, and not to use too much sugar, otherwise the delicate flavor of this exquisite summer fruit is impaired. If, by any chance, your preserves do not set (you can use this tip for jams, too), try adding 1–2 teaspoons of fresh lemon juice to every pound of fruit, and bringing to gel point again. The pectin in the lemon should do the trick.

MAKES 5 POUNDS

4 pounds strawberries

3 pounds (6¼ cups) granulated sugar

Choose a sunny day to gather the strawberries, and leave them in the sun until ready to use: This treatment preserves the color perfectly. Use fruit as fresh as possible, and wash it carefully, being careful not to bruise the berries. Remove the hulls and discard any bruised or damaged fruit before use.

Put the strawberries and sugar into a kettle and cook briskly for 15–20 minutes. Then remove the strawberries and spread them out in flat dishes in the sun. Boil the syrup until it is thick and clear, then return the strawberries. Pack in hot jars, seal, and process.

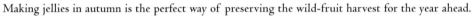

Making jellies in autumn is the perfect way of preserving the wild-fruit harvest for the year ahead.

Pear, Orange, and Walnut Conserve

The best conserve in the world. The recipe was given to me years ago by a woman who lived in a village in the depths of Burgundy, France, and I have made it over and over again. I shall never forget how it first tasted on baguettes from the *boulangerie* for breakfast, with a pot of fresh coffee.

MAKES 5 POUNDS	3 pounds (6¼ cups)
2 oranges, peeled and finely	granulated sugar
chopped	1 pound (3 cups) golden raisins
3 pounds pears, peeled,	1¼ cups water
cored, and finely sliced	1½ cups roughly chopped walnuts

Place the fruit in a preserving kettle with the sugar, raisins, and water, and simmer for 1½ hours. Add the chopped walnuts and cook for another 15 minutes. Pack into jars, seal, and process.

Plum Jelly

I make this superb jelly with my neighbor's Victoria plums, when she has a glut that she cannot cope with: It is a memorable tea-time treat on scones. One of the problems with jelly-making is losing the wooden spoon in the pan, however long its handle. An American lady gave me this tip: Clip a wooden clothes pin to the handle of the spoon and it will lodge securely on the edge of the pan.

MAKES 8 POUNDS	Juice of 1 lemon
6 pounds plums, stems	Water and granulated sugar
removed	

Slit the plums and put into a preserving kettle with the lemon juice and enough water to cover. Simmer gently until the fruit is tender, about 30 minutes. Place a jelly bag over a large bowl and tip the contents into it. Allow to drip for an hour or two. Do not squeeze the bag because this will strain impurities into the jelly and make it cloudy.

Measure the strained juice and for every 2½ cups, allow 2 cups sugar. Return the juice to the clean preserving kettle, bring to a boil, then remove from the heat, and stir in the sugar. Dissolve it over a low heat and then simmer until gel point is reached (see page 140).

Remove the pan from the heat, skim off any scum, and pour the jelly into hot, clean jars. Cover with two-piece screw-on lids and process (see page 140), unless using old-style jelly glasses and sealing with paraffin.

Japonica or Quince Jelly

I have a flowering quince (*Chaenomeles japonica*) trained to the front of my cottage, and it rewards me with exquisitely elegant salmon-pink blossoms in the spring, and a surprisingly abundant harvest of yellow fruit in October. So there is an annual ritual of jelly-making for our winter breakfasts: Inimitable on toast, and a weekend treat with croissants. It is the most heavenly dark pink.

japonica fruit or quinces	granulated sugar
water	

Wash the fruit and discard any over-ripe or damaged ones. Cut in half, or into quarters if they are large. Put into a preserving kettle with water to cover and simmer until tender—about 45 minutes. Pour into a jelly bag, suspended over a large bowl. Leave to drip until dry—anything from 2 hours to overnight. Do not squeeze the bag, or impurities in the fruit will cause the juice to become cloudy.

Measure the juice into the clean preserving kettle. For every 2½ cups juice add 1¾ cups sugar. Allow it to dissolve over a gentle heat, then bring to a boil, and simmer to gel point (see page 140). Cover with two-piece screw-on lids and process (see page 140), unless using old-style jelly glasses and sealing with paraffin. Store in a cool, dark place.

An alternative to carrot marmalade can also be made with a 50:50 mixture of rhubarb and carrots.

MARMALADES

Although "marmalade" nowadays means a kind of jelly made from citrus fruit, its origin lies in preserves of other fruit, usually quince. *Marmelo* is the Portuguese for quince, and in early days a thick quince paste, not unlike the cotignac at right, was a common sweetmeat around the Mediterranean. From there it must have traveled to South America, because a friend brought up in Brazil with Portuguese maids, told me he remembers it from his childhood in Rio. Sixteenth- and seventeenth-century recipe books contain numerous recipes for "marmalades" using quinces and other fruit, without a trace of oranges or lemons.

It was not until the eighteenth century that oranges began to appear in the recipe as a characteristic feature: The Keiller family had the idea of including strips of orange peel in their preserves, a famous brand-name to this day. In 1870, a certain Mrs. Cooper, a grocer's wife from Oxford, England, took up making orange marmalade on a commercial scale and created the famous product that epitomizes the British breakfast at its best.

So although many families have their favorite treasured recipes for citrus marmalades, I have chosen some very old country recipes that show their ancestry in the use of unusual fruits and even vegetables.

Cotignac Special

When I was a child, the old quince tree in our garden leaned dangerously out of a bank. I loved to sit in it where nobody could find me, reading a book. My mother made full use of the crop of fruit, and every year gleaming jars of this quince "butter" lined the cold marble shelf in the pantry. There is no need to peel the quinces.

MAKES 10 POUNDS
6 pounds quinces, sliced
About 1¼ cups water
About 4 pounds granulated
   sugar
⅔ cup whole almonds

1 pound (3 cups) golden raisins
⅔ cup candied cherries
⅓ cup chopped mixed candied peel
⅓ cup finely diced candied stem
   ginger (optional)

Place the quinces in a preserving kettle and add enough water to just cover. Place over a gentle heat and cook them to a pulp, about 1 hour. Stir from time to time to prevent them from sticking to the bottom and burning. Pass the pulp through a sieve. Weigh the pulp, and for every pound add 1¾ cups sugar. Return to the pan, along with the almonds and raisins, and cook to a thick purée. Boil until it reaches gel point (see page 140). Add the candied cherries and peel. Stir in the ginger, if using. Put into jars while still hot, cover, and process. Store in a cool, dark place.

Carrot Marmalade

A stunning "marmalade," delicious on wholewheat toast for breakfast. The zing of ginger is superb with the lemony flavor.

MAKES 3 POUNDS

2 pounds (about 8 cups) grated carrots
1½ pounds (3⅓ cups)

granulated sugar
2 lemons, quartered and sliced
2 teaspoons ground ginger

Cook the carrots with a little water until tender. Add the sugar and stir until dissolved. Add the sliced lemons and cook all together slowly until the mixture thickens and reaches the gel point (see page 140). Pack in hot, clean jars, cover, and process. Store in a dark, dry, cool place.

Apricot Marmalade

This thick apricot conserve contains the apricot kernels, which give a nutty flavor as well as a crunch to the finished product. A great summer favorite, simply delicious with hot croissants. I have not given quantities because the joy of this recipe is that you can use any quantity you want to as long as you follow the proportions.

Ripe apricots   *Granulated sugar*

Cut the apricots in half and remove the pits. Weigh the fruit, and for every pound allow 1 pound (2¼ cups) sugar. Sprinkle the sugar over the apricots and leave for 12 hours. Break the pits with a nutcracker, and blanch the kernels in boiling water for 3–4 minutes.

Put the fruit, sugar, and kernels into a preserving kettle and simmer very gently until the gel point is reached (see page 140)—

about 45 minutes. Remove any scum with a slotted spoon, then pack in clean, hot jars. Cover and process. Store in a dark, dry, cool place.

Tomato and Lemon Marmalade

This highly unusual combination makes a surprisingly delicious "marmalade." A tip for lemons: Store them in a jar of cold water in the refrigerator, and they keep for weeks. Also, you can freeze cut quarters of lemon in plastic bags.

MAKES 3 POUNDS

12 medium-sized ripe tomatoes, peeled and thinly sliced

1 pound (2¼ cups) granulated sugar
1½ lemons, quartered and thinly sliced

Put the tomatoes into a preserving kettle and bring to a simmer. Cook gently until they are soft. Add the sugar and stir until dissolved. Add the lemons and continue to cook slowly until thick, stirring from time to time, until gel point is reached (see page 140). Pack in hot, clean jars, cover, and process.

Cotignac is a rich, dark butter made from quinces.

BEES AND HONEY

More flies are caught with honey than with vinegar. Dutch proverb

Ever since antiquity, the busy bee has been producing the sublime and justly world-famous honey from wild herbs on the slopes of Mount Hymettus in Greece, and the celebrated honey from Mount Hybla in Sicily. A pound of honey requires 37,000 bee-loads of nectar, the equivalent of traveling 148,000 miles! Small wonder that bees have inspired mankind with a sense of awe.

Today there is hardly a country in the world that does not produce honey. The USA, Russia, China, and Central and South America produce 100,000 tons of honey each, a world production of 500,000 tons. Australia and New Zealand are well known for their honey, too: Black bees from Europe were thought to have arrived in Australia on the convict ship *Isabella* in 1822, and missionaries took bees to New Zealand in 1839. In the USA, the only indigenous bee, the stingless Meliponinae, was domesticated by the Mayans. Utah now calls itself "The Beehive State" and the seal of the Mormons, who brought in the honey bee, is a beehive surrounded by flowers beneath the crowning word "Industry."

Honey has acquired legendary status. It has been used in ointments, as a taste-killer for medicines, as a cosmetic that softens the skin, and as a disinfectant. Honey was the principal sweetener in cooking until the eighteenth century, although in the Middle East, syrup of figs or dates was an alternative. Honey was and is useful as a preservative: It keeps indefinitely because of its high sugar content. The rinsings of the combs were used to make mead, and mead-drinkers were renowned not only for their vigor but also for living long and healthy lives. Beeswax has been used in candles, cosmetics, and industry, and has had many household uses including polish, waterproofing, and sealing bottles. The famous waxworks of Madame Tussaud's are made of beeswax. And royal jelly—a hormone that unfortunately decomposes fast outside the hive—has given rise to international beauty legends.

Honey gives energy quickly and is the food most easily absorbed by humans.

Baklavas

Making your own baklavas—those deliciously fragrant Greek pastries (made all the more delicious if you use Hymettus honey)—is nowhere near as difficult as you might think.

MAKES 8	
6 tablespoons unsalted butter or margarine	Melted butter for brushing
	Ground cinnamon
¼ cup honey	SYRUP
2 cups chopped walnuts	½ cup honey
8 ounces phyllo pastry	½ cup water
	Juice of ½ lemon

Preheat the oven to 350°F. Heat the butter or margarine with the honey. Add the chopped nuts.

Line a well-buttered 7-inch square baking pan with 3 layers of phyllo, brushing each one with melted butter. Spread a thin layer of the filling on the pastry, sprinkle with cinnamon, and cover with 2 more layers of buttered phyllo. Repeat, and finish with 3 layers of phyllo on top. Tuck in the ends and sides to contain the filling. Brush the top with melted butter, and score into squares or diamonds with a sharp knife.

Bake until golden and crisp, 25–30 minutes. To make the syrup, boil the honey, water, and lemon juice. While still hot, pour it over the baklavas. Let cool before cutting into pieces for serving.

Honey Cookies

A month of celebrating, drinking honey-based wines such as mead, metheglin, or hydromel, is the source of "honeymoon." Attila the Hun greatly overdid the celebrations at his wedding by drinking too much of these potent wines during his honeymoon—and died. These honey cookies, however, should be safe enough: Light, wafery, and crisp, they melt in the mouth.

MAKES 18–20	
4 tablespoons margarine	3 tablespoons all-purpose flour
¼ cup raw brown sugar	Pinch of salt
2½ tablespoons honey, melted	½ teaspoon ground ginger
½ cup wholewheat flour	A squeeze of lemon juice

Preheat the oven to 325°F.

Put the margarine, sugar, and honey into a pan and stir over a

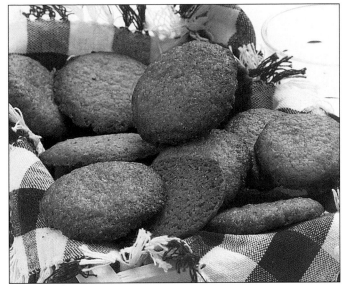
Honey cookies

gentle heat until the margarine has melted. Remove from the heat and stir in the flours, salt, and ginger. Then stir in the lemon juice.

Place teaspoonfuls of the mixture on a well-greased baking sheet, allowing room for the cookies to spread. Bake for 8–10 minutes until they are a light, golden brown.

Leave to cool for a minute or two, then carefully lift off and cool on a wire rack.

Honey-Baked Figs

From Turkey, here is a dish redolent of Mediterranean sun. Poaching ripe figs in white wine, honey, and a little lemon is a gastronomic delight. These are then served cold, covered with a thick layer of whipped cream and sprinkled with toasted almonds.

SERVES 4–6	
1 pound fresh figs	2 teaspoons lemon juice
1¼ cups white wine	Strip of lemon zest
¼ cup honey	1½ cups heavy cream, whipped
	¼ cup toasted sliced almonds

Preheat the oven to 400°F.

Arrange the figs close together in a shallow baking dish. Put the wine, honey, lemon juice, and zest into a pan and heat gently until the honey has melted. Pour over the figs. Cover and bake until tender, about 10–15 minutes depending on the ripeness of the figs. Cool before covering with the cream and almonds.

WILD FOOD CALENDAR

The food-for-free season starts in spring, with blossoms and young leaves and the spring crop of mushrooms. Throughout the summer you can pick a wide range of greens, herbs, and flowers with which to make salads, cordials, pies, and ice creams. Come the autumn, the harvest becomes a serious business, with the plentiful annual yields of fruit, nuts, and mushrooms that cloak the autumn hedgerows and fields. This calendar is a general guide to how you can make the most of the wild harvest by freezing or storing seasonal foods. It also gives advice on which plants are available at which times of the year.

For the Freezer
soups, quiches, pies and tarts, ice creams, cakes and cookies, sauces, sorbets, gratins

For the Cupboard
cordials, preserves in brandy, vinegars, teas and herbal tea, dried mushrooms

For the Pantry
jams, jellies, chutneys, ketchups, wines, cheeses and butters, pickles, curds, syrups, relishes

Spring

- amaranth
- birch
- bistort
- chickweed
- comfrey
- corn salad
- crab-apple
- dock
- blossom
- dandelion
- fiddlehead fern
- hawthorn blossom
- mulberry
- mushrooms
- pokeweed
- ramp
- stinging nettles
- violets
- wild garlic

Summer

- angelica
- bittercress
- borage
- chamomile
- chives
- clary
- comfrey
- corn salad
- elderflower
- glasswort
- goldenrod
- lady's mantle
- linden
- mallow
- marigold
- marjoram
- meadowsweet
- mint
- mustard
- nasturtium
- plantain
- purslane
- rose petals
- salad burnet
- sorrel
- sow thistle
- stinging nettle
- tansy
- thyme
- watercress
- wild grape
- wild raspberry
- wild strawberry
- yarrow

Autumn

- blackberry
- black walnut
- blueberry
- butternut
- cherry
- chestnut
- crab apple
- cranberry
- dewberry
- elderberry
- hickory
- juniper
- medlar
- mushroom
- pecan
- sloe
- walnut
- winter cress

Blackberry and apple tarte tatin

WILD FOOD THROUGH THE SEASONS

The long tradition of gathering wild food is associated mainly with autumn, when fruit and berries mature in the hedgerows, and a feast of fungi is to be found in the woods. However, there are many spring shoots and summer leaves that make excellent ingredients, too, offering a rich wild harvest for free: Country walks through the seasons can furnish you with baskets full of tasty and unusual flavors. I took to "hedgerow cooking," as I call it, when I first moved to the countryside from the city in my twenties. It seemed like a dream come true to be wandering the lanes and fields instead of rushing around a supermarket. This selection of dishes, both savory and sweet, consists of my favorites among the many that I have used over the years to make the most of the wild harvest.

Blackberry and Apple Tarte Tatin

Blackberry and apple is one of the longest-lasting marriages in gastronomy. This upside-down tart is inspired by a French classic, and is divine.

SERVES 4

1 pound (about 3 cups) blackberries

8 ounces apples, peeled, cored, and sliced (about 2 cups)

¼ cup granulated sugar

Pinch of ground cinnamon

8 ounces puff pastry

Milk for brushing

Preheat the oven to 425°F.

Mix the blackberries with the apples, sugar, and a pinch of cinnamon. Put into a 10-inch tart pan. Roll out the puff pastry to a circle measuring ½ inch larger than the rim of the pan, and place it over the top. Brush with milk. Bake for 25–30 minutes, until the pastry is risen and golden.

To serve, turn the tart upside down onto a serving plate. Cut into wedges and serve immediately, with thick strained yogurt or whipped cream.

Comfrey and Wild Mushroom Puffs

Majestic comfrey, with its beautiful bell-shaped flowers, contains all the mineral richness of spinach, plus vitamin B12—the only vegetable to do so—and also has a high protein content. Gather it from June onward, usually from damp, shady places. Wild mushrooms grow freely from spring through autumn: The Romans deemed them food for the gods.

SERVES 4 (makes 8 triangles)
2 pounds comfrey leaves, cooked and drained
1¼ cups béchamel sauce (see below)

8 ounces wild mushrooms such as chanterelles, puffballs, or cèpes, sliced
4 tablespoons butter
2 garlic cloves, minced
2 teaspoons dried mixed herbs
1 pound puff pastry

Mix the cooked comfrey with the béchamel. Sauté the sliced mushrooms in the butter until soft, then stir in the garlic and herbs. Let cool for 5 minutes, then drain off the juices. Add the mushrooms to the comfrey mixture.

Preheat the oven to 400°F. Roll out the pastry and cut into eight 5-inch triangles. Place a tablespoon or so of the filling in the center of each. Moisten the edges of the pastry and fold over one corner. Press the edges together firmly with a fork. Brush with beaten egg, and bake for 25 minutes, until risen and golden brown.

Chickweed Sandwiches

One of the great surprises of wild food is how delicious chickweed is. It is such an abundant and common weed, found much of the year round from Greenland to Tierra del Fuego, Lapland to Capetown, Siberia to Tasmania. It makes a stunning summer soup as well as being delicious in salad, and makes a highly nutritious drink when juiced, as my friends in Pennsylvania do. In sandwiches, it tastes not unlike watercress—a delicate version.

Wash the chickweed leaves, and chop them a little. Lightly spread slices of fresh whole-grain bread with a mixture of cream cheese and softened butter, and place the leaves between the slices, adding a little lemon juice, if you like. Cut off the crusts and cut each sandwich into four small squares.

Glasswort with Melted Butter

Glasswort, or samphire (*Salicornea europaea*), is a succulent annual found along the Atlantic and Pacific coasts of North America. Equipped with waterproof boots and large plastic bags—it grows in huge abundance—you can gather this muddy harvest at low tide. It is definitely worth it: Glasswort is, in my view, worthy of being rated a kind of sea asparagus. Serve with melted butter and you have a dish fit for a king.

Wash the glasswort well. Cook it—roots and all—in boiling water for 10 minutes. Serve on a hot plate, since it loses its heat very quickly. Holding the root, dip the fleshy leaves into melted butter (to which you can add a little minced garlic or a few drops of fresh lemon juice) and strip the fleshy part off the stem. Alternatively, you can wait until it is cold, and use it in salads and sandwiches.

Béchamel Sauce (medium thickness)

MAKES ABOUT 2 CUPS
½ cup all-purpose flour
4 tablespoons butter or margarine

2 cups milk
Salt and white pepper
Pinch of nutmeg (optional)

Put all the ingredients into a heavy-bottomed saucepan and whisk continuously over a medium heat until the mixture thickens and is smooth. Bring to a boil and simmer gently for 5 minutes to cook the flour, stirring with a wooden spoon. Season to taste with salt and pepper, plus a pinch of nutmeg, if desired.

Garlic Crisp of Nettles and Mushrooms

Stinging nettles grow almost everywhere, and have been used by the country housewife for generations, both in cooking and in herbal practices. They make a superlative soup, prepared just as you would spinach soup. So abundant and common are nettles, that there is nothing to stop you from picking masses of them from spring onward—wearing rubber gloves, of course. Pick the top shoots—the top six leaves—for the most tender flavor.

SERVES 4	CRISP TOPPING
2 pounds nettle tops	1 cup bread crumbs
3½ cups sliced mushrooms	2 garlic cloves, minced
3 tablespoons olive oil	½ cup grated cheese
1¼ cups béchamel sauce	2 tablespoons butter, diced
(see page 151)	Salt and pepper
Salt, pepper, and a little nutmeg	

Preheat the oven to 350°F.

Wash the nettles and cook like spinach, with just the water remaining on the leaves. Drain well. Sauté the mushrooms in the oil. Fold both into the béchamel and mix thoroughly. Season to taste with salt, pepper, and a little nutmeg. Place in a baking dish.

Mix the topping ingredients together, season, and sprinkle over the nettle mixture. Bake for 40 minutes, until the topping is crisp. Serve hot.

Cranberry Relish

From a friend in New York, this adaptation of a traditional Thanksgiving relish shows how multi-cultural influences have been integrated into much Western cooking: Mexican, Canadian, Indian, and Mediterranean tastes all add to the humble New England cranberry. This makes a serious amount, for a large party at the very least, but the leftovers freeze well.

1 pound (about 4½ cups) fresh cranberries	2 fresh jalapeño peppers, seeded
Grated zest of 1 orange	2 tablespoons maple syrup
1 orange, peeled and sectioned	2 tablespoons grated fresh ginger

Put the cranberries into a blender with all the other ingredients and process to a purée. Serve with roast turkey (this is also delicious with pre-dinner nibbles).

Almond Plum Tart

My neighbor has a Victoria plum tree in her garden, which I love to raid for this recipe each autumn. The golden-brown crust of almonds that tops the plums in a light pastry case makes for an irresistible dessert. My neighbor doesn't possess a rolling pin: She rolls her pastry out with a wine bottle filled with chilled water, which, she swears, keeps the pastry light.

SERVES 6	1 egg white, lightly beaten
1⅔ cups ground almonds	1 pound plums, halved and
6 tablespoons granulated sugar,	pitted
plus extra for sprinkling	Pinch of ground cinnamon
Pie dough for an 8-inch tart pan	A little butter or margarine

Preheat the oven to 400°F.

Mix together the ground almonds and sugar. Roll out the pie dough and use to line the tart pan. Brush with lightly beaten egg white—this is a useful tip, to stop the pastry from becoming soggy. Sprinkle one-third of the ground almond mixture over the bottom of the pastry shell to form a thick layer. Arrange the plums on top and add a little extra sugar. Spread the rest of the almond mixture over the top and dot with butter or margarine. Bake on the bottom of the oven for 35–40 minutes, covering the tart with a piece of foil after 10–15 minutes, to prevent the almonds from burning. The base of the pastry shell will cook crisp by being on the oven floor.

Season of mists and mellow fruitfulness,
Close bosom-friend of the maturing sun;
Conspiring with him how to load and bless
With fruits the vines that round the thatch-eves run;
To bend with apples the moss'd cottage-trees,
And fill all fruit with ripeness to the core;
To swell the gourd, and plump the hazel shells
With a sweet kernel; to set budding more,
And still more, later flowers for the bees,
Until they think warm days will never cease,
For Summer has o'er-brimm'd their clammy cells.

John Keats, *To Autumn* (1819)

Sorrel picked from the wild makes an elegant summer soufflé.

French Sorrel Soufflé

Wild sorrel can be found in grassy places and banks. The Laplanders use it instead of rennet—its sourness curdles milk. Its name comes from an old French word meaning "sour," and it found its culinary way into refreshingly sharp sauces to go with rich meats. It makes a stunning soup or soufflé. This one is based on a classic French recipe.

SERVES 4

12 ounces fresh sorrel

¾ cup béchamel sauce
  (see page 151)

½ cup grated Gruyère cheese

4 extra-large eggs, separated

Black pepper

A little sea salt

Preheat the oven to 375°F. Wash the sorrel and cook like spinach, with just the water that remains on the leaves, for 3–4 minutes. Drain thoroughly. Mix into the béchamel with the cheese, and season to taste. Cool a little, then stir in the well-beaten egg yolks. Beat the egg whites until very stiff, then fold carefully into the mixture. Pour into a buttered soufflé dish and bake for 25–30 minutes, until risen and golden, and still slightly moist in the center when a clean sharp knife is inserted. Serve immediately.

WILD MUSHROOMS

The incomparable thrill of mushrooming is akin to a treasure hunt. The place: The silence and stillness of the autumn woods, or the early-morning fields as a low sun struggles through gentle mist. The scene: Falling leaves, the smell of damp ground, that first chill in the air as summer relinquishes its hold.

Mushroom-hunting is pretty well a global pursuit: Fungi have no respect for boundaries and spring up abundantly wherever conditions are right. So the woods of Russia, the USA, China, and Europe all have their secret harvests hidden away for the delight of the enthusiast. Even the desert gives up treasure: The Kalahari in Botswana contains some of the richest truffle harvests of the world.

Mushrooms are best gathered into smooth woven baskets—the specially made ones are flat, so as not to damage the delicate flesh of the fungi. If you are going to eat your wild mushrooms fresh, cover them with damp paper towels as soon as you get them home, and store in the refrigerator until you are ready to cook them.

Sweet and Sour Mushrooms

There are two hundred meatless days required by the Russian Orthodox calendar, and this is when the mushroom comes into its own. Fresh or dried, pickled or salted, they provide both protein and a satisfaction-factor in the absence of meat. My friends in Moscow served me this dish one autumn, using fresh wood oyster mushrooms from their *dacha* in the country. A delicious way of cooking mushrooms, served cold as a first course or as a light snack.

SERVES 2

6 ounces wild mushrooms such as chanterelles, cèpes or boletus, meadow mushrooms, etc.

3 tablespoons each olive oil and tarragon vinegar

2 tablespoons sugar

2 whole cloves

1 bay leaf

Salt

⅔ cup sour cream

Wipe the mushrooms clean and slice. Heat the oil with the vinegar, sugar, cloves, bay leaf, and a pinch of salt, and simmer over a low heat for 5 minutes. Add the mushrooms and simmer, covered, for 3 minutes, stirring from time to time. Leave to cool, then mix in the sour cream. Serve with blinis, the little Russian pancakes, to mop up the juice.

Easy Mushroom Curry

When wild mushrooms are so abundant that you are hard-pressed to know what to cook next, this is a useful option. I wouldn't use chanterelles or cèpes, because of their delicate flavor, but the honest taste of giant puffballs or oyster mushrooms, or even beefsteak fungus (*Fistulina hepatica*), all lend themselves to this simple dish. Easy to make, using garam masala paste, this is a wonderful warming dish for an autumn evening, as the weather grows chilly.

Before eating wild mushrooms, always check with a good field guide, or ask an expert.

SERVES 3–4

4 tablespoons butter

2 large onions, chopped

2 teaspoons garam masala paste

1–2 teaspoons each ground ginger
    and turmeric

1 large bunch fresh cilantro

4 canned tomatoes with their juice

1 pound wild mushrooms,
    chopped

Salt

1 tablespoon lemon juice

Melt the butter in a pan, add the onions and spices, cover, and cook over a gentle heat for about 10 minutes, until soft. Add the chopped cilantro and the tomatoes with their juice, and stir well. Add the mushrooms and mix in. Season with salt and lemon juice, and cook for 8–10 minutes.

Serve with basmati rice and popadoms.

Fungi alla Crema

This recipe was given to me by an Italian woman living in the Tuscan hills near Florence. She told me how her father had shown her where her grandparents before him had hunted for cèpes (porcini) and chanterelles, following the time-honored tradition of keeping secret the best places for mushroom-hunting. The Italians, she said, take it all with the seriousness it merits, holding numerous festivals in the villages and towns to show off their treasures, a staggering array of many varieties of wild mushrooms neatly stacked in woven baskets lined with the leaves of the sweet chestnut tree.

SERVES 4–6

6 tablespoons butter

2 pounds assorted wild
    mushrooms

1 medium bunch fresh tarragon,
    minced

Sea salt and freshly ground black
    pepper

1¼ cups heavy cream

Melt the butter in a pan, add the mushrooms, and stew over a gentle heat, covered, for 10 minutes, or until they are soft. Add all but 1 tablespoon of the chopped tarragon and season to taste. Turn up the heat a little and allow to bubble, to evaporate some of the liquid, then add the cream and bring back to a simmer. Stir well, bubbling, for 2 more minutes, then serve in individual dishes with the remaining chopped tarragon sprinkled over the top.

Delicious with warm Italian slipper bread to mop up the juices.

Oyster mushrooms

Identifying Fungi

There are people around the world who take great pride in their expertise in identifying fungi. The Aborigines, for example, have a vast knowledge of wild plants and fungi, and know which ones are dangerous. You need to be absolutely sure of correctly identifying the mushrooms you pick from the wild: You cannot be too careful since eating some fungi can have fatal results, and death by mushroom-poisoning is spectacularly unpleasant. Never eat a mushroom unless you are 100 percent sure which one it is. The following fungi are easily identifiable and completely safe to eat, but always check with a field guide before you do so, or consult an expert.

Blewit (*Lepista nuda/Clitocybe nuda*)

Cèpe/King bolete (*Boletus edulis*)

Chanterelle (*Cantherellus cibarius*)

Fairy ring/Scotch bonnet (*Marasmius oreades*)

Giant puffball (*Calvatia gigantea*)

Black trumpet/Horn of Plenty (*Craterellus fallax*)

Morel (*Morchella* sp.)

Oyster mushroom (*Pleurotus ostreatus*)

Parasol mushroom (*Lepiota procera*)

Shaggy mane/Shaggy ink cap (not with alcohol) (*Coprinus comatus*)

Deep-Fried Puffballs

If you are lucky enough to find puffballs in the meadows or woods in late summer, this is one of the most delicious ways of cooking them. Mouthwatering, crisp, and irresistible. Serve them as soon as possible after cooking, with a little soy sauce for dipping.

SERVES 4

1 medium giant puffball

Fritter batter (see page 132)

Oil for deep-frying

Wipe the puffball clean and cut into cubes about ½ inch square. Dip in the fritter batter and deep-fry in very hot oil until the batter is crisp and browned. Drain on paper towels and cool a little before serving.

Stuffed Mushrooms

I made these after an expedition to a field on the Welsh Borders early one misty morning: Large meadow mushrooms (*Agaricus campestris*) were thick on the ground where none had been visible the evening before. One of the intriguing characteristics of this mysterious creature—neither plant nor animal but microbe— is how it appears so suddenly, as if from nowhere. I filled my basket to overflowing, and made this very simple recipe for supper, delicious with a crisp salad, warm whole-grain bread, and a glass of red wine.

SERVES 4

*4 very large, or 8 medium,
meadow mushrooms*

½ cup breadcrumbs

3 tablespoons milk

3 tablespoons butter

1 large onion, chopped

1 large garlic clove, minced

2 tablespoons chopped parsley

*Salt, pepper, and a pinch of
cayenne (optional)*

Grated Parmesan cheese

Preheat the oven to 425°F.

Cut the stems off the mushrooms and mince them. Soak the bread crumbs in the milk. Melt the butter in a pan, add the onion, and cook, covered, for 10 minutes, until soft and translucent. Add the minced garlic and mushroom stems and stir well for a couple of minutes longer. Then add the bread crumbs and the parsley. Season to taste with salt, pepper, and cayenne. Pile the stuffing into the mushroom caps, sprinkle with Parmesan, and bake for 15–20 minutes.

Wild mushrooms provide rich feasts from spring through autumn.

DESSERTS, CAKES, AND COOKIES

Autumnal puddings and cakes made with the annual glut have a special appeal. Our grandmothers the world over made the most of nature's harvest, and much of this "food for free" has become legendary. My mother's gardener, Mr. Williams, used to say that after a frosty winter there would be a good fruit harvest, and his advice was to pick the crops at full moon, so that the fruit would not lose its plumpness. He also used to swear that wallflowers planted around an apple tree made it fruit better.

Windfall Cake with Nuts

"An apple a day keeps the doctor away," goes an ancient saying—a good excuse to make this wonderful cake as your apples drop onto the grass and the evenings draw in. To help unmold it—and other moist cakes like it—place a strip of foil across the bottom of the cake pan before putting the batter in; this keeps the center intact as you invert the pan.

SERVES 8–10

1⅔ cups self-rising flour

Pinch of salt

⅔ cup (1½ sticks) butter or margarine

½ cup granulated sugar

1 cup chopped hazelnuts or walnuts

3 cups peeled, cored, and diced windfall apples

2 eggs, beaten

Sugar for dredging

Preheat the oven to 350°F.

Sift the flour with the salt into a large bowl, then rub in the butter until it resembles crumbs. Stir in the sugar and the nuts, then fold in the apples. Stir in the eggs with a metal spoon until thoroughly amalgamated. Pour the batter into a greased, deep 8-inch cake pan. Bake for 50 minutes, or until a skewer inserted into the center comes out clean. Leave to cool in the pan for 10–15 minutes, then unmold onto a wire rack. Remove the pan and let cool for another 30 minutes. Dredge the top with sugar and serve warm.

Windfall cake with nuts

Blackberry Bread and Butter Pudding

Misty mornings, followed by low, clear sunlight casting long shadows over the fields—and it is blackberrying time again. This is an autumnal version of English summer pudding, as described to me by a friend in the village. It is sensational.

SERVES 6

1½ pounds (about 4½ cups)
*   blackberries*
Squeeze of lemon juice

⅓–½ cup granulated sugar, to taste
1 teaspoon ground cinnamon
10–12 slices of bread, crusts removed
Butter for greasing

Cook the blackberries with a very little water over a gentle heat, just until the juice runs. Add the lemon juice, sugar, and cinnamon and cook until the blackberries soften. Cool.

Butter the bread lightly on one side. Line a bowl with the slices, buttered side out, and fill with the blackberries, adding enough of their juices to moisten the bread. Cover the top with more slices of bread. Press down with a plate, put a weight, such as a can of food, on top, and chill for several hours or overnight.

Unmold onto a platter and cut into wedges. Serve with thick yogurt or whipped cream.

Walnut Cake

If you soak fresh walnuts in salted water overnight they will be easier to crack, and the flesh will come out whole. If you are using dry ones that taste a bit stale, cover them with boiling water, drain, then put on a baking sheet in a low oven to warm for 20 minutes.

SERVES 10–12

1½ cups all-purpose flour
1 teaspoon baking powder
14 tablespoons (1¼ sticks)
*   unsalted butter*

1 cup granulated sugar
3 extra-large eggs
¾ cup chopped walnuts

Preheat the oven to 325°F.

Sift the flour with the baking powder. Cream the butter with the sugar, then beat in the eggs one at a time until the mixture is fluffy. Fold in the flour and add the chopped walnuts. Mix well.

Bake in a greased 8-inch cake pan for 30–40 minutes. Cool for 10 minutes on a wire rack, then remove from the pan and allow to cool completely. Frost with coffee butter icing, if desired.

Apple Dumplings

My neighbor's tip to ripen apples: Put them into a brown paper bag with one already ripe apple, pierce a few holes in the bag, and store in a cool, dark place for 24 hours.

SERVES 4

4 baking apples
8 ounces (1½ cups) blackberries
Granulated sugar to taste

½ teaspoon each ground
*   cinnamon and ginger*
1 pound pie dough
1 egg, beaten

Preheat the oven to 375°F.

Core the apples and cut the center out to make a good-sized hole. Mix the blackberries with a little sugar to taste and the spices, and pack into the center of the apples. Roll out the pie dough and cut into 4 large squares. Place an apple in the center of each square, and bring opposite corners together. Moisten with cold water and pinch the edges so that they stick together. Do the same with the other 2 corners. Pinch the edges together and brush all over with beaten egg. Bake for 25–30 minutes, until the pastry is golden and the apples inside soft. Lovely with thick yogurt, or English custard sauce (see page 131).

Hazelnut Cookies

Irresistibly crunchy, these cookies come from the country kitchen of an American living in Normandy, France, where the annual crop of wild cobnuts—from a tree related to the hazel—is abundant.

MAKES 12–14

1⅔ cups all-purpose flour
6 tablespoons granulated sugar
10 tablespoons (1¼ sticks)

butter or margarine, softened,
*   plus extra for greasing*
1 cup chopped hazelnuts

Sift the flour with the sugar. Rub the softened butter or margarine into the flour until the mixture resembles fine crumbs. Mix in the nuts. Knead to a soft, smooth dough on a wooden board. Roll into a sausage shape about 2 inches across, and chill for 1–2 hours.

Preheat the oven to 350°F.

Cut the roll into ¼-inch slices and place on a well-greased baking sheet. Bake for 15 minutes until lightly browned. Cool on a wire rack.

Plum Cobbler

This is my slightly unorthodox version of a traditional cobbler that my American mother always used to make, as her mother had taught her in their home in the glorious woods of Pennsylvania.

SERVES 6

3 tablespoons butter or
    margarine

TOPPING

6 tablespoons butter or
    margarine

¼ cup granulated sugar

1 egg, beaten

¼ cup packed brown sugar

2 pounds plums

A little grated lemon zest

1⅔ cups all-purpose flour

2 teaspoons baking powder

1 teaspoon ground cinnamon

Pinch of salt

1 cup milk

Preheat the oven to 350°F.

Melt the butter or margarine and pour into an 8-inch cake pan. Sprinkle the sugar over the top. Pit the plums, cut into quarters lengthwise, and arrange on the bottom of the pan with the lemon zest.

To make the topping, cream the butter and sugar and add the beaten egg. Sift together the flour, baking powder, cinnamon, and salt, and stir gradually with the milk into the butter mixture to make a smooth batter. Spread this batter over the plums. Bake for 30–35 minutes, until a knife plunged into the center comes out clean. Let cool a little on a wire rack before cutting into squares and serving with thick yogurt or custard sauce.

Wild Strawberry or Raspberry Vacherin

The extremely delicate flavor of wild strawberries makes it one of our most sought-after wild fruit. I grow a patch in my herb garden to provide me with its inimitable fruits. If you find wild raspberries growing, try them in this superb vacherin once prepared for me by my French friend, Emanuele.

SERVES 6
MERINGUES

2 egg whites

½ cup superfine sugar

A few drops vanilla extract

A few drops lemon juice

FILLING

½ pound (about 2 cups) wild
    strawberries or raspberries, hulled

1¼ cups crème fraîche

2 tablespoons granulated sugar

1 egg white

Preheat the oven to 250°F.

To make the meringues, beat the egg whites until they are stiff, then gradually beat in the sugar with the vanilla and lemon juice until they are thick and shiny and hold their shape. Place 12 tablespoon-size blobs on a well-greased baking sheet and bake for 1 hour. Leave in the oven to cool overnight, with the door slightly open.

Mash the strawberries and fold into the crème fraîche with all their juices. Stir in the sugar. Beat the egg white until stiff and fold in.

To serve, place 2 meringues on either side of each dish, and spoon the filling in between. Serve at once.

Spicy Pecan Cookies

Pecans are native to the Mississippi valley and neighboring states, and are the richest and oiliest of all the nuts—and in many people's view the most delectable. On a trip to New Orleans, my daughter came across the ultimate dessert: maple syrup and chopped pecans over vanilla ice cream (see below). A glorious idea, served with these cookies.

MAKES 12–14

⅔ cup all-purpose flour

6 tablespoons granulated sugar

5 tablespoons soft butter or margarine

1 teaspoon apple-pie spice

3 tablespoons rolled oats

½ cup pecan halves

Preheat the oven to 350°F.

Sift the flour into a bowl with and add the sugar, butter, and spice. Mix thoroughly with your fingertips until it resembles bread-crumbs, then knead until smooth on a wooden board. Divide into 12–14 pieces and roll into small balls. Spread out the oats on a plate. Press each ball into the oats, making a disk 3 inches in diameter, covered in oats on both sides. Press 2 pecan halves into the top of each cookie. Bake for 15–18 minutes, until lightly browned. Lift off while still warm and cool on a wire rack.

Mississippi Sundae

PER PERSON

3 scoops vanilla ice cream

1 tablespoon pecans, chopped and toasted

3–4 tablespoons pure maple syrup

Put the ice cream into a tall glass and sprinkle with the nuts. Pour the maple syrup over the top and serve.

Blueberry bake (above) and blueberry slice (below)

SERVES 8	4 extra-large eggs
Butter for greasing	⅔ cup pure maple syrup
8 cups white bread with the	1¼ cups milk
crusts cut off, cut into tiny cubes	2 teaspoons ground cinnamon
1 cup light cream cheese, cut into	1–2 tablespoons granulated sugar
tiny cubes	

Arrange half of the bread cubes in a buttered 8-inch soufflé dish. Scatter the cream cheese, then sprinkle over with the blueberries. Arrange the remaining bread cubes over the top.

Beat the eggs to a froth, then continue to beat while adding the maple syrup, milk, and cinnamon. Pour the mixture evenly over the bread and press down with a plate over the top. Refrigerate for several hours or overnight, so that the liquid is absorbed into the bread.

Preheat the oven to 350°F. Just before baking, sprinkle the top thickly with sugar. Bake for 1 hour, until puffed and golden brown. Eat either hot, warm, or cold, with whipped cream or yogurt.

Blueberry Slice

In Europe, bilberries are more common than blueberries, but the bigger and juicier blueberries are becoming very popular, just as they are in North America. Either berry can be used here. This scrumptious treat is delicious served with thick yogurt.

SERVES 6	¾ cup packed brown sugar
10 tablespoons (1¼ sticks)	2½ cups rolled oats
softened butter or margarine,	½ cup all-purpose flour
plus extra for greasing	2 cups blueberries

Preheat the oven to 375°F. Place the butter, sugar, oats, and flour in a bowl and rub together until evenly mixed. Press half of the mixture into the bottom of a small greased loaf pan. Cover with the blueberries. Spoon the remaining mixture over the top and press down lightly. Bake for 30–35 minutes until lightly browned; cool on a wire rack. Loosen the edges while still warm, then unmold when completely cold. Cut into slices to serve.

Blueberry Bake

Blueberries and bilberries (*Vaccinium* spp.) are among the first wild fruits of the season. From the mountains of western Maryland comes this unusual and delectable dessert, given to me by a woman who runs a bed and breakfast business there and who cooks evening meals for her clients. This is an established favorite, and no wonder.

CUPS
AND THEIR
CUSTOMS

Wine has come to symbolize full communion with life, as sung by Edward Fitzgerald in *Rubaiyat of Omar Khayyam:*

Awake, my little ones, and fill the Cup
Before Life's Liquor in its Cup be dry.

The grapevine is an age-old symbol of peace and prosperity. Wine was cultivated by the ancient Persians, and enjoyed by the Egyptians, who also used it in temple rituals and who believed that Osiris was the first god to make wine. The Greeks went on to develop the fine art of wine-making, and thus it took root in western civilization. Plato recommended it as "a comfortable medicine against the dryness of old age, that we might renew our youth." The Romans took their wine-making skills all over Europe as their empire increased, and today most of the world's wine is produced in Italy, France, Spain, Germany, Argentina, Algeria, Russia, Australia, New Zealand, South Africa, USA, and Portugal. The "blood of the grape" still retains its ancient sacrificial origins in the communion service of the Christian church, a spiritual drink that was also, in ancient times and in differing cultures, offered to the dead as a revivifying force.

The "fruit of Dionysus," god of wine and worshiped by some as lord of souls, is widely illustrated in myth as a symbol of a happier life in the other world. Dionysus represents the productive abundance and intoxicating power of nature, which transforms man from his usual gray way of living, stimulating his mystical faculties, which are habitually subdued by the trivial concerns of living. The Hebrews gave credit to Noah who, having discovered the delights of the grape, carried several young vines to safety with him on the Ark. To Noah was ascribed the wisdom that man, before drinking wine, is as gentle as a lamb. When he drinks moderately, he becomes as brave and as strong as a lion. When he drinks to excess, he resembles a swine.

Wine harvests throughout the world are an occasion for celebration, and every country has its tradition. In France, the *vendange* takes place in late September, with hired workers who are given simple meals in the spirit of a bacchanal: a *pot au feu* and local cheeses washed down with the regional wine. In Spain, the *vendimia* is marked by flamenco dancing and singing, and *tapas* are offered as refreshment. In Italy, the *vendemmia* workers are rewarded with a pasta soup, boiled stuffed beef or roast chicken, or both, and tomato and radicchio salad. The *Weinlese* in Germany offers public tastings. In Hungary, traditions that go back hundreds of years were still unchanged at the beginning of this century. The Tokay harvest—Hungary's inimitable honey-sweet wine—is accompanied by the music of gypsy fiddlers, and the workers are rewarded with a paprika goulash and stuffed cabbage, washed down with peach brandy. A huge and heavy bouquet of grapes is carried on a pole by two men leading a festive procession.

Joy is our greatest asset, just as fear ever was and still is our greatest curse .... The wine instinct is the natural urge for joy. The joy that is wine is the joy of sunshine. It has nothing in common with the many drugs and poisons which some people crave for and turn to in their search for peace of mind or relief from frayed nerves. Wine is not a drug, it never is a craving and rarely becomes a habit .... Wine is a symbol and it is an instinct, Man's time-honoured urge for joy.

André Simon, *Let Wine Be Mine* (1946)

CEREMONIAL CUPS

Frequent cups prolong the rich repast
Alexander Pope, *The Rape of the Lock* (1714)

Grace Cup

The grace cup was reputed to have been devised by Margaret Atheling, wife of Malcolm Canmore, King of Scotland, to induce the Scots to remain at table for grace to be said. It was filled with the choicest wines, and each guest was allowed to drink as much as he wanted as the cup was passed around after the saying of grace.

Early drinking cups were made of gold or silver by master craftsmen, and elaborately decorated with precious stones or fine chasing. The Howard Grace Cup in the Victoria and Albert Museum in London is made of ivory set in gold with the inscription: *Drink thy wine with joy.* The London City Companies possess fine grace or loving cups for use at their banquets, some of them with four handles. They were typically filled with a mixture of wine and spices or sack, to be drunk according to the loving-cup ritual.

Loving Cup

Loving cups go back to the pagan custom of wassailing (see page 169). As Christianity spread, the monks renamed the cup "*poculum caritatis,*" or Loving Cup. The custom still remains at British state banquets, City of London company dinners, and in some of the university colleges. A loving cup is still served at St. Catherine's College, Cambridge University, at the Commemoration Feast of the college's foundation in 1474, in a ceremony dating from the seventeenth century. The recipe is a mixture of 1½ quarts each of white wine and sparkling wine and ¼ bottle of Cointreau or Curaçao.

Four two-handled cups made of silver, of great antiquity and value, are used to serve the loving cup toward the end of the feast, passed around clockwise. When the head of the table rises to drink, his neighbors to his left and right also rise. The drinker bows to them, first to the right and then to left, with the toast to the Founders. Bowing to your neighbors keeps the right, or dagger, hand employed, rendering you defenseless, so the name "loving" cup took on a secular symbolism, that of guarding your friend who was drinking from harm: a bonding ritual in the masonic tradition.

The man with the loving cup (for this is essentially a male ritual) then drinks, and the other two turn their backs to protect him from attack: Using both his hands precludes him from drawing his sword in self-defense. With another bow, he passes the cup to his left-hand neighbor. As soon as the right-hand neighbor sits, the person on the left of the left-hand neighbor rises so that there are still three people standing, the center one of whom holds the cup. And so the cup circulates around the table, a napkin around the right handle of the cup.

The loving cup

Good glass should be fine, not coarse, perfectly clean, and well-polished.

The libation varied: Sometimes the beverage was "sack," sometimes a spiced wine. Sack was a wine imported into England from Spain and the Canaries, usually sherry or malaga. An eighteenth-century record tells how at Temple Bar the loving cup was strictly observed and that only one draft was allowed per person. At one feast, however, 45 quarts of the liquor were consumed by 70 people.

If sacke and sugar be a fault, God help the wicked.
William Shakespeare, *Henry IV, part i* (1589–90)

Glasses

The shape, size, and color of wineglasses can make or break the appreciation of good wine: A good glass should be fine, plain, perfectly clean, and well-polished. Wash in hot soapy water, then rinse under hot water and then cold before setting upside down to drain. When dry, polish with a soft cloth until crystal clear. Glass retains smells of all sorts and these can easily affect the flavor of the wine. Ideally, a glass should be large enough to hold a fair measure of wine when only half full, and curved in at the top to retain the bouquet.

"Lamb's wool" is a traditional English country drink made with apples and spices.

CELEBRATORY CUPS

There was laughing and chattering, and "pass the cup round,"
Bargains and toasts and rounds, and so till Evensong.
Wilham Langland, *The Vision of Piers Plowman* c. 1367

Rural traditions are rich in celebratory cups: Special brews to mark particular festivals have been going on for centuries, and many rural areas of Europe continue these customs, which give rural life its vitality and individuality. Celebratory wine cups used to be part and parcel of feasting, near-lethal libations passed around with traditional rituals to drink a health or a toast. The term "toast" probably derived from the seventeenth-century custom of floating a piece of toast spread with nutmeg or other spices on top, to give the wine flavor. Yet drinking a toast in company also has a sinister origin, which comes from triumphing over your enemy: A cup or goblet containing drink was called the *skull* or *skoll*, from the barbarous Nordic practice of converting the skull of an enemy into a drinking cup. Hence the toast: "*skoll!*"

Lamb's Wool

This English Christmas drink is made with baked apples in strong ale, spiced with nutmeg and ginger, and sweetened with sugar. It was traditionally made in earthenware vessels, and was originally dedicated to the angel presiding over fruits and seeds. Some of my friends still make it every winter to an original recipe, and for them Christmas would not be the same without it.

PER PERSON	½ teaspoon ground nutmeg
2 apples, quartered	1 teaspoon groud ginger
2½ cups ale	½ cup packed brown sugar

Preheat the oven to 350°F.

Cut the apple quarters crosswise, put into a metal pan, and bake for 30 minutes. Warm the ale gently, and add the spices and sugar. Stir until dissolved, about 3–4 minutes, being careful not to overheat. Float the apples on top and it is ready to serve.

Wassail Cup

Wassailing the apple trees is a pagan ceremony to bring good crops and good fortune to the house. *Waeshael!* means "be whole, be well," and the ceremony was enacted around the New Year. A wassail song was sung, a wassail cup of spiced ale drunk, then pieces of toast were dipped in the drink and placed in the fork of the tree. Shotguns were fired through the branches to frighten off evil spirits, or trays banged to make a loud noise. Toasts were drunk to the tree as if it were a person.

This is what they would drink, from Sir Watkin William Wynne's recipe dated 1722:

Put into a quart of warm beer one pound of raw sugar, on which grate a nutmeg and some ginger; then add four glasses of sherry and two quarts more of beer, with three slices of lemon; add more sugar, if required, and serve it with three slices of toasted bread floating in it.

It is traditionally served with hot baked apples floating on top.

Glögg

This mulled wine from Sweden keeps out the winter cold, and is a popular drink for parties and celebrations around Christmas.

A Norwegian version, called skrub, was sent to me by a friend. This is made more simply, with cinnamon infused in water and sugar, then added to brandy and heated again; this mixture is added to red wine and heated for the third time.

SERVES 6–10	6 whole cloves
1 quart aquavit or vodka	¼-inch piece of cinnamon stick
1 bottle red wine	4 strips orange zest
6 cardamom pods	8 ounces lump sugar (about 45 lumps)

Place the aquavit and wine with the spices and orange zest in a pan over a medium heat. Simmer very gently for 1 hour, covered, to infuse the flavors. Put the lump sugar on a wire rack and balance it over the pan. Fill a ladle with the glögg, light with a match, and pour over the sugar. Continue this process until the sugar has dissolved, then stir thoroughly. Serve hot.

A tip: Put a small metal spoon into the glass before you pour in the hot liquid; this will prevent the glass from cracking.

MEAD

*Meade is made of honney and water boyled together, if it be fyned
and pure it preserveth helth.*   Anon

Mead is fermented honey water, a by-product of beekeeping. It
evolved from metheglin, which in turn came from hydromel, a
favorite drink of the Greeks and Romans. According to Lord Holles,
an Elizabethan gentleman, a cup of this honey mixed with spring
water and ginger, taken at night, "will cure thee of all troubles."
Metheglin was also said to promote and preserve good health. As
early as the sixth century, it was an important drink in Russia, and it
seems to crop up in many parts of the world: The Indian word for
mead is *Madhu*, the Lithuanian *Medus*, the German *Meth*.

Whereas metheglin used a strong-flavored honey, the best
mead was made with a mild one. It was made from the washings
of honeycombs after the honey had been extracted, and rainwater gave the best results. Beebread—a mixture of pollen and
nectar predigested by the bees—was used as a fermentation
agent. Monks took pride in developing special cultures of yeast for
their mead, which they guarded jealously down the years.
Everyone's mead had a subtle difference to it, the flower fragrance
was selected to enhance the brew, and much pride was taken in
its culture.

Eighteenth-Century Recipe for Mead

*To 1 gallon of water take 1 pint honey. Boil it, and after boiling,
immediately plunge in a handful of rosemary, sweet briar or a little
lemon balm. A bay leaf, or some cloves and bruised ginger, may be added
if liked, but we do not care for mead in which the taste of the honey is
burnt out with ginger and spices.*
Dorothy Hartley, *Food in England*

The brew was then fermented until it stopped "working." After
skimming, it was poured into a cask with some raisins, bunged, and
left to rest for 3 months. It could be "drawn off in frosty weather,
when it will be found very clear and bright, with a fine froth."

A Finnish friend makes hers with the addition of lemon zest,
which sounds delicious.

An apiculturist in traditional protective costume

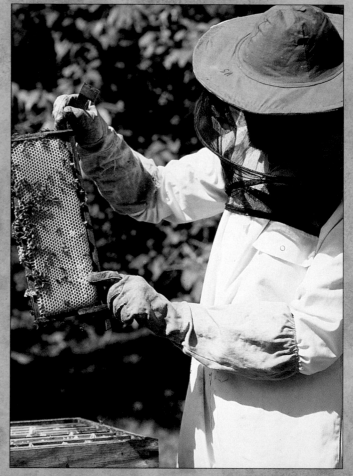

POSSETS AND CAUDELS

A posset was drunk from a posset-cup, a specially made china dish with a cover. It is a drink of hot milk curdled with ale, wine, or some other liquor and often flavored with sugar and spices. It was prescribed for catarrh, colds, and other minor ailments, as described in a couplet by Dryden:

A sparing diet did her health assure
Or sick, a posset was her cure.

Dr. Johnson describes posset as "milk curdled with wine and other acids," and they came in various forms: Milk-possets, pepper-possets, cider-possets, or egg-possets.

A Simple but Brilliant Posset

2 ½ cups milk
⅔ cup white wine
2 ounces cube sugar (about 10 cubes)
1 lemon
1 teaspoon ground ginger
Grated nutmeg

Bring the milk to a boil in a pan, then add the wine. Set aside for 10 minutes to curdle. Strain off the curds. Rub the sugar over the lemon, to absorb the oil from the skin, and stir into the hot curds. Flavor with the ground ginger and nutmeg to taste.

A richer recipe suggests heating raw cane sugar with sherry and nutmeg, adding eggs until they cook, then milk. The mixture is heated through and served thick and hot.

Caudels

These are a kind of gruel, a mixture of eggs, cereal, and malt, serving as a food-drink combination to see folk through long journeys or extended gaps between meals. Sometimes they were made with beer, sometimes with whisky or other spirits. Caudels were warming and nourishing and kept you going until you landed a solid meal. They were made in countless ways, but here is one based on a description by Charles Dickens:

A Victorian posset-cup

A Dickensian Caudel

2 tablespoons medium-ground oats
2½ cups hot water
Thinly pared zest of ½ a lemon
¼ cup granulated sugar
¼ teaspoon ground nutmeg
½ teaspoon ground ginger
1 egg, beaten
1–2 tablespoons brandy

Stir the oatmeal into the water with the lemon zest and boil until thick. Strain, then add the sugar and spices and mix in the beaten egg. Return to the pan and heat very gently for 2 minutes. Finish with the brandy.

Alternatively, according to a Scottish recipe, you can cook the oatmeal in milk, and use Scotch whisky rather than brandy. Or, you can use cinnamon and a blade of mace to spice it, and use mild ale or porter, a dark brown malt beer, instead of water.

A feminine version was made with ground rice, port, and ginger.

SYLLABUBS

"Bub" is sixteenth-century slang for a bubbling drink, traditionally made by mixing wine and brandy with whipped frothing cream. Sill was a region of Champagne that provided the bubbles. An instant "syllabub under the cow" was made by drawing the milk from the cow directly onto the wine. An Irishwoman told me of a family tradition, dating back to the seventeenth century, whereby·her ancestors used to attend a well-dressing in May. Every member of the family would gather at the well early in the morning, with a flask or vessel containing a measure of whisky, onto which the cow was milked.

In the seventeenth and eighteenth centuries, the syllabub developed various forms: A punch bowl of cider or ale, spiced with cinnamon and nutmeg, was sweetened with sugar and the milkmaid milked the cow onto it to produce an alcoholic whey, which was sometimes served with cream on top. A syllabub made with wine or spirits was a richer mixture, containing four-fifths cream, and spooned rather than drunk out of glasses. Then someone discovered that if you reduced the proportion of wine and sugar to cream, it would not separate: This became the basis of the "Everlasting Syllabub."

You can also make syllabubs with syrups rather than alcohol (see page 176). In the nineteenth century, they were sometimes made with the juice of Seville oranges.

An Everlasting Syllabub

Most syllabubs are as delicious to drink as they are to eat from a spoon. I have thickened this one with cream, for a luxurious satin texture.

1 lemon
½ cup sherry or white wine
2 tablespoons brandy
¼ cup granulated sugar, plus extra for sugaring petals
1¼ cups heavy cream
Whole nutmeg
2 egg whites
Small edible rose petals, to decorate

Pare the lemon zest thin and put into a bowl with the wine and brandy. Leave for several hours or overnight.

Strain into another bowl. Add the sugar and stir until dissolved. Pour in the cream slowly, whipping all the time with a wire whisk. Grate in a little nutmeg, then fold in one stiffly beaten egg white. Spoon into small glasses and keep in a cool place until ready to eat. The syllabub can be made 2–3 days in advance. Decorate just before serving with rose petals dipped in egg white and frosted with sugar.

Syllabub Trifle

Completely irresistible, this is a variation of a traditonal British dessert.

SERVES 6–8
1 homemade sponge cake, broken into pieces
1¼ cups sherry
6 tablespoons brandy
1¼ cups light cream
½ cup granulated sugar
4 eatra-large eggs
5 tablespoons mango purée, sweetened to taste
Juice of ½ lemon
1¼ cups heavy cream
¼ cup slivered almonds

Line the bottom of a large glass bowl with the cake pieces. Moisten with a mixture of 3 tablespoons sherry and 2 tablespoons brandy. Heat the light cream. Beat half of the sugar into the eggs until creamy, then pour on the hot cream. Return to the pan and cook over a low heat, just long enough to thicken to a custard, taking care not to let it boil and curdle. Cool, then pour over the cake layer. When cold, spoon the mango purée over the top.

Mix together the remaining sherry, brandy, and sugar with the nutmeg and lemon juice. Beat in the heavy cream slowly with a wire whisk until it thickens. Chill the syllabub for several hours or overnight.

Just before serving, pour the syllabub over the top of the trifle and sprinkle with slivered almonds.

An everlasting syllabub

PUNCHES

The origin of the word punch is thought to come from the Persian *punj*, or the Sanskrit *panca*, meaning five, denoting the number of ingredients—spirits, sugar, lemon, spices, and water or milk. Special punch bowls of silver and china became quite an artform, with ladles to match made of silver, mounted on wooden handles so as not to conduct heat. Families had their own special recipes for punch, which were handed down through the generations, and which were served on special family occasions.

Mrs. Beeton comments in her original volume of *Household Management* that "it is thought to be very intoxicating . . . but its strength does not appear to the taste to be so great as it really is. Punch, which was universally drunk among the middle classes about 50 or 60 years ago, has almost disappeared from our domestic tables, being superseded by wine."

This is her recipe (I decorate it with slices of orange):

½ pint rum	*1 large lemon*
½ pint brandy	*½ teaspoon nutmeg*
¼ lb sugar	*1 pint boiling water*

Rub the sugar over the lemon until it has absorbed all the yellow part of the skin, then put the sugar into a punchbowl. Add the lemon juice (free from pips), and mix these two ingredients well together. Pour over them the boiling water, stir well together, add the rum, brandy and nutmeg; mix thoroughly, and the punch will be ready to serve. It is very important in making a good punch that all the ingredients are thoroughly incorporated; and to insure success, the processes of mixing must be diligently attended to.

German Punch

This recipe, a favorite of my German friend Inge, is traditionally served on Christmas Eve as the family gathers for the festive rituals.

SERVES 10	
¼ cup granulated sugar	*2 small sticks cinnamon*
1¼ cups water	*6 whole cloves*
Pared zest of ½ lemon	*1 bottle Moselle or Hock wine*
and ½ orange	*1 bottle red wine*
	3 wineglasses of brandy

Heat the sugar, water, zests, and spices in a large pan, stirring until the sugar dissolves. Cover and leave to infuse over a very low heat for 30–40 minutes. Add the wine and the brandy, heat through again, remove from the heat, and serve.

Mrs. Beeton wrote, in her original edition of *Household Management*, that punches are "very intoxicating."

A Norwegian non-alcoholic punch

Jesus College Milk Punch

This is served on the annual occasion of the Audit Feast in Jesus College, Cambridge University, at the end of a considerable intake of food and fine wines. According to the Manciple (head steward), not all that much is drunk, and it sits on the side cooling, acquiring a crust on top. It is, however, a delicious drink.

SERVES 10
1 lemon
1¼ cups brandy
½ cup noyau (amaretto)
Freshly grated nutmeg
3 egg yolks
7½ cups milk
1 heaping cup granulated sugar
⅔ cup rum

Peel the zest of the lemon thin and place in a glass. Pour over it a little brandy and noyau, add a little grated nutmeg, cover with a saucer, and let it stand for about 8 hours. Beat the egg yolks with a little cold milk. Put the remaining milk in a pan and bring to a boil. Stir in the yolks, sugar, rum, remaining brandy and noyau, and the lemon zest mixture. Continue to stir until it thickens. Strain into a punch bowl and grate a little nutmeg over the top.

Non-Alcoholic Punch

If you prefer a non-alcoholic punch, this recipe from friends in Norway is a delicious drink.

6 cups confectioners' sugar
2 quarts water
Juice of 8 lemons
Grated zest of 4 lemons
1 teaspoon grated nutmeg
1 quart boiling milk
Frozen grapes, to serve

Place the sugar and water in a pan and bring to a boil. Boil, uncovered, for 5 minutes. Cool, then add the lemon juice, zest and nutmeg. Allow to stand overnight.

Stir the boiling milk into the lemon mixture, and leave to stand for 24 hours. Strain through cheesecloth and pour the cold punch into bottles.

Serve cold, adding this mouthwatering touch: Freeze some grapes in advance and float them in the drink.

Whisky Punch

From a friend in Scotland, who was interested in this section of the book and wanted to share an ancestral recipe. "The most fascinating tipple ever invented," goes his message. Just mix the ingredients together.

2⅓ cups Scotch whisky
2 glasses brandy
Grated zest and juice of 1 lemon
1 wineglass of boiling ale
1 heaping cup granulated sugar
5 cups boiling water

Syrups and Cordials

You can make a range of old-fashioned syrups from fruits and herbs to use in contemporary ways, such as sodas, wine cups, and certain dessert sauces. They are simple to make, and can be stored indefinitely in a cool place. They should be poured into sterilized bottles while hot, and corked immediately. Keep cold or refrigerated for up to six months.

Almond Syrup

Miles of almond groves line the road in parts of California. A friend made us a soda with her homemade almond syrup when we visited, and it was sublime.

1½ cups whole almonds,
blanched and skinned
2 tablespoons almond extract

2½ cups cold water
1¼ cups granulated sugar

Grind the almonds roughly in a food processor. Place in a pan with the almond extract and stir in the water. Add the sugar and bring to a boil. Simmer for 3 minutes, then strain through a linen bag. It may need straining twice.

Coffee Syrup

An Italian friend sent me this amazing recipe from Venice. Try pouring it over praline ice cream, or mixing it with crème fraîche to serve with a chocolate cake.

1 pound freshly ground coffee
2½ cups water

2¼ cups granulated sugar

Bring the coffee and water to a boil in a pan and boil for 20 minutes. Strain through cheesecloth and stir in the sugar. When it has dissolved, return to the pan and simmer, skimming until the syrup becomes thick.

Crème de Cassis

Black-currant syrup is widely used in France: a dash in white wine for *kir*, or a splash over ice cream to transform it. A good friend who lives in Cucuron, in southeast France, sent me her version, to which she sometimes adds brandy before bottling. In autumn, she makes it with blackberries, or bilberries if she can find them.

Coffee syrup is delicious poured over ice cream

5 pounds black currants
2 pounds (4½ cups)

granulated sugar
1¼ cups cold water

Put the berries and sugar into a stoneware jar or crock. Bruise the fruit, then leave overnight, covered with a cloth.

Stir the fruit, add the water, and stand the jar in a pot of boiling water. Boil gently for 2½ hours. Strain through cheesecloth, then boil for 5–10 minutes.

Lemon or Orange Syrup

One of the most refreshing of all syrups, this is wonderful in summer weather. My uncle, who lived for a while in southern Spain, sent me this recipe.

3 pounds (6¾ cups)
granulated sugar

2½ quarts boiling water

Juice of 5 lemons or oranges

Finely pared zest of 3 lemons
or oranges

4 ounces citric acid

Put the sugar and water into a preserving kettle. Add the juice and zest. Dissolve the citric acid in a little hot water and pour into the mixture. Let stand for 24 hours, then strain and bottle.

Rose-Red Syrup

A delightful and delicious combination from the grandmother of a Frenchwoman who now lives in Normandy. It is a rich red color and has a heavenly flavor.

1 pound red currants

5 cups cold water

2 pounds (4½ cups)

granulated sugar

1 pound scented red rose petals,
trimmed of the white "heel"

Simmer the currants in the water for 20–25 minutes until all the juice is extracted, then strain. Add the sugar and the rose petals. Simmer gently for 15 minutes, then strain to remove the rose petals. Boil until the syrup thickens.

Elderflower Cordial

For many years now I have been making elderflower cordial for my family. Every June, when the elder produces its plentiful crop of flowers, I am out there to gather them—although European folklore warns against the elder mother, who will wreak her revenge if you harm the tree. So it is as well to appease her before you pick.

20 heads of elderflower

3½ pounds (8 cups) granulated sugar

7½ cups boiled water, cold

2 ounces tartaric acid

1 lemon, sliced

Put all the ingredients into a large bowl and leave to steep, stirring occasionally, for 24 hours. Strain and bottle. It is ready to drink immediately, but keeps for several weeks. Dilute with sparkling water.

Bramble Cordial

The bramble gets its name from "brom," or thorny shrub, and in Germany it is still called brombeere. As well as its culinary uses, the root of the bramble provides an orange dye.

4–5 pounds blackberries

For every 2½ cups blackberry juice (below) you need:

1 heaping cup granulated sugar

1 stick cinnamon

3–4 whole cloves

Pared zest of ½ lemon

For the blackberry juice: Wash the blackberries and put them into a preserving kettle with no water. Heat slowly until the juice runs freely, but don't let them boil. Pour into a jelly bag and leave to drip.

Measure the juice into a large pan. Add the sugar, spices, and lemon zest and boil for 30 minutes. Strain and bottle. You can add Scotch whisky or vodka, if you want an alcoholic version.

Summer Cordial of Soft Fruits

A stunning way of using summer fruit in high season. You can add a quantity of brandy, to taste, to make an alcoholic drink.

Black currants, red currants, raspberries, strawberries, and so on

Water   Brandy   Granulated sugar

Put the fruit into a stoneware jar and stand it in boiling water until the juice has run from the fruit. Strain and measure. Add 1 pound (2¼ cups) sugar for every 2½ cups of juice. Mix well. Allow to stand, covered, for several days, then strain again and bottle.

Rose-red syrup

DRINKS TO CHEER THE ILL

When I was writing a book about village life, I came across a woman who had worked "below stairs" as a maid in the manor house nearby during the 1920s and '30s. Although she is now frail and her memory poor, she handed me a couple of handwritten notebooks with all the tips and recipes she had collected from those long-gone days. "Invalids require variety," she had been told. "The drinks succeed each other in different forms and flavors." Evidently looking after invalids was an art-form in those days. I tried the drinks and they are excellent. Give your patient a selection of these stunning recipes.

Three Agreeable Drinks
• Into a tumbler of cold water, pour 1 tablespoon of lemon juice.
• Scald currants or cranberries, strain, and add a little sugar to taste.
• Serve buttermilk with cookies or rusks, and ripe or dried fruit, raisins in particular.

Apple Water

Slice and bake 2 large apples and pour on 5 cups of boiling water. Leave to stand for 2–3 hours, then strain. Sweeten lightly with honey.

Barley Water

Wholesome and nourishing, lovely when you feel too ill to eat much.

Wash a handful of barley, then simmer it gently in 7½ cups of water with a bit of lemon zest.

Or, boil 2 tablespoons pearl barley in a little water for a few minutes, to cleanse, then drain. Put the barley in a pan with 5 cups of water and simmer for 1 hour. When half done add a piece of fresh lemon zest and a cube of sugar. If it seems to be too thick, you may add another ½ cup of water. Lemon juice may be added if chosen.

Hot Chocolate

This is the best hot chocolate I've ever tasted. Sure to lift the spirits and strengthen a weak body.

Break 7 ounces of dark chocolate into very small pieces. Heat 1¼ cups of water in the pot and, when it boils, put in the chocolate. Stir it off the fire until quite melted, then heat on a gentle fire till it boils. Pour it into a bowl. It will keep in a cool place for 8–10 days, or more. When wanted, put a spoonful or two into a cup of milk, boil it with sugar, and stir it well.

Artificial Asses' Milk

This is wonderfully soothing and settling.

Mix together 2 tablespoons of boiling water, 2 tablespoons of milk, and an egg, well beaten. Sweeten with 2 tablespoons of white sugar. Take twice or thrice a day.

Coffee Milk

A beautiful way of reviving the ill—a sweet "caffe latte."

Boil 2 teaspoons of ground coffee in 1¼ cups of milk for 15 minutes. Then set it on the side of the fire to grow fine. Strain, and sweeten to taste.

CUPS AND THEIR CUSTOMS

Egg Wine

Not unlike zabaglione, this is soothing, comforting food.

Beat an egg, and mix with a teaspoon of cold water. Set on the fire a glass ⅓ cup of white wine, half a glass of water, 1 tablespoon sugar, and ½ teaspoon nutmeg. When this boils, pour a little of it onto the egg by degrees till the whole be in, stirring it well. Then return the whole into the

saucepan, put it on a gentle fire, stir it one way for not more than a minute, for if it boil, or the egg be stale, it will curdle. Serve with toast.

Ground Rice Milk

Comforting for the stomach, pleasant and easy to drink, with delicious spicing.

Boil 1 heaped tablespoon of ground rice with 1¼ cups milk, and ¼ teaspoon each of cinnamon, lemon zest, and nutmeg. Sweeten to taste when nearly done.

Lemon Water

A delightful pick-me-up. It's like lemon tea, and makes a nice change from ordinary tea.

Put 2 slices of lemon into a teapot with a little bit of zest, and a cube of sugar. Pour in 2½ cups of boiling water and leave, covered, for 2 hours before drinking.

Lemon Whey

This cleansing drink is an excellent remedy for a queasy stomach.

Pour into 1¼ cups boiling milk the juice of half a lemon. Leave to stand for 15 minutes until a small quantity is quite clear. Strain off through muslin and put in a cube of sugar.

"Soft and Fine Draught for Those Who are Weak and Have a Cough"

A lovely potion, light and flowery, yet nourishing and comforting. Far nicer than most cough mixtures.

Beat an egg and mix it well with ½ cup of warm milk, 1 tablespoon each of rose water and orange-flower water, and a little grated nutmeg. Do not warm it after the egg is put in. Take it first thing in the morning and last thing at night.

Pleasant to Drink

Sharp and uplifting, and full of vitamin C.

Put a teacupful of cranberries into a cup of water and mash them. In the meantime, boil 5 cups of water with 1 tablespoon of oat meal and a bit of lemon zest, then add the cranberries and sugar to taste. Add about ½ cup of sherry, or less, as may be proper. Boil the whole for 30 minutes and strain.

NIGHTCAPS

Fine orange well roasted, with wine in a cup,
They'll make a sweet bishop when gentlefolks sup.
Jonathan Swift

One of the oldest recipes for a nightcap is bishop, famous in—among other places—the University of Oxford. It was, and is, a drink of sweetened wine or port with oranges and lemons and sugar. The following recipe comes from *Oxford Nightcaps*, of 1827. My father, who was a proctor in the university for a short term in the 1930s, recalled a similar drink being served after a Feast at High Table.

Using sherry instead of port, this drink was curiously called "lawn sleeves." For cardinal, use claret, whereas for pope use champagne. Norwegian friends make what they call old-fashioned bishop (*Gammeldags bisp*), using sweetened red wine with oranges.

Bishop

1 orange	*6 allspice berries*	*6–10 sugar lumps*
15 whole cloves	*Piece of fresh ginger, bruised*	*1 lemon*
Short stick cinnamon	*1¼ cups water*	*Nutmeg*
1 blade mace	*1¾ cups port*	

Prick the orange in several places and stick with the cloves. Roast in the oven at 400°F for 30 minutes. Put the spices in a pan with the water and boil until reduced by half.

Heat the port to drive off some of the alcohol, then add the roasted orange and the hot spice mixture. Leave to warm over a very low heat for 10 minutes.

Rub the sugar lumps over the lemon, to absorb the oil from the skin, and add to the mixture. Stir, grate a little fresh nutmeg over the top, and serve.

Rumfustian

This is a thick drink enriched with egg yolks. The mixture of spirits would knock anyone unconscious and I'm not sure that I would recommend it. For purely academic interest, the recipe goes:

12 egg yolks, 5 cups strong beer, 1 bottle of wine, 2½ cups of gin, and cinnamon, nutmeg, sugar, and ginger to taste. Beat and warm (without boiling, which would curdle the egg yolks) until thick.

Oxford Nightcaps also recommends:

Brown Betty

Brown sugar, dissolved in 1 pint of hot water, a slice of lemon in it. Add cloves, cinnamon, brandy and a quart of strong ale. Heat it up, and float a round of brown toast on top of it—and on the toast grate nutmeg and ginger root. Serve hot.

Bishop

BEER

Pliny advises that five almonds consumed before drinking ale will preserve sobriety. Hops were not used in beer-making until the sixteenth century. Before this the traditional country drink in many parts of the world was ale, which was brewed from malt and yeast and flavored with herbs. Forty percent of the Sumerian grain crop went into beer production, so popular was ale, and the brewers were women. In Russia, "kvas" has been an important national drink since the sixth century A.D., made from malted barley or rye.

Malt is made by steeping barley grains in water so that they begin to germinate, then heating them to arrest the process: The longer they are heated, the darker the malt. Soft water was generally considered to give the best results in beer-making, and the flavorings used before the arrival of hops included hay, bog myrtle (sweet gale), mugwort, wormwood, rosemary, and ground ivy, which had a common country name of ale-hoof.

Eventually, ale and beer became synonymous. The strongest beer was brewed for special and festive occasions, whereas the light beer brewed for harvest workers was as inoffensive as barley water. Every household would make its own beer to serve its own purpose, and the brewing copper was used as regularly as the bread oven.

Nettle Beer

A light, tasty beer for hot summer days, this beer has been a tradition in country households for centuries.

A large basketful of fresh young stinging nettle tops	*1 pound (2¼ cups) sugar*
	1 ounce ginger
1 lemon, cut up	*1 ounce cream of tartar*
4½ quarts water	*1 ounce brewer's yeast*

Put the nettle tops and lemon in a large pan with the water, and boil for 25 minutes. Strain into a wooden tub, add the sugar, ginger, and cream of tartar, and stir until dissolved. Add the yeast, and leave in a warm place to ferment for 3 days, or longer if the weather is chilly. Store in a small cask or bottle for immediate use.

Bell-Ringers' Beer Flip

To drink before a long peal—presumably to warm, sustain, and inspire. Adapted from Dorothy Hartley's *Food in England*.

8 eggs, separated
Sugar, orange juice, and spices
5 cups strong beer, heated

Beat the egg yolks with sugar, orange juice, and spices, and pour on the hot beer. Then pour it back into the pan from a great height so that it froths. Add the stiffly beaten egg whites to the froth, and serve immediately.

Tankards

The serious beer *aficionado*, keeps his beer tankard—pewter, of course—in the same place as the beer, because pewter at room temperature will make the beer seem unpleasantly warm. Traditionally, pewter tankards, with a jug of beer, were served on a wooden tray for the effect of the musical sound of pewter on wood. The tankards were kept well-polished, the trays well-scoured.

Pewter tankards should be washed in warm soapy water, dried, then polished with a soft cloth. In the old days they were cleaned with fine sifted sand and coarse rushes. Today a scouring pad will do the job, but do not use metal polishes or chemicals on pewter since it retains odors and will contaminate the beer.

Bell-ringers' beer flip

CIDER

Cider on beer makes good cheer
Beer on cider makes a bad rider.

Cider often replaces beer in apple-growing areas. English country lore has it that late frosts on May 19th–21st, which often destroy the year's crop of apples, occur because a brewer named Franklin, from Devon, sold his soul to the Devil for frost on those three days, so that people would buy his beer instead of drinking cider. Cider-making was the domain of the farmer's wife, and a cider press was as often as not shared in a district, trundled around from farm to farm during the autumn. The farmer would sometimes give cider to his workers in part payment. Cider-making is a far simpler process than brewing beer: All you need is apples, something to pulp them with, and a wooden barrel. Traditionally, apple-pressing began on November 1st, although it now begins in September. Most of the work is done by Christmas, although it can continue until March if there are enough apples.

There are numerous varieties of cider apples, but Northern Spy is considered by many to make the best cider. Cider needs no addition—although some ghastly "improvers" have been used in the past, from blood, milk, or cream to a rain-soaked rag and a dead sheep. No sugar is added to fresh cider, but hard cider may have sugar added before it is left to ferment.

Hard Cider

Pulp the apples, press out the juice, and put it into wooden barrels. Allow to stand in the orchard for 6 months.

Cider Cup

In a pan heat 2½ cups hard cider, 2 wineglasses brandy, 3 tablespoons sugar, and the juice of half a lemon, and stir over a low heat for 5 minutes. Grate some nutmeg onto 2 slices of lemon and float on top of the cup. Serve chilled.

FARMHOUSE WINES

Ever since the principle of fermentation was discovered, way back in antiquity, wines have been made by country people the world over. Homemade wines were always, and still are today, made from almost anything plentiful in the garden: Berries, rhubarb, plums, apples, pears, and quinces. From the vegetable patch, beet, carrots, celery and pea pods all make excellent traditional wines.

In the early days, rural winemaking equipment was simple: An earthenware "panshon" to start the wine, a mortar and pestle to bruise and break the spices, old spirit casks for fermentation, and whatever bottles were around—always sterilized. Today, winemakers prefer large glass jars or plastic buckets, fitted with fermentation traps. Be sure to sterilize all equipment and keep the first ferment well covered against fruit flies—they turn the wine to vinegar! Use a yeast nutrient to make sure of a good fermentation. Country wines make full use of natural yeasts found on plants and fruit, so many of the recipes do not add yeast; when they do, they traditionally spread it on toast and float it on top of the working wine. Even this was not wasted, as an eighteenth-century manuscript tells us: "The toasts taken out of ale and wine should always be given to the hens—it will encourage them mightily."

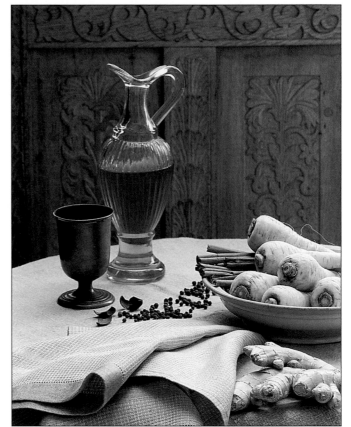

Parsnip wine (see page 186)

Bread Wine

Records show that the ancient Egyptians made wine from bread, and this very early manuscript recipe gives a version made with rye bread and honey, to produce a sweet wine resembling mead. This version was passed down through a family living near Tours in France.

> *2-pound loaf of homemade bread, broken up*
> *1 pound (2¼ cups) granulated sugar*
> *3½ quarts water*

Brown the bread lightly in the oven at 300°F for 30–40 minutes. Cool, then put into a wine jar. Dissolve the sugar in the water and pour over the bread. Keep the jar in a warm place until well fermented. Drain off into a cask. Bung lightly until the fermentation is complete, then bottle.

Keep for 3–4 months before drinking—it will improve with time. It is a lively, heady wine.

Dandelion Wine

This recipe comes from the man to whom I owe the idea for this book. He is now in his nineties, so this wine has seen many successful seasons. Thank you, Harry!

> *1 orange*　　　　　　　　*3 pounds (6¾ cups)*
> *1 lemon*　　　　　　　　*granulated sugar*
> *7½ pints dandelion flowers*　*1 ounce brewer's yeast*
> *5 quarts water*

Peel the orange and lemon, taking as little pith as possible. Put the peel and dandelion heads into a cheesecloth bag and boil in the water for 20 minutes. Remove the bag, squeezing lightly. Dissolve the sugar in the liquid. Pour into a plastic bucket (not metal), and when lukewarm (not cold), add the juice of the orange and lemon. Mix the yeast with a little of the liquid, pour back into the bucket, and cover.

Irish "poteen" or potato wine

Leave to work for 3 days, then syphon into a fermentation jar, and leave until it has finished fermenting. When fermentation has completely finished, bottle. The longer the wine is kept, the better it will taste.

Parsnip Wine

One of the oldest and most traditional of country wines. This recipe is from a Dutch friend living on a farm in the southern Netherlands.

> 4 pounds parsnips, cut up
> 5 quarts boiling water
> 1 ounce fresh ginger, cinnamon,
>   allspice, and mace, to taste
>
> 3 pounds (6¼ cups) raw brown
>   sugar
> 1 tablespoon compressed fresh yeast
> A slice of toasted bread

Boil the parsnips in the water for 15 minutes. Add the bruised or broken spices and stir gently for 10 minutes more. Strain, add the sugar, and stir to dissolve. Leave it until lukewarm. Spread the yeast onto the toast and float on the liquid. Allow it to work for about 36 hours (longer if the weather is cool), then pour it into a cask and let it ferment. As soon as fermentation ceases, bung securely and leave for 6 months. Rack off into bottles and store for a year before using. It improves with time—a 10-year-old parsnip wine is very fine.

Potato Wine

This recipe was sent to me by an Irishman, who described the "poteen" (potato spirit) that his grandfather brewed (illegally!). This wine is the legal version.

> 2 pounds potatoes, scrubbed clean
> 2 pounds (6 cups) raisins
> 4 pounds (9 cups) raw brown
>   sugar
>
> 2½ cups fresh wheat,
>   husked
> 20 quarts boiling water
> 1 ounce brewers' yeast

Grate the potatoes into a large container, add the rest of the ingredients, and stir at regular intervals for 3 weeks. Strain off into a keg to ferment, then rack and bottle.

Hedgerow Wines

Our ancestors always made wine from what grew around them in the wild: Nettles, gorse, coltsfoot, and clover made fragrant flower wines. Cowslip was the most famous of all, but these flowers, so over-picked, are no longer abundant enough to use. Hawthorn, rowan, bilberry, damson, sloe, and crab apple make heady fruit wines. Picked at the peak of their ripeness, they were used as soon as possible after picking. Autumn berries are considered best after the second hard frost; spring water is used whenever possible; and it is important never to use aluminum or iron pots because they spoil the color of the wine. A wooden cask was traditionally thought best for fermentation, or earthenware, although nowadays it is usually glass. The weather dictated the time to rack the wine: "When the frost has stilled and cleared the standing water in the pond, it will have stilled and cleared the wine in the cellar," says country wisdom. For utmost clarity, decant hedgerow wines before drinking.

Elderberry Wine

Every winemaker appears to have his or her version of how to make this excellent hedgerow wine. This particular version comes from a German doctor, who inherited the recipe from his grandfather. There are many superstitions about the elder tree, including the one that a powerful Dryad, the Elder-mother, inhabits it and you should respectfully ask her permission to gather its fruit or flowers.

4 pounds elderberries

5 quarts water

8 ounces (1½ cups) raisins

1 tablespoon citric acid

1 sachet wine yeast (Port type)

3½ pounds (8 cups)

granulated sugar

Strip the berries from their stems, wash them clean in cold water, and remove every trace of stem and unripe berry. Place the berries in a suitable sterilized vessel, crush them, and pour boiling

Elderberries

water over them. Chop the raisins and add to the vessel along with the citric acid. Cover and leave until cool.

Add the wine yeast and ferment the pulp for three days, then strain, pressing the fruit; discard it. Stir the sugar into the juice and pour into a sterilized fermentation jar. Fit an airlock into the jar and leave in a warm room until the wine is still—about three weeks.

Move the wine to a cold place for a few days to help it to clear, then siphon it into a sterilized storage jar. Bung tightly and keep for one year before bottling, then keep for another six months before drinking. This is a strong, slightly sweet wine to serve after meals.

Blackberry Wine

One of the most frequently made of hedgerow wines, because of the abundance of the blackberry harvest. This version was given to me by a local farmer's wife whose grandmother made it before her. It is invaluable, she swears, as a tonic, and as a medicine for winter ailments.

Crush the berries, and pour on 5 cups boiling water for each 5 quarts of fruit. Let the mixture stand for 24 hours, stirring occasionally. Strain and measure into a keg, adding 2 pounds (4½ cups) sugar and 2½ cups rye whiskey to each 5 quarts. Cork tightly, and let it stand for about 2 months before drinking.

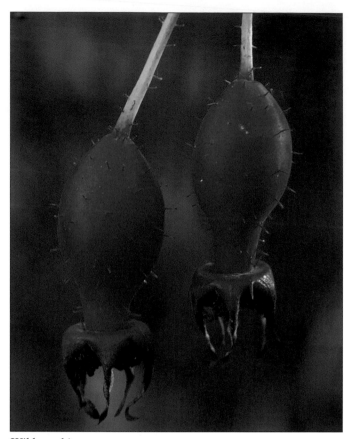
Wild rose hips

Wild Rose-Hip Wine

Here is one answer to using up the abundant annual harvest of rose hips. A fine hedgerow wine, dry and distinctive. From a villager in East Anglia, England.

Rose hips   *Water*   *Granulated sugar*

Pick the rose hips when quite ripe. Take off the stems, mash them, cover, and leave for a day. Drain well in a fine sieve, squeezing out all the juice. Measure, and to every 5 cups juice add 8 ounces (1 heaping cup) sugar. Cover, and leave for a day, stirring now and then to make sure the sugar has dissolved. Put into a cask that just holds the amount of wine. Bung the hole lightly. When it no longer hisses, close the bunghole tightly and leave for 3 months. Then bottle and leave to mature for 6–9 months at least. It will improve the longer it is kept.

Blackberries

LIST OF RECIPES

INDEX

Photographic acknowledgments

All photographs by Michelle Garrett except for:
A–Z Botanical Collection Limited: 8–9, Björn Svensson; 10, Mark Bolton; 14, Houses and Interiors; 110–11 (bee skep) Kellie Castle.
Christie's Images: 166 Loving Cup by Daniel Maclise R.A.
Melanie Eclare: 57, 78–9 (background).
Ecoscene: 25 top, Ian Beames; 46 top, David Wootton.
FLPA: 88, Cath Mullen.
Foulsham Press for facsimile of Old Moore's Almanack on page 47.
The Garden Picture Library: 40, Juliette Wade; 50–1 John Miller; 54, JS Sira; 55, John Glover; 98, Clive Boursnell; 114 and 116, John Glover; 118 (above), Jerry Pavia;
    119 and 148 (right), Ron Sutherland; 149 (left), Tim Spence, (right), Nigel Francis; 156 (above), Vaughan Fleming; 184, Tim Macmillan; 187, Sunniva Harte; 188 (top)
    Linda Burgess, (bottom), Howard Rice.
Michelle Garrett Archive: 6 (bottom), 7 (bottom), 13, 26, 30, 37, 41 (above), 42–3 (top and bottom), 45, 56 (bottom right), 58–9, (all three pictures), 61, 128, 148 (left)
    and 157.
Holt Studio International: 44, Willem Harinck; 115 (bottom left and right), 56 and 146 (bee), 164 and 170 (bee-keeper), Nigel Cattlin; 117, Primrose Peacock;
    118, (below) Bob Gibbons; 154, Phil McLean.
Jacqui Hurst: 28.